Penguin Books
Solid Bluestone
Foundations

Kathleen Fitzpatrick was born at Omeo but has spent most of her life in Melbourne. She was educated at the Universities of Melbourne and Oxford and until her retirement was an Associate Professor of History in the University of Melbourne. She is a Fellow of the Australian Academy of the Humanities and of the Australian College of Education, and in 1983 was awarded an honorary Doctorate of Laws by the University of Melbourne.

She has travelled widely in the United States as a Carnegie Scholar and has paid many visits to Italy. Her previous books include *Sir John Franklin in Tasmania, Australian Explorers* and *PLC, Melbourne, the First Century.* She has contributed articles to *Meanjin* and many book reviews to the *Age*. She has also written entries for the *Australian Dictionary of Biography* and book reviews for *Historical Studies.*

Solid Bluestone Foundations

Memories of an Australian girlhood

KATHLEEN FITZPATRICK

Penguin Books

Penguin Books Australia Ltd.
487 Maroondah Highway, P.O. Box 257
Ringwood, Victoria, 3134, Australia
Penguin Books Ltd,
Harmondsworth, Middlesex, England
Viking Penguin Inc.,
40 West 23rd Street, New York, N.Y. 10010, U.S.A.
Penguin Books Canada Limited,
2801 John Street, Markham, Ontario, Canada L3R 1B4
Penguin Books (N.Z.) Ltd,
182-190 Wairau Road, Auckland 10, New Zealand

First published 1983 by the Macmillan Company of Australia Pty Ltd
with the assistance of the Literature Board of the Australia Council
Published in Penguin, 1986
Reprinted 1987

Offset from the Macmillan Company of Australia Pty Ltd edition
Made and printed in Australia by
The Book Printer, Maryborough, Victoria

CIP

Fitzpatrick, Kathleen, 1905- .
Solid bluestone foundations, and other memories of a
Melbourne girlhood 1908-1928.

ISBN 0 14 0087419.

1. Fitzpatrick, Kathleen, 1905- —Childhood and
youth. 2. Historians—Australia—Biography. 3.
Melbourne (Vic.)—Social life and customs—1901-1945.
I. Title

994'.007'202

To my sister Lorna and my brother John

To my sister Laura and my brother John

ACKNOWLEDGEMENTS

I thank the members of my family who have helped me to write this book: my sister Lorna Maneschi and my brother John Pitt, who shared their memories and papers with me, my cousins Dick and Frank Buxton for information about the Buxton side of the family, and my cousin David Pitt, to whom I am heavily in debt for his permission to use his research into the history of the Pitt family. I alone, however, am responsible for any opinions expressed. My youthful impressions were not necessarily the same as those of my relations and my effort has been to record those impressions truthfully rather than to ascertain and record hard facts.

CONTENTS

SOLID BLUESTONE FOUNDATIONS

I

The house where my mother's parents lived, called 'Hughenden', was the most solid and permanent fact ever to be known to me. It was my rock of ages. My own home was more like a camp for transients: I was born in a hotel and before I was out of my teens I had lived in another hotel, four houses, a boarding-school, three guest-houses and a flat. The parental caravan sometimes made long halts, but sooner or later we got our marching orders, packed up our rather sketchy household goods and moved on. But while we came and went 'Hughenden' stood firm: there the ground never quaked under our feet, we felt safe and could count on everything. At 'Hughenden' life was orderly, the gong announced meals at exactly the same time every day, Grandpa sat at his end of the table and Grandma at hers, with the uncles and aunts in between, and it would have been as astonishing if there had not been roast beef for Sunday dinner as it would have been in our house if we had predicted correctly what we might have to eat on any given day.

'Hughenden' was not, in fact, an old house. It was little more than thirty years old when I first knew it, but to me and all the other grandchildren it was historic. We knew, from family legend, that before Grandpa built 'Hughenden' Mother's people had lived in South Melbourne, but to us that was prehistory; for all we knew 'Hughenden' might have dated from that Renaissance which its architecture dimly recalled.

'Hughenden' is still standing and is now the Danish Club. Grandpa, John Robert Buxton, was wont to say that he had built his house on solid bluestone foundations and indeed he had, for, to make assurance doubly sure, he had built a whole bluestone house under the house proper, so that it was like a partly submerged iceberg. This basement proved a treasure-trove for the Danes, who now have it gaily lighted and heated, with card tables, a bar and other aids to jollity. But in my childhood this spacious catacomb was simply the cellar, and it was dark and chill. The entrance was inside the house, by a door giving on to a steep stairway and from it we could make our way to the exit to the garden through all the dim rooms and corridors intervening. 'Down the cellar' was a place of mingled fear and fascination for children. I would not have dared to enter it alone and even when led by the hand by an adult or by my fearless elder sister Lorna, I was never sure whether the thrill was worth the dread it cost.

The cellar was used as a dumping ground for unwanted domestic objects which, when seen through the murk, took on enigmatic and fearsome meanings. Some light entered a central chamber in the cellar through a sliver of window. There it was safe to pause and inspect many objects of interest. One was a large wax model, under glass, of a Hindu temple, complete with its surrounding garden of pure white palm trees. This, I always understood, was a gift from Mr Rudd, a merchant engaged in the importation of Ceylon tea, a widower who married Grandma's elder sister, Kate. I thought the wax temple the most beautiful thing I had ever seen, and wondered why it was not displayed upstairs, in the drawing-room.

'Hughenden' was what used to called a handsome house, which meant, I suppose, that although it was not really beautiful it was solid, commodious and expensive. It was certainly more imposing than comfortable. Built in the Italianate style, much favoured in Melbourne in the eighties of the last century, it was two-storeyed and grey-stuccoed, with heavy balconies supported by arches and columns, and ornamented with pilasters and Corinthian capitals. For a cool windy city such as Melbourne, 'Hughenden' was incorrectly sited and badly designed, because none of the main rooms faced north and the heavy balconies kept the sun from the rest.

Grandpa was an Englishman, who did not mind the cold but dreaded the hard colonial light and the arid heat of the few hot days of summer. When he decided to move his growing family from the long-settled district of South Melbourne, where he felt that the air was not fresh enough for children, Middle Park was a pleasant, almost rural place, with plenty of open spaces where tea-trees and wildflowers grew. It was also convenient to South Melbourne where Grandpa's business was situated, because during a depression in the seventies the Government had provided employment by constructing a boulevard, Beaconsfield Parade, to replace the old rough road which had hitherto linked South Melbourne with St Kilda. This facility encouraged settlement in the intervening wilderness of Middle Park, but not for long, as building came to a standstill when the land boom burst. When it was resumed, at the turn of the century, the age of ostentation was over and Middle Park became a lower-middle class suburb, crowded with speculative builders' mean houses on minimal frontages, among which Grandpa's boom mansion was as incongruous as a ship stranded on dry land, alone and out of hailing distance of its own kind.

The main facade of 'Hughenden' was built close to Beaconsfield Parade, a broad, bleak, wind-swept road facing Port Phillip Bay, which, during the equinoctial gales, sometimes dashed over the sea wall. There was an attempted plantation of discouraged grass down the middle of the road, but none of the English trees (which were the only ones then considered suitable for streets) could survive the wind.

In my childhood 'Hughenden' had a garden on the west side and a tennis-court, but much of the land had already been sold to keep a roof over the heads of the family during the bitter nineties and houses on each side had diminished the palatial effect. There was a high galvanized iron fence and a hedge of coprosma, that coarse, unpleasant shrub whose only virtues are greenness and the capacity to survive in the teeth of gales. At the front gate there was a flagstaff from which, on patriotic occasions, Grandpa flew the Union Jack, never our own Australian flag because he thought it disloyal of us to have a different flag from the mother country. He was not too keen on our new Commonwealth either, and was still apt to refer to Victoria as 'the colony'. It was considered a mark of Grandpa's Englishness and his view that his home was his castle that the front gate at 'Hughenden' had to be locked at night, a distrustful procedure unknown to real Australians. If one could stand the wind, it was fun to watch from the

3

front terrace as the ships passed to and fro across the bay.

The front door of 'Hughenden' was not at the front, but halfway along the west side. After we rang the door bell, we huddled with our backs to the breeze until someone came, a wait which was often longish as there were considerable distances to be traversed. The front door was huge and opened into a fine hall, broad enough to be furnished with sofas and arm-chairs and an oval walnut table, on which there stood a green jardiniere, containing an aspidistra with polished, shiny leaves. The hall led to a wide staircase with cedar banisters and brass stair-rods. The hall and stairs were covered by a carpet which was never replaced in my time and never shabby either; I have only to close my eyes to see again the precise shade of yellowish-green with a spidery red design. There was a stained glass window on the stairs but the house was rather dark, and in the dining-room, whose windows faced a high fernery, artificial light was needed even at lunch time.

The first room on the right of the hall as you entered was Grandma's drawing-room, which was charming. The carpet was green, which came to seem to me, and still does, the only proper colour for a drawing-room carpet. The mantelpiece was white marble and the snowy curtains of Nottingham lace. There was a piano, with no fingerprints on its gleaming surface, although it was constantly used; the furniture was light and graceful and included a love-seat, which I thought the very height of elegance. There were pictures on the walls, and on small tables many objects to entrance the eye of a child: pretty pieces of china and the marble statue of a beautiful lady who lacked both arms and a dress and which was, I ultimately learned, a copy of the Venus de Milo. I still see her in my brother John's drawing-room, where she lives now. As well, there were lovely flowers, the work of aunty Doone, the eldest unmarried daughter of the house. With a taste far in advance of her time, she disliked stiff arrangements and undue profusion, preferring, for the adornment of the mantelpiece, one well-shaped vase with a single bough of blossom casting an enchanting shadow on the wallpaper and, for the tables, silver christening mugs with a few primroses or a single camellia with its leaves, or even, if aunty Doone had been to the country recently, some wildflowers, a rare sight indoors in those days, when they were hardly more esteemed than weeds.

The drawing-room was essentially a feminine realm to which the men of the house rarely penetrated, except on state occasions or when there was music.

The men's chief habitat was the billiard-room, immediately beyond the drawing-room on the right of the hall. It was huge, with ample room for a full-sized billiard-table, with plenty of space left over for the family's summer sitting-room. The billiard-room was so large as to tempt the uncles, when they were children, to amuse themselves on wet days by riding round and round the billiard-table on their bicycles and legend told of a fine old row when one of them rode right through one of the closed windows on to the verandah. Billiards was frequently played at 'Hughenden' by Grandpa, his sons and sons-in-law and male guests but no female ever took cue in hand. I do not know whether billiards was thought 'fast' for women or if it was merely inconvenient for the men to share the game with them. Children were welcome everywhere and anywhere at 'Hughenden', and we had the run of everything with two exceptions, one of which was the billiard-table, which was taboo. We were told that there was a danger that we might rip the cloth and that if we did Grandpa's wrath would be terrible, a threat sufficiently alarming to keep Lorna and me from meddling with the billiard-table, but I have always suspected that my cousin Mark Pitt and my brother John, the senior grandsons, took the risk occasionally when Grandpa was known to be safely out of the house. Bridge was also much played at 'Hughenden' but, like billiards, was only for male players. I do not remember resenting this, because cards never interested me, but I did note it and wondered why men, who seemed to be so important, should spend so much time playing games, just like children.

On the left of the hall was the morning-room, very snug with its red velvet sofa and armchairs, one of which was Grandpa's, the second of the sacred artifacts at 'Hughenden'. I would as soon have thought of seating myself in one of the dread electric chairs of an American penitentiary as in Grandpa's armchair, for I was sure that a thunderbolt, similar in effect to the electric current, would certainly have followed such a blasphemy. The morning-room was worthy of its name as sunlight reached it in the morning and when that was gone we were at liberty to light the coal fire which was set for six months of the year. That huge, roaring coal fire at 'Hughenden' gave me a strong sense of luxury. In our own frugal home the grate was partly filled with bricks, to limit the consumption of coal, but Grandpa could not abide a mean fire and his will was law at 'Hughenden'. The drawing-room, as we have seen, was chiefly the province of the ladies of the house, and the billiard-room, though open to all, had a touch of a wild male tang about it, but the morning-room was the social centre of the house, where male or female might be encountered and where afternoon tea arrived punctually at half-past three and coffee at nine.

Beyond the morning-room came the dining-room, a huge room whose dimensions matched those of the billiard-room opposite. It was mostly occupied by a mahogany dining-table – at least, I believe it to have been mahogany, but never saw the wood because it was always covered with a white damask table-cloth. The table was set for the next meal immediately after the last one, just as in a hotel, with cruets and salt cellars as solid as the bluestone foundations. The fare was solid, too, for Grandpa could no more abide a poor table than a poor fire. Despite its being so dark because its windows faced the high fernery, once the electric light was on the dining-room was a cheerful place, with a red carpet, red velvet seats on the mahogany chairs, and white lace curtains. There were also two huge sideboards, bearing a well-polished array of gleaming silver, and a black marble mantelpiece with a marble clock and a procession of ebony elephants, probably the gift of that same Mr Rudd, the Ceylon connection who gave the heathen temple in the cellar. I suppose the admission of the elephants to the dining-room was intended to console him for the exile of the temple.

From the left end of the hall behind the dining-room a corridor set off on its long course to the scullery, passing the larder and the kitchen on the way. One wall of the kitchen was covered by a huge dresser, on which battalions of soup, dinner and dessert plates were ranged and scores of cups dangled from hooks, for, what with the family and the eternal visiting relations, there were rarely fewer than a dozen people for meals. There was a kitchen range kept shining with blacklead, although gas was used for cooking in my time. There was a large, scrubbed kitchen table and a smaller one at which Grandma sat to make cut lunches in the mornings, with a great joint of cold beef in front of her and all her equipment in orderly array: the loaves, a couple of pounds of butter, the mustard already mixed, the salt and pepper, a well-sharpened carving knife and a bowl of hot water, frequently renewed from the scullery, for heating the knife used for softening and spreading the butter. During this rite any grandchildren staying in the house clustered round to gobble up the crusts, rich with butter and fragments of cold beef, which Grandma sliced off so deftly and rapidly.

Beyond the kitchen was the scullery, where the maid washed and the aunts dried the dishes, occasionally with the reluctant help of grandchildren. Upstairs there were six bedrooms for the family and one for the maid, and a room for which I had a special affection, known as the schoolroom, which had once, I suppose, been the nursery. The schoolroom was one of the few rooms reached by the sun and, as well, was the most informal of the rooms to sit in. Although as clean and orderly as everywhere else at 'Hughenden' it was the repository for bits of furniture that were too good for permanent retirement to the cellar but too shabby for the more public rooms downstairs. There was nothing of which a child had to be careful in the schoolroom, where everything already carried what Grandpa used to refer to most unjustly, as 'the family brand', which was merely the inevitable wear-and-tear of continuous use by his nine children, followed by that of his nineteen grandchildren, of whom Lorna and I were the *avant garde*. I loved to sit in the schoolroom doing my homework where I knew my mother had done hers, and even better, to sit at my ease in the battered bentwood rocking-chair by the sunny window, having a quiet time reading a book. Upstairs was completed by a single bathroom for the whole household.

Miles away (as it seemed to young children) downstairs, past the fernery, along the verandah, out into the garden, past the shrubbery and on into the backyard, there was an outside lavatory where I could go if desperate, which happened sometimes as the only one in the house was in the bathroom. There was a whole complex of buildings in the backyard. There was a laundry with troughs, a mangle, an ironing-table, skirt-board and a copper which, from time to time, became a great centre of interest for children when it was used as a cooking vessel. There, gallons of tomato sauce and green tomato pickle were cooked and bottled and in the soft fruit season Grandma made enough damson plum jam to last a whole year. Into its bubbling waters were plunged, months before Christmas, the mammoth plum pudding and, in Christmas week, the ham for Christmas dinner. Beyond the laundry were the stables and a vast coachhouse, full of disused vehicles and harness, which became a garage in my time, and there were various other offices of which I never grasped the precise significance.

In the backyard, too, Grandpa carried on his cultivation of flowers in what could not really be called a garden. It was a rectangular excavation in a prevailing sea of asphalt, well filled with soil and smelly manure and bristling with stakes in precise measured rows, where the more boring types of flowers, such as dahlias and oversized chrysanthemums, were grown as if for the market. Everyone despised poor Grandpa's plantation, but not too openly, because the manual labour gave him needed occupation and exercise, and besides, it suited everyone to have him out of the house for a few hours every day.

II

Those who lived at 'Hughenden' were known to us collectively as 'the Hughendens'. To be a Hughenden, we thought, one had actually to live there and we did not regard as Hughendens members of the family who had forfeited the title by marrying and setting up domiciles of their own. When my memories begin, only two of the nine children had left home, Mother and her married sister, Kathleen, always known at Kit. So there were, in 1908, nine Hughendens. Grandpa and Grandma, aunty Doone, aunty Dot, uncle Ray, uncle Tom, uncle Jack and Astley and Len, the last two still schoolboys, to whom we did not give the title of uncle. As time went on, four of the boys married and ceased to be Hughendens proper, but aunty Doone, aunty Dot and uncle Jack were Hughendens right to the end.

The house that Grandpa built and Grandma administered was almost like a hotel, there were so many comings and goings. Grandpa's relations, being English, were rather formal and visited 'Hughenden' only at stated times and with their gloves on, so to speak. But Grandma's family, who were Irish-Australian, and the Australian grandchildren, were less home-loving and more prone to dropping in. 'Hughenden' was an ideal place for that, because ten to one both the host and hostess would be at home. Grandpa retired from business when he was fifty and throughout my childhood he was about the house all day. Grandma sometimes paid afternoon calls but otherwise her duties kept her at home. It was her organising ability which caused the house to run on oiled wheels. Not only was there the large family proper to be provided for and the married uncles and aunts and their children constantly visiting and being persuaded, without much difficulty, to stay for meals, but there were also Grandma's relations from the country: the O'Briens from Nar-Nar-Goon and the Bolands from near Maffra. When occasions brought them to town from time to time they put up, as a matter of course, at 'Hughenden'. There were also friends of the O'Briens and the Bolands, and friends that my parents made during the years they lived at Omeo, and relations of the relations and friends of the friends – they all came to stay at 'Hughenden'.

We, the grandchildren, all considered that we had a perfect right, whenever it suited us, to descend on 'Hughenden'. We knew that leaves could be added readily to the dining-table, and there was sure to be plenty in the larder. We drew up our chairs to the table with perfect assurance of our welcome and the knowledge that if we decided to stay the night, or any number of nights, we were at liberty to do so. As I look back, I am appalled at the amount of work we all caused and how we took the 'Hughenden' largesse for granted. Only one servant was kept and though additional servants came in for the washing and heavy cleaning, both Grandma and aunty Doone, her right hand help, led very hardworking lives. As for Grandpa, he must have had to pay frightful bills, but although not a man to suffer in silence any grievance, real or imagined, no one ever heard him complain of the cost of keeping open house.

'Hughenden' was a paradise for grandchildren. To begin with, we were never asked why we had come or how long we intended to stay. This made it an ideal place for the purpose of running away from home. Earlier attempts which I had made at running away to nowhere in particular had proved unsatisfactory. When one had eaten the bag of bananas bought with the idea that it would provide sustenance for weeks, and night was falling and there was no prospect of dinner, there was really nothing for it but to run tamely home again. The whole procedure was lacking in dignity and even in drama, because Mother, who was absent-minded, had probably not even noticed my absence. But if I ran away to 'Hughenden', as I soon learned to do, my enterprise was richly rewarded. Everyone seemed delighted to see me, I felt more highly valued than at home. It was true that Grandma or one of the aunts would soon be on the telephone to Mother. They lowered their voices but could still be heard because in those days telephones were always sociably located where everyone could hear the conversation. I did not really mind Mother's being told where I was, as being now comfortable and happy, I did not want her punished too severely for whatever she had done to cause my flight.

I could not analyse it when I was a child but was as aware then as now that part of the fascination of 'Hughenden' arose from its comprising a larger and more varied community and a richer storehouse of human experience than was available in what is now called the nuclear home. Our home was perhaps more restricted than most because Mother's shyness and her hatred of domestic chores meant that we had few visitors.

'Hughenden' stretched back into the past to the 'Old Country', to England itself, and specifically to Kent, where Grandpa had lived as a boy. He had also been to a boarding-school at Chiswick, where he had had ale for breakfast every morning. Ale, we knew, was English for beer – what an extraordinary thing to give a child for breakfast, we thought, really like something in a tale by Charles Dickens! Grandma, who was Australian born, represented another tradition, that of life in the bush in the olden days when there were blacks, even in Victoria.

But despite its backward reach, 'Hughenden' also represented for us the very frontier of modern progress. When our own home was still lighted by gas, which made an alarming pop when turned on, 'Hughenden' was already resplendent with electric light, and it was some years before we caught up with 'Hughenden' by having a telephone installed. At 'Hughenden' hot water came out of taps in the kitchen and bathroom, but at our place we had to boil kettles of water for washing dishes and wash ourselves in cold water except for the weekly plunge-bath on Saturdays, for which there was a rather anxious lighting of a temperamental bath-heater. When we wanted to get anywhere we walked or took the train or tram, but at 'Hughenden' they were pioneers of motor transport; Grandpa owned a Wolseley motor car and the elder boys dashed about on motor cycles. At 'Hughenden' they had the first gramophone I ever heard or saw: an Edison. The records were cylindrical and limited in number; bought, I imagine, by Grandpa when he acquired the machine and never added to, because he was like a child in the swift waxing and waning of his enthusiasm for new toys. His tastes were unsophisticated and songs by Harry Lauder and Peter Dawson and comic records by negroes pretty well exhausted the collection, but for us the medium was indeed the message and as long as the marvellous machine would sing and talk we asked no more.

Father was a public servant and so were all the male members of his family and their father before them. We heard a certain amount about *res publica* at home but nothing whatever about business: we were as remote from the operations of capitalism as if the government Father served had been that of the Lancastrian or Yorkist kings. At 'Hughenden', however, one heard the busy hum of the market-place because the Firm (as it was always called) was the family estate agency of J.R. Buxton & Sons, and the home was so interwoven with the Firm as to be inseparable. All the grown-up sons of the house worked for the Firm and often came home for lunch bringing the latest news from the business front. At lunch on Saturdays there were discussions as to what the properties to be offered at auction in the afternoon might bring. Grandpa was often spruced up on Saturdays in his best blue suit because, although so long retired from the Firm, it was conceded by his sons, who were by no means uncritical of him, that he was a dab hand at an auction and he was called on if the sale were an important one or likely to prove difficult. On Saturday nights and at midday dinner on Sunday there were post mortems about what the properties offered had brought or should have brought if things had gone better. Money was never a topic of conversation in our house, but at 'Hughenden' they talked about it often, referring to enormous sums with a familiarity that amazed us.

Pervasive as this urban and commercial atmosphere was, it was often diversified by the presence of primary producers, Grandma's relations from the country, the spud-growing O'Briens and dairy-farming Bolands with whose wholly different lives we also became familiar. Perhaps the most fascinating of all to me was the life of Mary O'Brien, one of the daughters of Grandma's brother Patrick, of Nar-Nar-Goon. Grandma called her Mary Pat in the Irish way, to distinguish her from the many other Marys in the family, but she was called Mary O. by the rest of us. Mary O. was the first middle-class woman I ever met who, instead of being supported by her husband or her father, earned her own living, because she was unmarried and the Pat O'Briens were poor. She was an itinerant dressmaker, working chiefly for her relations, and she used to stay in the house she was working in. Her base was a small rented room somewhere, which I never saw, and where she must have managed somehow between engagements. Mary O. had had no formal training in her craft, she had just picked it up and her grasp of it was somewhat infirm. She was to be relied on, the ladies of our family said, in the making of curtains and was really good at covering chairs and sofas, but she found the human form more intractable and the dresses she made lacked style and were apt to be too skimpy in some places and too full in others.

Mary O. loved children and was very patient with our constant presence underfoot among the fascinating snippets of material that strewed the floor around the whirring Singer sewing machine, and our constant demands to be told, all over again, about her life as a child at Nar-Nar-Goon. As an elder sister, that must have included a good deal of child-minding, because Mary O. knew a great many rhymes for children and I made her repeat my favourite, 'Little Kitty Cottontail', hundreds of times. I loved Mary O. but always noticed a shade of reserve in the relations between her and Mother and the aunts. I think now that they envied her status as a self-supporting, independent woman who did not have to put up with the selfishness of men or the tantrums of children. Although they knew that Mary O. did not earn much and never wasted a minute of the time she was paid for, they rather resented her professional attitude, which was that she came to their houses to sew and not to lend a hand in general. They never failed to remark, when Mary O. was not within hearing, how odd it was that she never offered to help with the washing up or to make a cup of tea. I hotly resented this criticism and pointed out that other people who earned their livings, like the uncles and Father, did not wash up or make tea either. That, my elders told me, was beside the point; women's work did not count in the same way as men's and they should always be willing to postpone it when good manners demanded. This argument infuriated me, but Mary O. may have been somewhat at fault, too; resentment against women who had fathers and husbands to provide them with good homes and pay the bills may have made the poor seamstress, whose lot it was to spend her life in other women's houses, a bit prickly and inflexible in a family situation.

Dear Mary O! She lived to a great age and continued her hardworking, solitary life almost to the end. In her old age she lived in a house of her own, bought out of her savings, God knows by what miracles of economy, for even her critics admitted that 'her terms were reasonable', meaning cheap. She never went for holidays or outings or had any fun, but year in year out was chained to her machine, or down on her knees wrestling with hems that were never, for all her efforts, perfectly straight, or dealing, in a way everyone acknowledged to be masterly, with a refractory bulge in a sofa-cover. Mary O. was tall and thin and bony, very Irish-looking, with dark hair and dark blue eyes. Well dressed she would have looked handsome, but although always clean and neat she never had any clothes that suited her for the simple reason that she never had any that were bought or made expressly for her. She had only old ones given by her customers and altered, more or less to fit, by herself in periods of unemployment.

III

Both Grandma and Grandpa loved and indulged their grandchildren. Grandpa in particular, who had a good deal of the child still about him, had a natural affinity with us and knew the kind of treats that delight children most. When we were staying at 'Hughenden' we knew that, before he went to bed, generally at some weird hour such as 3 am, Grandpa would have set out on the smoking table beside his bed a bar of Cadbury's Mexican chocolate for each child in the house and that we might go into his room as soon as we woke up, even if it were at first light, to take our share. Grandpa also had very comfortable ideas about bedtimes: he did not see why we should go to bed before we wanted to, he never had himself. On Saturday mornings we were entitled to claim 'Saturday money' from Grandpa of a penny each, a most welcome doubling of the same stipend accumulating for us at home. Sometimes when the first course of dinner was being served at 'Hughenden', Grandpa would say: 'What if we all went to the theatre?' 'All', in this context, meant him and us, the children, and it must have been maddening for Grandma and the aunts to see us gobbling our meal and bolting from a table in disarray in search of coats and hats. The famous Wolseley was never driven at nights – perhaps because it was driven only by the chauffeur, who had probably gone home by then. This chauffeur was rather an exotic, a Frenchman, it

14

was said, and his name was Ganard (or that is how it sounded to us). He had been the coachman before he was the chauffeur and had been in Grandpa's service a long time when one day he suddenly disappeared for ever. The grown-ups refused to tell us what had become of him, but somehow we found out that poor Ganard had committed suicide, but were never able to learn why. In any case, we went to the theatre by public transport, sprinting along Beaconsfield Parade to The Avenue, where there was a cable tram to the city. There was no need for all this haste and drama. Grandpa had had all day to decide on going to the theatre and dinner could have been served earlier, which would have been more convenient for everyone, but that would have spoilt Grandpa's surprise and our delirious joy at a treat falling straight from heaven.

Going to the theatre with Grandpa was great fun because he took the child's view that an outing is an outing, and his pleasure in an entertainment – any entertainment, but especially a comic one – was not sicklied o'er with the pale cast of *l'esprit critique*. He laughed at the funny bits just as heartily as we did and much more loudly, because he was entirely uninhibited, whereas Lorna and I were convent-bred and on our best behaviour in public. In summer we were taken to *The Pierrots* instead of to the theatre. *The Pierrots* were a troupe of entertainers who appeared regularly, every summer, in the gardens at the Esplanade, St Kilda. They always wore pierrot dress for the opening and closing choruses, but in between the men affected white trousers, blazers, straw hats and twirling walking-sticks, and the girls had saucy summer dresses in bright colours. An evening at *The Pierrots* combined the delights of entertainment with those of a picnic. Our second-best clothes were good enough and we could lick ice-cream cones to our heart's content, a plebeian delight which Lorna and I knew to be *infra dig.* in the grandeur of a proper theatre.

I do not associate Luna Park, at the other end of the Esplanade, with Grandpa, and I think our visits there must have come later: Grandpa tended to lose interest in children when they turned into girls and boys. Luna Park was a treat on a more sophisticated level than *The Pierrots* because there the inevitable 'refreshments' which formed such an important part of our youthful outings were not consumed in a gross, ambulatory fashion, but at the first soda-fountain bar I ever saw. The Luna Park soda-fountain was a place of unimaginable splendour, where one sat at little round marble-topped tables and watched the marvellous speed and skill with which the men behind the counter, on which lamps of many colours glittered like jewels, made ice-cream sodas and peach Melbas and banana splits and glorious complicated sundaes with enormous dollops of whipped cream and elaborate, edible decorations.

Going to the theatre or *The Pierrots* were special treats, but even without such peaks of experience there were always lots of interesting things for children to do at 'Hughenden'. We did not frequent the beach much. In winter it was too cold and windy, and in summer it was feared that we would get sunburnt, even in the mushroom hats with the detested gossamer veils which Lorna and I were compelled to wear to protect our complexions. There was also still some doubt in the minds of our elders as to the propriety of the new 'mixed bathing' that was coming in at the time. I well remember the municipal notices which prescribed, for this frolic, the wearing of 'neck to knee' bathing gowns, with dire penalties for those who offended against modesty. But we could collect the eggs in Grandma's poultry yard, or feed the canaries in the aviary, or potter among the tree-ferns in the fernery, all amenities which did not exist in our more modest home. We loved roaming in the shrubbery, a controlled wilderness full of sweet-smelling flowers, such as violets, jonquils, primroses and daphne, and it was from a pink-and-white striped specimen in the 'Hughenden' shrubbery that I gained my life-long love of camellias. The shrubbery was ideal for all games which included the practice of hiding. My sister Lorna had a spice of the devil in her, although she was considered a perfect child by our elders, as indeed she nearly was. Bad boys used to steal the figs that grew in the shrubbery. Lorna invented a very imaginative game of climbing the fig-tree and hiding in it until the robbers came when she revealed herself, uttered weird shrieks and pretended to be raving mad, a performance which, I remember, frightened her little sister much more than the horrid, hardened boys.

On wet days we played at dressing-up in the schoolroom, because it was there that the big box was kept. This was a huge wooden trunk with brass corners in which, it was said, Grandpa's possessions had come out from England with him in 1869 in the *Great Britain*. It contained scraps of material from all the dressmaking that had ever gone on at 'Hughenden', together with lengths of ribbon, bags of sequins, feathers, artificial flowers, silk cords and cards of gimp. If I stayed long enough I could furbish up my doll's wardrobe by making her woollen dresses for winter, muslin ones for summer and splendid evening gowns or a wedding dress of silk or satin.

Another special treat for little girls was watching our beautiful aunty Dot, Mother's youngest sister, getting dressed for the races or a ball. This was a lengthy process because aunty Dot, who adored clothes and fashion, had many garments to choose from in her closet, racks of dresses, piles of band-boxes containing hats, parasols, innumerable shoes in boxes and, in her chest of drawers, gloves and scarves of many colours, all carefully done up in white tissue paper. Aunty Dot was hard to please, so each occasion was a fashion parade, in which she tried on, if she were going to the races, hat after hat, while Lorna and I oh'd and ah'd, preferring this one and looking with disfavour upon that. Preparation for a ball was even more protracted because aunty Dot had to apply a sticky fluid to all the parts of her that were to be bare, in order to make her skin look white, and then soften the effect of this icing with abundant powder. When all was done and the flower was fastened in her hair and her ear-rings were screwed on, aunty Dot added the finishing touch by rubbing her lips with red geranium petal; more than that would have been 'fast' in the days before the First World War.

We knew that once upon a time when Mother was a little girl, Grandpa and Grandma had been rich, and then they had been poor, but when we were children they were what was then called 'comfortable'. Housekeeping at 'Hughenden' was on a more lavish scale than in our own home, where there was enough but not to spare. Grandma was to be heard regularly on the telephone giving splendid grocery orders to the Mutual Store and to the butcher, and, on Friday, to the fishmonger.

Fruit and vegetables were bought, in huge quantities, at the South Melbourne market. In the larder, the door of which was always open, there were tins of biscuits and a well-stocked cake-box. We were at liberty to ruin our teeth by taking whole handfuls of loaf sugar from an earthenware crock. In summer we were allowed endless swigs of ginger beer that came in stone jars from that Mutual Store whence, it seemed to us, all blessings flowed, and which Mother did not patronise because it was too dear for us. In the davenport in the morning-room there was an abundance of wonderful writing-paper, the thickest of cream bond, which we used lavishly for writing and drawing and even for playing noughts and crosses. Brought up as we were in severe economy, 'Hughenden' gave us the occasional luxury of full and plenty.

A lax attitude prevailed at 'Hughenden' towards book-learning, a subject which was taken very seriously by our parents. Mother and Father were at one in their determination that we should go beyond their frontier, matriculation, and absorb every scrap of education of which we were intellectually capable: it was for this that they were saving. We were never pushed nor punished for not distinguishing ourselves at school, but we were expected to try and our parents would stand no nonsense from us in matters scholastic. If we pleaded indisposition in order to avoid going to school, we were told that the doctor would be called, and if we were not really ill that got us up and off to school without more ado. There was no possibility of an escape from homework or school attendance by way of a note of excuse from Father or Mother; if we had failed to do our homework or played the wag we were told to accept the responsibility and face the music alone. Schooling was taken less seriously at 'Hughenden'. If, while staying there, we hinted at a cold or even a headache, Grandma was only too ready to pen that excuse that could never be gouged out of our parents; we stayed in bed and read books and were pampered with good things to eat on trays. None of the family at 'Hughenden' ever aspired to higher education and when, in the course of time, all Mother's children went to the university, we were regarded as prodigies of cleverness and learning at 'Hughenden', and Grandma was always afraid we would overstrain our brains or at least ruin our eyesight. At heart I thought all this was silly and was on my parents' side in the matter of education, but an occasional change to the indulgent atmosphere of 'Hughenden' was very enjoyable.

Except for Mother and aunty Kit, none of the 'Hughenden' family was bookish. There were two books in Grandma's bedroom, her prayer-book and *The Imitation of Christ,* and I never saw her read any other. Grandpa was said to have been a great reader of Dickens in his youth, and owned the *Works* in a good illustrated edition, on which I feasted before the morning-room fire, but I never saw him reading them. Aunty Doone read weak, silly novels from a circulating library. Aunty Dot went in for bouts of self-improvement and for years, it seemed to me, she carried Carlyle's *French Revolution* about with her, hoping, I suppose, to take it in by osmosis. She was always settling down, with much arrangement of a comfortable chair and a good light, to get on with Carlyle, but her concentration was poor and she did not get on and I am sure she never finished it. The uncles read magazines and sometimes light books with paper covers. But the whole family read the daily papers with passion, the *Argus* and the *Age* in the morning and the *Herald* at night. At every hour of the day or night some member of the family was engaged in reading the papers. They also read items from them aloud, a habit as unnecessary as it was maddening, as everyone had either read the news already or was just about to. The uncles, I suppose, omitted the fashions and the recipes, and Grandma and the aunts did not read the sporting pages, but everything was covered by someone. Grandpa fulminated over the leading articles and the political news, and never failed to observe that the country was going to the dogs, and Grandma was an authority on births, deaths and marriages. Aunty Dot was addicted to the social columns, which were very extensive in those days, furnishing detailed descriptions of what everyone wore to every ball in Melbourne, and she had a faculty, mysterious to me to this day, of knowing who was related to whom and how, so that, after observing that she saw in the paper that a Mrs Daly, say, had given a party, she would add that of course Mrs Daly had been one of the Brennan girls and her mother a Madden.

At 'Hughenden' the advertisements were read with the

same unfailing relish as the news. Real estate was in the blood, but I never could see why it was of so much interest to everyone to learn that there was a four-bedroom house for sale in Hawthorn or a weatherboard, single-fronted cottage to let in Fitzroy, when neither of these dwellings was of pro-fessional interest by reason of being in the hands of the Firm nor was anyone in the family in need of a house in Hawthorn or a cottage in Fitzroy. No reason, of course, was necessary. They just loved the papers and were *virtuosi* of the news. As well as all the newspapers delivered at the house there were spare copies brought home by the uncles or by anyone who, being from home, was suddenly taken with a craving to read the paper. There were always mountains of old newspapers at 'Hughenden', which had to be smoothed out and stacked up for the greengrocer and the fishmonger, or cut into neat oblongs by us, the children, for use in the outside lavatory.

IV

'Hughenden', I somehow understood quite early, was not an intellectual treat; what it provided for was our social and sensuous life. No children, we were sure, had Christmases to equal ours at 'Hughenden'. We knew the routine by heart and loved it and would have found any variation as distasteful as changes in reading aloud of 'Cinderella' or 'Snow White and Rose Red'. All the married Buxtons and their spouses and children arrived at 'Hughenden' in the morning, in good time for Christmas dinner at one o'clock. About twenty could be accommodated at the dining-table and there were sometimes small tables for the very little children. The table was all snowy damask and holly and greenery and silver dishes filled with dried muscatels and blanched Jordan almonds. The immense turkey and the ham were already in place before Grandma, who always carved. She was a wonderful carver and the great bird seemed to recognize the hand of a master and to attempt no resistance. The meat fairly flew from the bones under Grandma's surgery and each helping, with its correct ratio of dark to light meat, its just share of seasoning and its slice of ham, was passed to Grandma's left where aunty Doone presided over the vegetable dishes, frequently refilled from the kitchen. What the adults drank at Christmas dinner I do not remember, because it was of no interest to me. Doubtless they had good alcoholic cheer for 'Hughenden' was by no means a teetotal establishment. The children drank nectar, or so it seemed, the rosy blissful raspberry vinegar of yesteryear.

Of course there was plum pudding, and its blazing entrance and triumphal march round the dining-table to Grandma's end was a stirring spectacle, as one had only to turn the light out to make the room dark enough, even at midday in summer. I have always disliked plum pudding but would not have dreamt of refusing my portion, which I pushed round my plate till I found the treasure. One could be sure of finding a shining new threepenny bit and might be lucky enough to find a second one, pudding-encrusted. It seemed odd that no child ever failed to receive one of those shining silver coins, while a puddingy one was all that adults could hope for, and did not always get. As one grew older and sharper, one suspected Grandma of sleight of hand, which of course she did practise, but so skilfully that even when I meanly watched I never caught a glimpse of her silver hoard or saw her adding a coin from it to a child's designated portion.

The time between Christmas dinner and afternoon tea was the least satisfactory part of the day for Lorna and me. Our plan was to disappear quickly and to begin reading the books our parents had given us for Christmas. As the eldest grand-daughters, however, we had little or no chance of escaping the obvious duty – at least it was obvious to Mother – of lending a hand at drying dishes in the scullery. That done, we made our second attempt at disappearance, but usually in vain. Our married aunt, and the wives of our married uncles, soporific after Christmas dinner and a day that had begun at dawn, wanted a good lie-down and were on the prowl for baby-minders and our mother, basely and untruthfully, asserted that Lorna and I would be only too pleased to oblige. We were not pleased but furious, but could hardly refuse on Christmas Day. Our ordeal seemed long, but cannot have been, for soon the gong would announce that afternoon tea was ready, and our sufferings were recompensed with abundant Christmas cake and as many slices as we wanted of aunty Doone's famous sponge, with thin, crackly, white coconut icing.

During the interval between Christmas dinner and the ending of afternoon tea, the morning-room was out of bounds to children. As we ate our cake, always in the hall on Christmas day and never in the drawing-room or billiard-room, for reasons I cannot now recall, we could hear queer bumping noises, lowered voices and suppressed laughter behind the closed door of the morning-room. We knew it would open soon, but it was hard to wait and the grown-ups were dreadfully selfish, wanting second cups of tea and sipping them slowly and chattily instead of drinking them down and having done. Finally, however, the gong rang again, the door of the morning-room was thrown open, and in we all filed, youngest children first, to the Christmas tree. Santa Claus was always in the very act of arriving, from the chimney obviously, as he was just stepping out of the fender. As we grew older he seemed, despite his red robes and white whiskers, to look more and more like uncle Ray, but as older children we knew better than to say so. The old familiar morning-room was transformed into fairyland on Christmas Day. It was in darkness, except for the Christmas tree in the bow window, on which the sparklets had just been lit and were now spilling in brilliant crystal streams down the green branches of the tree, a wild cherry which our O'Brien relations at Nar Nar Goon always cut down and sent by rail to Melbourne for the 'Hughenden' Christmas. Christmas trees were not common when I was a child, at least not in the circles in which we moved. We never had one in our own home, nor were there any in those of our cousins or school-friends; in my earliest years I regarded them as peculiar to 'Hughenden'. Santa Claus gave everyone a present from the Christmas tree. I think they must have been very modest little offerings, for I do not remember attaching any importance to them as possessions: they were more in the nature of symbols of participation. To me, certainly, the tree was not a source of material wealth, but a vision of beauty.

It might be thought that after the dinner and the Christmas

tree we would have had the decency to go home. Not a bit of it. We were in our Christmas stride and nothing could halt the rites of our tribe before their appointed time. We were all hungry again by now and it was time to go back to the dining-room for our cold evening meal. More turkey and ham, many plates of thin bread and butter (white tin loaf, cut diagonally and arranged in double rows, according to the 'Hughenden' ritual); bowls of salad made of finely shredded lettuce and hard-boiled eggs and dressing, and jars of pickles and chutney. This laid a solid foundation for the puddings, which were glorious. Apple Snow, Floating Islands, mince pies and trifle with pints of cream. We had some of each and rose from the table feeling sickish. We soon forgot that, however, because now, for the first time in the day, we were all going into the drawing-room to sing.

Aunty Dot was in charge of this part of Christmas Day and her social genius made everything go with a swing. She and Mother and aunty Kit played the piano and nearly everyone could sing. The exceptions were Grandma, aunty Doone and I, the difference between them and me being that they knew their limitations and remained silent, while I did not and brayed happily out of tune. We began and ended with a mass attack on *Adeste Fideles,* sung (by even the smallest child, who did not understand a word of it) in Church Latin: Grandpa, who was Protestant, did not attend this Popish manifestation. Aunty Dot had a lovely voice, a sweet but quite powerful mezzo-soprano. She always gave us a solo, usually *Down in the Forest* or *Four by the Clock* by request. Uncle Jack had a pleasing tenor voice, but was too shy for solos: we noticed the quality of his voice in our choruses. Uncle Astley (always known as 'Ack') was not in the least shy; in his good but untrained baritone he obliged with *Trumpeter, What Are You Sounding Now?,* which I thought tremendously dramatic and affecting. Then we all sang round the piano, Gilbert and Sullivan and some Christmas carols, and ended with *Adeste Fideles* all over again, as aunty Doone brought in the coffee tray that signalled the end of Christmas. It was time for all the babies to be taken up and the toddlers to be awakened and for the whole flock of now rather fretful children and their parents to take themselves off home by public transport, reached after a good long walk. How tired we all were! It never occurred to us to think how tired the family was at 'Hughenden'. They had been preparing for weeks and had entertained us the whole day.

V

In the earliest 'Hughenden' days that I remember, Grandma had a little pony-cart in which she went once a week to the South Melbourne market, and took any resident grandchildren with her. Ganard the chauffeur did not attend on these occasions. Grandma took the reins herself, and very capably because she had been a country girl brought up to horses. Oh, the bliss of these excursions, and the feeling of ineffable superiority it gave us to spank along Beaconsfield Parade behind the plump little pony, to the accompaniment, one felt, of the envious sighs of the pedestrians, mere plodding peasants as they appeared from our elevation. It was fun at the market, too, to follow Grandma around the fruit and vegetable stalls, in those days all kept by slant-eyed Orientals, each and every one of whom seemed to have, or anyway to be addressed by, the same name, which was 'John'.

On the way home we would be sure, if it were summer, to hear the merry tinkle of the ice-cream cart. Grandma had strict views on the subject of ice-cream carts. Most ice-cream carts, she averred, were dirty and dire results, such as tummy-ache or even going to hospital, could follow indiscriminate patronage. One ice-cream cart, however, she assured us (as if we cared!) was clean and wholesome and the owner of it was called Joe the Liar. Even at a tender age that struck me as an odd name for a man considered by Grandma to be of such exceptional integrity, but Joe the Liar she called him and so did everyone else. I suppose the poor man was an exiled Neapolitan and that his name was a corruption of some Italian name considered unpronounceable in the days when Britannia really ruled the waves and it was not thought necessary even to try to give foreigners their real names. For us there was always a slight element of worry about whether we might fail to encounter Joe the Liar and come home from our visit to the market without ice-cream, but Grandma would never have allowed children to be disappointed and I am sure she knew where to find him in what were, to us, the trackless wilds of South Melbourne.

To the family at 'Hughenden', South Melbourne did not represent trackless wilds but the cradle of their race. The solid bluestone foundations of 'Hughenden' rested on a still deeper foundation, the Firm, whose headquarters were in Clarendon Street, South Melbourne. This estate agency had been founded by W.P. Buckhurst, Grandpa's uncle, in 1861. Mr Buckhurst prospered and built himself a fine house in St Vincent's Place, South Melbourne, and also as a speculation the splendid Rochester Terrace on the opposite side of the Place. In 1869 Grandpa – John Robert Buxton, a lad of seventeen – was sent out from England to join his uncle in business. He must have been industrious and capable, because within six years he was in a position to marry, and in the 'eighties he was admitted to partnership and the Firm became Buckhurst and Buxton. Like other estate agencies it throve during the Land Boom. Mr Buckhurst moved away from South Melbourne and built himself a mansion, 'Goodrest', in Toorak Road, South Yarra, which is still standing and in good order, but its fallen status to that of business premises is proclaimed by the grounds now being used as a car park.

When W.P. Buckhurst retired Grandpa became the head of the Firm, and as son after son followed him into the business it was called J.R. Buxton & Sons. It still flourishes, as J.R. Buxton Pty Ltd, and is still a family business: the managing director is now Frank Buxton, one of the younger grandsons, and some of the great-grandsons are members of the Firm. In my day, and until recent times, the Firm had an office in town in Collins Street, but now, like many other businesses, it has retreated from the city proper. It has branches all down the Bay, but the South Melbourne office, which still exists, was the original one and South Melbourne is the Buxton heartland.

It was in South Melbourne that Grandpa lived when he first came to Australia, though it then bore the more romantic and now inexplicable name of Emerald Hill. It was to South Melbourne that Grandpa's family came out from England to join him as colonists, his father and mother, and his sisters Lizzie and Polly and, afterwards, his brother Dick, who tried life in Ceylon first. I remember my great-grandfather, Richard Raymond Buxton, very well, as a frail old man in perpetual dressing-gown and a black velvet skull-cap, by then a widower living with his daughter Polly, Mrs Len Lloyd. I was very proud of having a living great-grandfather when many girls I knew were already so death-denuded as not to have even a grandfather; but I suspect now that the poor old gentleman was not fully *compos mentis* in the days when I used to brag about him for I do not remember his ever speaking a word.

Grandpa's mother, known in the family as Granny, died before my time, but Mother had been devoted to her and told us so much about Granny that I felt as if I had really known her. When Mother was a child her Buxton grandparents had lived in Sutton Place, South Melbourne, at Sutton House, which was not the grand place its name suggests, but a sweet little cottage with snowy white curtains and potted geraniums on the window-sills, and the loveliest garden, laid out so artfully by Grandpa's brother, uncle Dick, with a grape arbour, winding paths and cleverly contrived vistas, that it looked much larger than it really was. Granny's was a frugal little establishment, but so spotless and Granny so good a manager that the simplest meal at Sutton House was a banquet for her eldest grandchild. Poor Mother! I do not think she was ever so happy as when visiting Granny. She spoke of Sutton House as of a paradise lost until the day she died. What Mother really loved, I think, was the peace and quiet and getting away from 'Hughenden' for a while. She was the eldest of nine children and from her earliest childhood until her marriage there was always a baby in the house or on the way; her youngest brother, Len, was only three years older than her own eldest child, my sister Lorna. The coming event was never openly alluded to at 'Hughenden' but Mother learnt to expect one when the bassinet was brought up from the cellar again and Grandma did it over in fresh white muslin. Mother was a dreamy, bookish girl with no vocation for domestic life. When the hubbub of the younger children and the bore of baby-minding became too much for her, the quiet and order of 'Sutton House' and her Granny's undivided attention was her ivory tower. Her own mother loved her children dearly, but could never give undivided attention to any one of them.

Grandpa's two sisters, Lizzie and Polly, both remained for life in Melbourne. Polly, the younger and pretty one, married a prosperous business man, Leonard Lloyd, of the firm of Eliza Tinsley & Co. The Lloyd family lived close to the Albert Park station in a very queer house with the very odd name of 'Lo-e-lo'. The house was queer because it consisted of two terrace houses joined together, so that it had four staircases and the drawing-room was like a tram car, very long, though, I suppose, not really narrow, but it looked so because the proportions were wrong. Why the house was called 'Lo-e-lo' and what the name signified I never thought to enquire. 'Lo-e-lo' always seemed to me the epitome of Englishness, I do not remember it as at all pretty. Indeed, the brown velvet-covered chairs and sofas in the drawing-room struck me as dismal, but the standards of housekeeping were of the highest and had it not been rather dark one could have seen one's face in all the mahogany and cedar; a detail that sticks in my mind is that at 'Lo-e-lo' all the electric light bulbs were taken down and thoroughly washed every week. I remember hearing that despite the sparkle of all the woodwork, no furniture polish was used, only elbow-grease. It was years before I discovered what that was and I often wondered why Mother did not buy some for use in our house since it was so efficacious.

There was plenty of elbow-grease available at 'Lo-e-lo' where two servants were kept, of whom one, an elderly retainer, was known by the extraordinary name of 'Waah'. The Lloyds went in for very odd names. The daughters of the house were called Toots and Goo, misleading names because they were very ladylike women. Toots was the domestic one: she dusted every ugly object in the drawing-room every day. Goo was the artistic one. She was really musical, a good performer both on the violin and piano; she played the violin in Alberto Zelman's orchestra and gave music lessons. She was devoted to music and taught it literally for love because, as the Lloyds were well-to-do people, her father would not allow her to accept payment for lessons. She taught Lorna the piano and was a very important influence in her life. She tried to teach me, too, but I was so lacking both in talent and in application that Mother soon withdrew me, thinking, quite rightly, that a serious artist's time ought not to be wasted on hopeless material. Goo had a very sweet nature and every morning, while Toots did the dusting, Goo entertained her by playing popular songs and bits from comic opera in which her sister, who had no musical culture, delighted.

I never, alas, knew my great-aunt Lizzie, who was dead before my time, but I wish I had. She was Mother's favourite aunt and Mother often told us about her. Aunty Lizzie was, according to Mother, highly intelligent and sensitive. She had been a governess in the Old Country, and had developed the letter-writing habit as a homesick girl in other people's houses. Her earliest post had been at an establishment called Swale House, where she had been very unhappy and whence she had written home at great length. In our family a very long detailed letter is still called a Swalehouser, and it is sad to think that when Lorna and I are dead this useful term will vanish for ever from the language. Aunty Lizzie married in Australia, rather late in life, and had no children of her own. Mother always waxed indignant when she spoke of aunty Lizzie's married life. She married a clergyman and was his third wife. The Vicarage abounded in children of the first and second marriages, who, according to Mother, did not appreciate their stepmother's superior intelligence and refinement. Mother, however, appreciated them and aunty Lizzie loved Mother and, as in the old days in other alien houses, wrote her Swalehousers which Mother treasured and used to read to us long years after poor aunty Lizzie's trials were over.

Grandpa's brother, Dick, was known to me only by hearsay. Of that there was plenty and it has taken me the best part of a life-time to form some opinion of what uncle Dick must really have been like. Two characteristics emerge unmistakeably – his conviction that he was made of finer grain than the common run of men and his determination that the world should recognize his superiority by making life easy and pleasant for him. He sounded his authentic note early in life, on an occasion of family legend when, while still a toddler, he was asked if he would like some bread and gravy and replied that he would, but only if given 'crumb without crust, gravy two sides'. That would have been a perfect inscription for his tombstone.

Uncle Dick was not exactly a black sheep but the Hughendens did not regard him as a wholly edifying character. He did not accompany his parents and sisters when they migrated to Australia in the wake of Grandpa, no doubt having a well-founded suspicion that life might be rather strenuous and crude in the bustling colony of Victoria. Instead, he went to Ceylon, where there were natives to do the dirty work and he could keep cool and clean while supervising them on a tea plantation. For some reason unknown to me the Ceylon experiment was not a success and uncle Dick rejoined his family in Melbourne. There he created a sensation by riding about on a horse, followed by a 'black boy' in the capacity of a groom. I always pictured the black boy as having looked like the attendant of one of those eighteenth-century grandees I had seen in reproductions of paintings, a shining Negro in red satin and a turban, but I suppose that the black boy was no African but a native of Ceylon. Uncle Dick had a gift for falling on his feet, and in Melbourne he met and married a rich widow. The Hughendens said it was for her money, because the bride was neither young nor fair. The poor lady was head over heels in love with her elegant new husband, who was not very nice to her. At least, that was what was said at 'Hughenden', but I have a treacherous inclination to uncle Dick's side, at least in the matter of the final incident which led to his desertion of his wife. It seems that they went to the theatre one night and Mrs Dick utterly maddened him by watching his face all night instead of what was happening on the stage. Uncle Dick decided that he just could not stand the woman, sailed away to England and never came back. His marriage had not reached his standard of 'crumb without crust, gravy two sides'. His wife loved him all the same and obligingly died and left him all her money, on which he lived in great comfort ever after. His family thought that he had behaved like a cad, and no doubt he had, but they did not understand that the drama is really important to some people, not just a show, and that what uncle Dick must have realized that night, and been unable to accept as a life-sentence, was that he was married to a Philistine.

Uncle Dick was an eccentric and a *poseur*. When his Australian nephews, my uncles Jack and Ack, were on leave in London during the First World War, they went to see him and wrote home startled accounts of his appearance in a silk dressing-gown with a lace collar and his hair worn in long curls. Perhaps they meant to imply something they would never have dreamt of stating clearly in a letter to be read by Grandma and the aunts. It is more probable, I think, that uncle Dick was simply an aesthete to whom it was fun to startle the bourgeoisie, and who could be more bourgeois than his nephews from Melbourne? Uncle Dick's gifts were minor, a little sketching, a little landscape gardening, and a good deal of taste; in short, he was artistic rather than an artist. But I cherish his memory because the aesthetic flame burned bright and clear in him and suggests the existence of some unknown ancestor from whom the aesthetic impulse, so strong in Mother and her children, was transmitted. It certainly did not come from Grandpa, who was as much a Philistine as uncle Dick's wife: it would never have occurred to him to use the word 'artist' without using its naturally accompanying adjective of 'long-haired'; nor did the love of beauty enter the family from the O'Brien strain. But it was certainly strong in us. When my brother John was a child and was asked by a visitor the usual question about what he meant to be when he grew up, he startled the questioner by failing to give any of the expected replies and said without hesitation, 'a patron of the arts'. None of us has any creative gift, but we are born appreciators, true kin of that deplorable dilettante, uncle Dick.

VI

The dominant personality at 'Hughenden' was that of

Grandpa, who was qualified, both by his position in the Firm and by nature, for the title of 'the Boss', by which he was known to his children. He was of medium height and weight and had an upright and sprightly carriage and a fine presence. He was handsome, with regular features, bright blue eyes and pink cheeks, and he must have had fair hair when young, but when I knew him he was bald and his pointed beard was white. Except when in his gardening clothes, which were deplorable, Grandpa was always very neatly dressed, in a pepper-and-salt suit for everyday and a navy blue for best. He had a gold watch on a chain and often took it out to check the clocks, which he usually found inaccurate. His linen was snowy and his boots gleamed, for Grandpa held that only effeminate men wore shoes. He might have risked the shoes, really, because there was never the slightest possibility of anyone's calling the Boss effeminate. He had fathered ten children, of whom nine grew to maturity, and his voice, when raised (as it frequently was) had a decidedly bull-like quality. He was outspoken and straightforward, and both in business and in private life a man of the utmost integrity. He was capable in business and practical matters and had been, before the breaking of the Land Boom, an active and useful member of the South Melbourne Council.

Grandpa was also emotional, unreasonable, arbitrary, quick both to laughter and to sudden gusts of ill-temper, and he was what people who have never had to live with one call a fine old English eccentric. He rose and went to bed at extraordinary times and never got up for breakfast which had to be carried to his bedroom, a long way from the kitchen, by some member of the family at whatever hour he signified his desire for it by ringing a bell. He was wont to observe that his needs were simple, merely tea and buttered toast and a dish of olives, but meeting his needs was less simple because the tea and toast had to be piping hot, despite the distance it had to be carried. The toast was put into a muffin-dish with boiling water underneath and as Grandpa did not like his tea in a pot but in a cup, ready poured and sugared and milked, the full cup had to be inserted into a covered basin of boiling water. It was quite a feat to carry these hot liquids at high speed without spilling anything, but it was possible, as I know from having carried Grandpa's breakfast tray many a time when I was a child. A strange feature of his bedroom was the amazing number of patent medicines, boxes of pills, and other health-promising nostrums that cluttered his dressing-table and shelves. Was he a hypochondriac or an experimentalist? Was his health so good and his life so long because of or despite all the medicines he consumed? Who can say? The Boss was *sui generis* and no one reasoned why. Sometimes he attended family lunch and sometimes he preferred to work in the garden and have it at about three instead. He did as he pleased. Once in his life, as I shall relate in due course, he had broken this rule and adapted himself to meet the requirements of others, but he had not found that it answered and never repeated the experiment.

I loved Grandpa when I was a child and although I knew that he had a hasty temper and wished he would not make scenes, I thought of him as being much like God the Father and entitled to let loose a few thunderbolts when he felt displeased. Besides, Grandpa was at his nicest with children; we were never the subjects of his denunciation and we got on with him swimmingly. He roared with laughter at primitive jokes, just like us, was a bit greedy at meals too, said whatever came into his head and was sometimes sorry afterwards. As well, his outlook on life was of the kind now called simplistic; it is an outlook which is very restful for children, to whom the whole world is new and puzzling. His politics were conservative, not to say reactionary. England was top nation and foreigners should thank Heaven fasting if England conquered them and gave them decent government, and that went specially for the ungrateful Irish, a devious, shiftless lot, a perfect nuisance, and quite incapable of looking after themselves. Although he had left England when he was seventeen and never went back, even for a visit, Grandpa never ceased to think of himself as an Englishman who happened, for his own convenience, to be living in the colonies. As for his wife and children and grandchildren, they were of course colonials and it was their duty to love, honour and obey the Mother Country which knew what was for their good. Grandpa was immensely loyal to the Crown, and even approved of Germans, because of the Teutonic origins and connections of the royal family. When 1914 came it must have been hard for him to take to hating the Germans whom he had always admired, and to start loving the flighty Frogs whom he had hitherto despised.

Disraeli was Grandpa's hero. He had called his house 'Hughenden' because that was the name of Disraeli's home and was so suitable in Beaconsfield Parade, named after Disraeli's title. I am sure Grandpa would have detested Disraeli had he known him; he would have found him too clever by half, not English enough in appearance nor manly enough in dress. But Disraeli had the right ideas, according to Grandpa, because he stood for the throne and the Empire, unlike the namby-pamby Gladstone, who was so weak about Ireland.

Grandpa was, in short, like a stage version of an Englishman in a play written by a foreigner. He belonged to the Church of England, Low Church, he always said, but his adhesion seemed more a matter of patriotism than religion, for he did not frequent his parish church, as was pointed out in an aggrieved letter from his sister Lizzie, the wife of the Vicar. Fate played a sorry trick on Grandpa, when he was a younger man, by causing him to fall in love with Mary O'Brien, an Australian-born girl of Irish Catholic parents. He proposed and was accepted but when he learnt that he must undertake to bring up his children in the Catholic faith he refused, and the engagement was broken off. No doubt he expected Mary – or Polly as he called her in his softer moments – to give in. Grandma looked and was a gentle creature, but her principles were made of steel and she did not give in. She was a great beauty, with black hair, creamy skin, dark blue eyes, a swan neck and a wasp waist. So it was Grandpa who gave in and they were married under a cherry-plum tree in flower in the orchard behind great-grandfather O'Brien's bush pub, the 'Limerick Arms' at Nar Nar Goon in Gippsland, when Grandpa was twenty-two and Grandma was nineteen. But they did not live happily ever after.

VII

Grandma's father, Daniel O'Brien, and his wife Brigid Walsh, and their first child, Ellen, Irish Catholics from

County Limerick, came to Victoria almost at the beginning of its history, in 1841, when it was still the Port Phillip District of New South Wales. Daniel was a builder and when he and Brigid left Ireland they had planned to stay in the newly-opened Port Phillip District, where work in the building trade was said to be abundant, for four years, by which time they believed they would have accumulated enough capital to return home and live there in reasonable comfort.

In the event, they were never to see Ireland again. On arrival they went to Geelong where builders were in demand, and they lived for a couple of years at Waurn Ponds. Inevitably the idea of 'taking up land' occurred to Daniel O'Brien, as it did to many migrants in the pastoral days before the gold discoveries. Had he become a landowner at Waurn Ponds or thereabouts, the O'Briens might have become colonial gentry and Brigid and her daughters might have gone to balls at Government House wearing dresses of satin and tulle and long white kid gloves. But the brown grass of the Western Plains, to which Waurn Ponds is the gate, though very nutritious for sheep, looked like a desert to the O'Briens from the Emerald Isle, and they welcomed the proposal of friends that they should follow their example and settle in Gippsland. So they bought a farm, rather ominously known as 'The Swamp' (and it was on the fringe of the Koo-wee-rup Swamp) at Mt Ararat, later known as Nar Nar Goon. There they had a proper Irish farm and raised cows and pigs and poultry and also a family of four daughters and four sons.

What with one thing and another, the O'Briens did not fare badly at Nar Nar Goon although they had to work and live hard. When the gold rush began Daniel found a good market for his dairy produce and meat and made periodical journeys by bullock waggon to the diggings to sell it. This was a profitable business but it meant leaving great-grandmother alone in the bush to cope with the farm and her young family, with no company but that of the blacks, of whom she was afraid. But Brigid was brave and resourceful. During one of Daniel's absences, as night was falling, she noticed that the blacks were lighting a great many of their little fires in the vicinity of the house and that the tribe was gathering and

something seemed to be afoot. It turned out to be a cor-
roboree, and after the blacks had been dancing for a while
they got worked up and noisy and began advancing, drawing
nearer and nearer to the house in which they knew there was
no man. Leaving the children in the care of her eldest boy,
Brigid took a stockwhip down from the wall and stole out of
the back of the house and ran some distance into the bush.
There she began to crack the whip very quietly, as if it were
far off, and then, at intervals, more loudly, as if Daniel were
coming home and giving his usual signal. The frightened
children saw the advancing line of blacks waver in the dance,
pause, confer and finally break off and withdraw. It was no
wonder that my Grandma, who was one of the youngest of
those children, always hated the bush. Even when she was
old, when we went for drives in the country she was always
the first to suggest that it was getting dark and that it was
time to go home to the safety and the lighted streets of town
because the bush, she said, was always so eerie at night.

Poor great-grandmother O'Brien had many other ordeals
to face, of which the worst, perhaps, was coping with the
bush fire of Black Thursday in the absence of her husband,
who had gone to the assistance of a neighbour. She kept the
children immersed in the water-holes to which the creek had
shrunk in the terrible summer of 1851, and soaked the
immediate vicinity of the house with water which she and her
eldest son carried from the water-holes, and with all the milk
from the dairy. Less dramatic but persistently wearing was
the difficulty of housekeeping when every item needed on the
farm or in the house had to be fetched from Melbourne by
bullock waggon. As the journey took at least a week each
way, and longer if the watercourses were flooded and man
and beast had to wait till they went down, it was not made
frequently and what one lacked one went without until next
time.

But the problem that worried Brigid O'Brien most was the
lack of schooling for the children. Indeed, it worried her so
much that she induced Daniel to let the farm and return to his
old trade as a builder in Melbourne. The O'Briens built a
house at Hotham Hill (now North Melbourne) and the
children went to the school run in connection with St

Francis's Church in Lonsdale Street. All went well at first and the O'Briens might have become an urban family like the Buxtons, but great-grandfather's partner skipped with the profits of the building business, and Daniel and his family were forced to fall back on the farm at Nar Nar Goon.

Somehow the losses had to be recouped and the O'Briens had the very Irish idea of opening a pub on the Gippsland Road, which now went as far as Sale. This was a successful venture because the 'Limerick Arms' soon became a haunt of owners and drovers of fat cattle, going to the sales in Melbourne and returning home again. The sleepy hollow of Nar Nar Goon was further enlivened when Cobb & Co. began a coach service to Sale and made it a stage for changing horses and for refreshments, provided at the 'Limerick Arms'. The work must have been terribly heavy for Brigid and her elder daughters, because drovers who had stayed the night had to be off at first light with a substantial breakfast inside them, and Cobb & Co., which prided itself on the speed of its operations, required quick service for its passengers. The 'Limerick Arms' must have been a blessed haven for weary travellers along the Gippsland Road, for not only was it spotlessly clean and famous for its good fare, but it had little touches of refinement rare in country pubs. Frances O'Brien, a grand-daughter of Daniel and Brigid, recorded as late as 1959 her childhood memories of the gleaming white tablecloths and napkins and the vases of fresh pink roses to be expected, along with abundant and delicious food, in the dining-room of the 'Limerick Arms'.

Nar Nar Goon and the Koo-wee-rup Swamp on which it borders have always been favourite places for the Irish to settle. I suppose they liked it for the same reason as Daniel O'Brien, because it was moist and green and more like home than the drier parts of the colony. One of the deprivations the Irish colonists felt most was that of the familiar offices of the Catholic Church. A priest came to Nar Nar Goon every six months, arriving on Saturday and staying until Monday morning. When it was known that he was coming Irishmen for miles around bundled their families into buggies and saddled their own horses and converged on Nar Nar Goon on Saturday, when they all went to confession and spent the night at the 'Limerick Arms' or with friends or just camping. On Sunday morning there was Mass, held alternately at the 'Limerick Arms' and the farm of Mr John Dore, a shipmate of Daniel O'Brien's in the olden days; and after Mass there were weddings and baptisms. When these were over there was a splendid banquet for everyone at the 'Limerick Arms'. A great day for the Irish, from which at last they returned to their lonely farms nourished spiritually and physically, socially and, no doubt, alcoholically.

Nothing astonishes me more, in the history of Daniel and Brigid O'Brien, than the tenacious campaign they waged to bring their children up as civilised people. That they were successful I can testify, for I knew their daughters Jo and Kate as well as Grandma, and they were all people of refinement. The men of the family I never knew, except one, uncle Jeremiah, and if the legend I was brought up on is true, he too had refined tastes. Mother used to relate the story as a cautionary tale to her daughters, of which the moral was the awful fate awaiting girls unless they learnt to be dainty in their ways. Uncle Jer had a mind to marry and, finding a girl who seemed to be suitable, began to court her. All went well, he decided to propose and asked her to go for a drive in his buggy for the purpose. As ill-luck would have it, his intended had a cold in the head and soon had to fish in her pocket for her handkerchief. When she brought it out it was, to uncle Jer's horror, not only crumpled but soiled. As soon as he decently could he turned the buggy round and drove home again with the question forever unpopped. Lorna and I regarded this as a tragic story and were very sorry for the poor girl who, instead of a lovely engagement ring and a white satin wedding dress and a house of her own and some sweet children just like us, got only a disappointment; but we did not doubt that uncle Jer was right and that the girl was impossible. It was about half a century later that the seditious thought occurred to me that perhaps uncle Jer might have had his faults too.

Great-grandfather O'Brien was an active agent in the refining process carried on behind the scenes at the 'Limerick Arms'. He was a stickler for good manners and woe betide anyone who came between him and the candle when he was

37

reading. He was an authority on deportment and I have often heard Grandma relate how, when she was a girl, he once noticed her sitting with her knees crossed and observed, in the Limerick brogue he never lost – 'Begad, Mary, that's an elegant attitude you have', with such withering scorn that she never repeated the offence for the rest of her life. I never saw Grandma in an inelegant attitude and learned from her to dislike the sight of people slumped or sprawled in their chairs. Like most Irishmen, Daniel O'Brien loved horses and he could not endure to see a woman on horseback unless she were well turned out; when not cooking for drovers, Brigid and the girls could be seen riding, side-saddle of course, in handsome and expensive habits ordered from Melbourne.

So that her children should be graceful, great-grandmother taught them to dance, and when she could not find a man about the place to play the dance music on a fiddle or accordion she sang the accompaniment herself. But the problem of schooling was very hard to solve after the O'Brien family returned to Nar Nar Goon. A procession of tutors came and went, mostly black sheep and remittance men, for whom the 'Limerick Arms' was not a very suitable residence. Great-grandfather still had, from time to time, building contracts in Melbourne and on one of his visits to town he at last struck it lucky when he encountered, working as a labourer, a well-educated fellow-countryman named Ahern and prevailed on him to go back with him to Nar Nar Goon in the capacity of a tutor. What Mr Ahern's background was I do not know, probably he was one of the many unsuccessful miners, as he was definitely not a black sheep but a well-educated person of considerable culture, and a wonderful teacher according to his pupils. The O'Briens soon became the envy of their neighbours, who begged to be allowed to send their children to join Mr Ahern's class. As Daniel O'Brien was already a farmer, a publican and builder, he felt he could hardly embark on a fourth career as the proprietor of a school. However, he and his faithful friend John Dore shared the expense of building a school for Mr Ahern at Seven Hills and soon all the children of the district were making their way there on ponies to learn their lessons from him.

The history of the rise and fall of the fortunes of the O'Brien family at Nar Nar Goon might well be treated as a footnote to the history of colonial transport, for what the road to Sale gave them, the coming of the railway took away. Cobb & Co. gave up the route, the coach stables were demolished and passengers were refreshed by the Victorian Railways and not at the 'Limerick Arms'. The drovers vanished too, because the cattle were now moved by rail, in cattle-trucks. So all the activity and hubbub died down, and the income died with it. When great-grandfather O'Brien died he left the 'Limerick Arms' to his eldest son, Michael, but as Michael preferred farming it was carried on by the next son, Daniel. The hotel was dying on its feet and was de-licensed in 1908. All the daughters married, and uncle Jer, now equipped with a wife whose handkerchiefs were irreproachable, moved to Melbourne and became the licensee of the 'Bleak House' Hotel in Beaconsfield Parade, the first roof I remember sleeping under when we moved to town from Omeo in 1908 and had not yet found a house. Michael, Dan and Pat remained on the land at Nar Nar Goon making a miserable living; hardly better, indeed, than they might have made if their parents had never left Ireland.

VIII

At 'Hughenden' Grandma, although much less conspicuous, was nearly as important as Grandpa, and how can she be understood without her proper background? Mary O'Brien and John Buxton were to spend more than sixty years of married life together. United they were to be in a sense – in the very important sense that I do not believe either of them ever even contemplated marital infidelity, and both had a strong sense of the responsibilities of married life and parenthood – but there was almost every other division between them, racial, religious, cultural and personal. The religious one had already revealed itself, and it must have been mortifying for Grandpa to be married by a Catholic priest, although he was lucky that there was no church at Nar Nar Goon, so that he was spared the humiliation of entering what was, to him, no better than a heathen temple. Grandpa was a man of his word and his children were all brought up Catholic, but he resented his defeat and detested the Roman connection and not silently. He was apt to drag it up when he was displeased, which was not infrequently. I remember an occasion when, thwarted in his desire for a third helping of a specially delicious pudding because it had all been eaten, he remarked bitterly that decent housekeeping could hardly be expected in a house dominated by the Pope of Rome.

Not that it was so dominated. Grandma was a practising Catholic but was not at all fanatical or bigoted. She was very tactful and no trappings of Popery ever affronted Grandpa's eye at 'Hughenden' in the way of holy pictures on the walls or prayer-books or rosary beads left lying about. Fridays were rather awkward, when Grandma and her children ate fish. If Grandpa were not offered the alternative of steak he was apt to point out that he, thank God, was not subject to the tyranny of the Pope of Rome and would not eat fish against his will; and if he were served steak without consultation he would want to know why he was deprived of the right to eat fish in his own house. On Sundays Grandma led her children and any resident grandchildren to Mass at the Carmelite Church in Middle Park, where we sat rather grandly in the front row, just under the pulpit, in a seat which bore a brass tablet saying that it had been donated by the Buxton family. I never failed to thank God that Grandpa had never seen it and never would. But, wayward creature that he was, Grandpa was great friends with the parish priest, Prior Kindelan, who was always welcome at 'Hughenden' although he fairly reeked both of Popery and of old Erin.

As in most mixed marriages, the 'Hughenden' children tended to be indifferent to religion and the boys were rarely seen in the Carmelite church once they grew up. Of the nine children, only one, Len, the youngest, went to a Catholic school for his secondary education, although I think that he, like all the rest, did his primary studies at the State School. The women of the family all observed their religious duties but only one of them, aunty Doone, was really pious. The family is still Catholic and there is even a Jesuit Buxton grandson, but they were Catholics who, because of their mixed inheritance, tended to be ecumenical before their time. All Grandpa's relations were Protestant and we knew and liked them, so Protestants never seemed queer or alien, much less wicked. Lorna and I went to convent schools for our religious education (about which the Church was much more exigent than when Mother had been a child) but we were sent to Protestant schools later, in case we should turn out narrow-minded. We made a kind of distinction between being Catholic, which was a private matter, and being 'RC', which we felt to be rather offensive, involving as it did wearing holy medals, displaying pictures of the Sacred Heart or the Little Flower, and saying grace, to the embarrassment of visitors not of the true faith.

To us as young children the solidity and cohesion of 'Hughenden' were absolute and unquestioned; we thought of it as all of a piece throughout, a family monolith. It came to me only gradually that it was really a complicated artifact. It rested, it was true, on solid bluestone foundations formed by the Firm and the integrity of character of our grandparents, but what kept it standing was a system of strains and balances, in which most of the strain was provided by Grandpa and most of the balance by Grandma. At 'Hughenden' Grandma came next in public importance to Grandpa, and in quiet, secret ways she was probably more important in holding the family together. No one ever mentioned her without adding that she was a wonderful woman, which indeed she was. She made a work of art out of the not very promising material of her life. No matter what storms might rage, Grandma remained composed and dignified. She was not without spirit but if she possessed any temper she must have decided, early in her married life, that she would never lose it.

When Grandpa raised his voice and made unreasonable complaints against her, she made no response. Her beautiful face showed strain and even, in the course of time, a touch of bitterness, but she remained calm. Many must have been the tears she shed in the privacy of her bedroom, but never one in public. She would have thought it ill-mannered to add to the unpleasantness of the moment, and besides, I suspect now,

41

she was determined not to give Grandpa the satisfaction of seeing her crack under the strain. Temperamentally the husband and wife were poles apart. Grandpa was English, frank and transparent and said whatever came into his head, but Grandma was Irish, opaque and reticent, her inner life defended by a mask of inscrutability. She was not talkative by nature, she kept her own counsel and held her peace. Grandpa, I fancy, found her baffling and could not guess what she thought or felt, and either fear, inarticulateness or black Irish pride prevented her from telling him.

The sons all adored their mother and as they grew older they could not stand hearing her abused; when Grandpa made one of his scenes one of them would jump to his feet and begin a counter-attack. Then, and only then, would Grandma speak, and what she said was spoken very quietly but with an authority which never failed to achieve its object – 'Sit down, Jack', or 'Ack' or 'Len' – as the case might be. From the point of view of family harmony I suppose her policy was right, for with no opposition forthcoming Grandpa's rages were short-lived. But I think it might have been better for Grandma herself if she had thrown a plate at Grandpa occasionally, since scenes usually took place at the dining-table. The iron discipline she imposed on herself for life must have galled her and it would probably have been better for Grandpa, too, if she had stood up to him. Her life-long moral triumph over him must have been humiliating. But she was not a fighter and could not act against her nature.

Grandma was very elegant. She kept her slender figure all her life and her well-brushed black hair did not go grey until her last years. Her clothes were always appropriate and in exquisite order, a missing button or a crumpled skirt was unthinkable. When I was a child other girls' grandmothers were old ladies, always dressed in black, and they wore bonnets and beaded capes when they went out. Grandma scorned the old ladies' uniform and always wore proper hats and coats, and although she wore discreet colours, she never dressed in black. I can see her now with her well-fitting gloves, her becoming veil with little dots on it, her neatly shod feet and the girlish flush of pleasure on her pale cheeks when someone remarked on her pretty ankles. Grandma was not a talker but she was an excellent and sympathetic listener with a real but unintrusive interest in everyone's problems: she was a very wise woman and someone was always going to 'Hughenden' to seek her advice. She never raised her voice but her children obeyed her instantly, and it used to amuse me to see how Mother, who was not tractable by nature, always did exactly what Grandma told her to, even when she was herself a middle-aged woman.

Grandma loved children, her own, her children's, anyone's. She must, I suppose, among nearly a score of grandchildren have loved some more than others, but I have no idea which were her favourites, because she seemed to find us all delightful. Grandma always had a store of small silver coins about her, the new, bright, shiny ones that children love, and she always remembered to slip one into our hands when we said goodbye to her. She never forgot our birthdays and used to ask me whether I would prefer a pair of kid gloves or half a crown for my present. This question always reminded me that even in the most understanding of grown-ups there was a strain of stupidity you never found in children. Fancy thinking that kid gloves and half crowns were comparable! I already had a pair of kid gloves, because Mother insisted on them for special occasions, and I loathed them. To buy them you had to go with Mother to a shop and put your elbow on a little velvet cushion on the counter while the saleswoman patiently fitted the gloves, after stretching the fingers a little with a wooden contrivance, on the same principle as a pair of scissors. Thereafter you had to put them on yourself, very carefully, a finger at a time, and work each one down, and when at last all four fingers were crammed in you had to begin the almost impossible task of inserting the thumb. If you lost your temper and rushed the donning of kid gloves you split them, and then there was the devil to pay.

How could a sensible woman like Grandma have imagined that I might prefer such instruments of torture to half a crown, which was simply a fortune when your economy was based on an income of a penny a week? Half a crown opened up a splendid vista of consumer goods at a halfpenny each, to be selected at leisure from a glass case at the lolly shop – Silver Sammies, made of toffee coated with chocolate,

Sherbet Suckers, which were paper packets containing sherbet, to be ingurgitated through a tube of licorice, Licorice Straps, rather dull but a lot for the money and, best of all Fizzoes, which were like white marbles, the outside made of a boiled sweet which, as you sucked, gradually released its contents of delicious sherbet and could be made to last for a long time provided you did not bite greedily through the hard shell.

In all things Grandma was disciplined, orderly and methodical, which was very reassuring and restful for a child brought up by a mother such as mine, who was unpredictable like Grandpa. Grandma's bedroom which, by my time, was not Grandpa's too, was an abode of peace and calm. It was spacious and its contents were fascinating, especially the square stool that was beaded all over and the double bed with spotless white curtains; but I was rather frightened by the print of Rembrandt's *Descent from the Cross,* which I thought gruesome. In the dressing-table there was a drawer full of beautifully ironed white linen handkerchiefs, all smelling of Cashmere Bouquet soap because Grandma kept a cake of it there for that purpose.

I never heard any of Grandma's nine children, even Mother and aunty Kit, in whom, alone among their family, *l'esprit critique* raged, utter a single adverse criticism of their mother. Indeed, I believe I was the only member of the family who ever even thought of one and as a member of a hopeless minority I had the sense to hold my tongue. It was not that I did not love and admire Grandma like everyone else, for indeed I did, but that I dissented for her view of the woman's role in life. This was that men can do as they like and women had better make the best of it. I would probably have made a greater success of life if I had knuckled down to this realistic philosophy, but I simply could not stomach it. Grandma herself, although it would have horrified her had she known, played a leading role in making me a feminist. One incident comes back vividly. It was Sunday night at 'Hughenden' and on Sunday nights there was always 'summer pudding', trifle without wine in it. Lorna and I adored summer pudding and as much as the delicious compound of custard and sponge cake and jam and lashings of whipped cream, we adored the plates on which it was served. I do not need a dunked madelaine to recall those plates exactly because they are mine now, my choice when the last of the aunts died and the remaining 'Hughenden' things were dispersed. The plates are of Rockingham china and are now at least a century old and probably more. The borders are a delicate grey, wavy and edged with thrice-laid gold, and there is a broad band of bluish-green. The centres are hand-painted and each represents a different flower. When our generous helpings of summer pudding reached us we had no idea what flower was under it, so the children used to race and the winner was the one who first yelled 'Carnation!' or 'Geranium!' or whatever. We must all have learnt the names of flowers from these plates, which were never considered too good for children. On this particular night Grandpa was out, a very rare event. The uncles were out too, but were expected back. There were only females left at 'Hughenden': Grandma, aunty Doone and aunty Dot, Lorna and me. It was time for the meal but we waited a little for the uncles. Then there was a telephone call from them, to say they would not be home. The summer pudding was already in the dining-room, on the sideboard, and I had been thinking about it for some time. Then Grandma whisked it away, saying, 'As there are no men we won't need this, it will do for tomorrow night.' I was not going to be there tomorrow night and at that moment a feminist was born.

During the first fifteen years of her married life it must have been felt at Nar Nar Goon that, except for Grandpa's being a Protestant, their Mary had married well. Between 1875, when they married, and 1890, when the Land Boom burst, the Firm was a very thriving concern, and by the 'eighties, when he built 'Hughenden', Grandpa was a rich man. Even then, of course, Grandma's life cannot have been easy. She bore her first child, my mother, when she was twenty and her tenth and last, uncle Len, when she was forty. As there were no twins there was little respite from maternity. Still, Grandma was young and strong and loving, and Grandpa's means made it possible for her to have plenty of help with the children and the housekeeping. Grandpa's family strongly approved of his wife and she found ready-made Melbourne friends in them and, as Grandpa was very hospitable, members of her own family came often to stay with her. Jack and Polly Buxton were a popular young couple who led a gay social life in the days of 'Marvellous Melbourne'. Mother recollected Grandma, in that golden age, as a great frequenter of balls, in the loveliest dresses made of yards and yards of costly materials. She herself, as an eldest child, came in for the largesse of those palmy days and there is an old hand-coloured photograph of her dressed for a children's fancy dress ball as a fairy queen, with a crown and a spangly, sparkly dress of pale blue tulle. When Mother died I found among her possessions a relic of those glorious days which she had treasured all her life – an exquisitely made white satin shoe which she had worn as a bridesmaid, so tiny that she cannot have been more than six years old when she wore it.

But suddenly, in 1890, when 'Hughenden' was still a new house full of new furniture purchased regardless of expense, the Land Boom burst and Melbourne was no longer marvellous. The calamity affected everyone, but none more dramatically than those whose very existence depended on the market for land. Buckhurst & Buxton, like every other estate agency, was in difficulties, but neither uncle nor nephew ever contemplated taking the easy way out, through the Bankruptcy Court. The only appearance the Firm makes in the book by Michael Cannon, *The Land Boomers,* which relates among other things the history of estate agents in the desperate 'nineties, is a single mention of W.P. Buckhurst as instrumental in pressing charges against Matthias Larkin, estate agent and building society secretary, for the embezzlement of £100,000. The judge who sentenced Larkin to eleven years gaol, addressed to him the terrible words – 'In the evil history of an evil time, your name and conduct stand as a monument of woe to multitudes of people'. Larkin's estate ultimately paid twopence in the pound, but Grandpa paid twenty shillings, gradually and with extreme difficulty. I was brought up to admire him for his integrity and I still do. So did his wife and children: it was a source of pride to them not to lack honour, whatever else they went without, but that was a great deal.

W.P. Buckhurst was a man of substance and the Firm weathered the storm of the 'nineties. But Grandpa's situation was different from Mr Buckhurst's in that he was not a man of established fortune, but was still only in his thirties when the Land Boom burst and his private financial commitments were very heavy. I have always understood that he supported his father and mother as well as his own family at 'Hughenden' but think it likely that, when his situation became difficult, this responsibility was shared with the husband of his sister Polly. There remained the support of his own large family and, worst of all, 'Hughenden' itself, because it had been built like most Land Boom houses, on credit when money was abundant and had to be paid for in a very different financial climate. Compared with most people concerned with the land market, Grandpa had been prudent, but he had not wholly escaped the euphoria of the time, as he admitted in a letter to Grandma, written in 1891, in which he told her of the downfall of that conspicuous spender of the 'eighties, Matthias Larkin, and went on:

'I have sometimes thought you blamed me in your own mind for not following more closely in his footsteps and being a bit more lavish, literal and lordly and creating more of a splash, but I am more convinced than ever that my policy of always endeavouring to live within my income and of trying, if possible, should anything happen to me, to leave you and the children not altogether unprovided for is the true and right one – no matter how unpopular it might be. Unfortunately of late I have not adhered so strictly to this policy as I should have done – but I trust, if I am spared a bit longer, to be able to weather through the present difficulties and be able to provide for your and their reasonable necessities.'

Grandpa was to be 'spared' until he was over eighty, but between the worries of the Firm and his private financial problems he must have been well nigh desperate in the first half of the 'nineties. In 1893 he wrote to two of his daughters, who were on holiday with Grandma's family in the country, a very typical letter in which he first scolded them and then was sorry, because they were only children. Their offence was that they had both written to him and instead of employing one envelope and one stamp, their letters had been sent separately. Grandpa wrote:

It is at all times well to be careful and frugal and avoid waste, but in our very altered circumstances it is absolutely necessary to be exceedingly careful of every penny we spend or we may run short of tucker as so many thousands of others have done – now I started this sermon in fun and have grown quite earnest about it.

From another letter we learn that a gardener was no longer employed at 'Hughenden' and that Grandpa was trying to keep its extensive grounds in order himself, but that he realised he could not go on doing so because he needed all his strength to cope with the harassing affairs of the Firm and, as he observed, 'Bread and cheese is more important than flowers, though not as pretty.' Grandpa must have been a pioneer of the low maintenance garden. Once, no doubt, he had dreamed of glorious herbaceous borders, as in his native Kent, but now the garden was reduced to nothing but a buffalo grass lawn, and a few hardy shrubs. Grandpa managed to sell off the land on the St Kilda side of 'Hughenden', on which some rather mean-looking terrace houses were built, which were damaging to its appearance, but cash in hand was now the only consideration.

As I changed from a child to a girl I did a good deal of sitting in mental judgement on Grandpa, because he was a domestic tyrant. It is only now, as my own life is drawing to an end, that I have fully grasped what the nervous strain of the 'nineties must have done to him. It was probably the cause of all those pills and patent medicines in his bedroom and the cause, too, of exacerbating his naturally hasty temper. His elder children, I always noticed, had more patience and affection for Grandpa than the younger ones, and I suppose that was because they had known him before the 'nineties and knew how he had changed and why. My mother, as the eldest, was the best informed, too early the sharer of her parents' anxieties: she was haunted, all her life, by the memory of Grandpa's footsteps, pacing up and down his bedroom at all hours of the night as quarter-day drew near and somehow or other he must pay the interest due on 'Hughenden' and still find tucker for his brood. Tucker they had and grew up pretty healthy on it, but the menu, according to Mother, placed strong emphasis on filling dishes, such as porridge, and butter was an unknown luxury, dripping taking its place. When the Land Boom burst, Mother was at the Presbyterian Ladies' College, then the leading girls' school in Melbourne, and Grandpa managed to keep her there until 1892 when she was sixteen and passed her Matriculation. But when her sisters finished primary school they had to make do with the South Melbourne College, which was cheaper than PLC and within walking distance of 'Hughenden'. There were no more splendid ball dresses or satin slippers; indeed, Mother used to recall the process of inking over the bald patches on her shoes on Sunday in order to be fit to be seen at Mass. Poverty in a mansion must have been a strange and puzzling life for children.

Up till 1893 Grandpa was still using writing paper which was a relic of better days. It bore the family crest, which depicts a very knowing-looking bird, which I take to be an eagle, perched aloft and looking down on the motto *Bene qui sedula,* which might be freely translated – You'd better look out. That cold, critical eye with its implied 'I told you so' must have got on the nerves of poor Grandpa, whose failure to look out had landed him in such difficulties. Although good writing paper was again abundant at 'Hughenden' in my time, the crest was never used again. The Buxton social pretensions did not survive the 'nineties. As a child I did not realise that they had ever had any pretensions, and was always puzzled by what seemed to me a snobbish streak in Mother and the aunts. It was a fact, though I did not know it, that in the Old Country the Buxtons had been, in a modest way, gentry, and that Grandpa's eldest children, four girls, had always thought of themselves in that light until the depression, when they fell down the social ladder.

For Grandma the change that had taken place at 'Hughenden' must have been hard to understand, for she was all woman, a wholly domestic person, who knew nothing of business or public affairs which were, in her experience, wholly the concern of men. What she had learnt from her own mother's example was the woman's part, to stick to her husband and children through thin as well as thick, to make the best of things and never to complain. Now the test had come and Grandma passed it but the cost was heavy. Among the family letters is one to Grandpa from his sister Lizzie, saying how concerned she was by 'dear Polly's' wan looks, the result of having now to care, single-handed, for all those children and do all the work of a house requiring two or even three servants. Aunt Lizzie begged Grandpa to contrive a single day's holiday for Grandma, to be spent resting under her care at her home at the vicarage.

More practical measures were taken at the 'Limerick Arms'. Great-grandmother O'Brien despatched her un-married daughter, Kate, to live at 'Hughenden' and help dear Polly with the children and the house. Aunt Kate proved a tower of strength and remained for many years as Grandma's right hand, beloved by all the household until, quite late in life, she married Mr Rudd, formerly of Ceylon, the source, as previously mentioned, of the 'Hughenden' ebony elephants and the wax temple. Aunt Kate was a charming person and it is pleasant that her whole life was not consumed by sisterhood and aunthood but that at last she had a home of her own. I knew it well: a small cottage kept as bright as a pin, with vases of fresh flowers from the garden, snowy tablecloths in the tradition of the 'Limerick Arms' and well-polished silver, some of which I still use every day of my life.

Although none of them would have agreed, I have some-times wondered whether it would not have been better for his family if Grandpa had swallowed his pride, gone through the Bankruptcy Court and paid a few pennies in the pound like so many others. The wound caused by the collapse of the family fortunes in the 'nineties never really healed, at least for the daughters of the house, who always felt they had been born for better things, of which they had been wrongfully deprived. The rest of Mother's life and, to some extent, that of her children, was dominated by the experience of her girlhood: she lived in fear of its happening again. By nature she was highly strung and had in an extreme degree the imagination of disaster, so that she lived in anxiety, which was communicated to her children. I do not think that any of us, to this day, can spend much on anything for ourselves without a sense of guilt and a strong desire to hide what we have done. Mother always felt that the world of appearances was deceptive and would probably betray you: with anyone but your blood relations, she said, it was safer to be 'civil but strange'. These attitudes were not conducive to *joie de vivre,* nor was Mother's settled belief, to which she often referred, that Father would die young like his own father, leaving her a poor widow and us as destitute children. In the event, Father died when he was eighty-three and did not leave his children poor. I wish Mother could have been spared unnecessary worry, but do not regret the consequent simplicity of our home and tenor of life nor that I had learnt that one can suddenly become poor, because I was not much dismayed when it was my turn to count pennies in the great depression of the 1930s.

IX

Implication in the subject, filial piety and the fact that one knows both too much and too little, make it difficult to depict one's own parents. Mother was the eldest of the family of nine children who had once lived at 'Hughenden' and a constant visitor to her old home. She was a woman of very original, interesting and difficult character. She was not strong, being prone to sore throats, headaches and fatigue and life was somehow always a bit too much for her: she did not really like it, I think. Mother was shy, withdrawn from the life of the world, which she mistrusted and feared. Perhaps she would have been happier if she had never married, for she shrank from the sexual aspects of life and I have no memory of a time when the relations between my parents were not cold, although they were always civil.

Mother loved her children but she was not naturally maternal. We got on her nerves and she had no patience with us, always expecting us to be small adults instead of beings of a related but different kind. I never learnt to ride a bicycle simply because at the first attempt I fell off and ruined my stockings. That, in Mother's eyes, was wanton waste and I was never permitted to try again. I wanted, as a child, to learn to use the sewing machine, which would have been easy as I am naturally neat-handed, but having no experience I broke a machine needle, was at once declared hopeless and forbidden to touch the machine again. Mother was, in some respects, very like Grandpa: she had a hasty temper and was irrational. Her tongue ran away with her and what she said was often provoking and occasionally very wounding. I was a trying child and my frequent clashes with Mother were often my own fault, but Lorna and John, who had angelic natures, also sometimes came into conflict with her.

Mother inherited Grandpa's eccentricity and as we, her children, were conventional, like Father's family, this was a frequent source of embarrassment. We wished she would behave like other children's mothers, but she could not see why she should. She was a great letter-writer but never wrote her letters, like anyone else, at a desk or table at home but at the GPO, in the Telegraph section, often on the forms so thoughtfully provided by the Post-Master General. She had absolutely no sense of time. We were always late for everything or worrying about the likelihood of being late, which was just as nerve-wracking. Our meals were rarely on time and, as Father was as punctual as Mother was the reverse, this was not conducive to peace in the home. Sometimes Mother would go into town and forget all about dinner until the shops were closing, when she would dash into Sargent's to buy some meat pies, and arrive home looking rather desperate and ask us, 'Is your father home yet?', which he always was, and with his eye on the clock. Mother's unpunctuality was not the result of a selfish disregard for the convenience of others, but an affliction, like blindness or deafness. Some inbuilt mechanism which enables most of us to know, pretty well, what o'clock it is and how much can be done in a given time had been left out of her composition. I remember once, when I was a university student, arriving home from a dance at two in the morning to find Mother, fully dressed and wearing a hat, reading a newspaper from which she glanced up in surprise, saying, 'Home already, dear?'

I have never known anyone whose social horizon was as closely confined to her family as Mother. She could have had many friends because people were attracted by her charm and unusual personality, but in fact she had none because friendship was literally but a word to her. She thought it unnecessary, a sheer waste of time. A girl she had known at school remained attached to Mother for life and always wrote to her on her birthday. Each year, when the inevitable letter arrived, addressed in the well-known hand, Mother would sigh and say, 'Poor old Elsie again! Why does she do it? I never write to her and I've no idea when her birthday is'. Lorna and I turned out to be rather given to making friends, a trait which Mother found mystifying, wondering why, with so many blood relations, we bothered with perfect strangers. This being her attitude, our social life was narrow and it was not until we went to the university that Lorna and I made a successful stand for our right to have friends and even to entertain them at home occasionally.

As well as being like Grandpa in some ways, Mother was like uncle Dick in others, a natural touchstone of aesthetic taste. Great names in letters and the arts meant nothing to her: she read and looked and judged for herself. She frequented exhibitions of paintings but never bothered to look at the catalogues, and when she was asked why this was so, she said that she was not interested in the name of the artist or the title of his picture but only in whether it was worth looking at or not. She lived largely in her eyes. When, as children, we walked along the street with her we danced with impatience, because she was forever stopping to look at something that seemed to us of no interest, such as the shape of a fanlight over a front door or the shadow cast by a tree on a brick wall. Like all the Buxtons, she loved physical beauty. In a cafe she would fall into an abstraction and stare at someone who looked to us quite old and dull and not a bit good-looking. She would then call on us to admire the back of this person's head, saying she had never seen anything so distinguished in her life. I still cannot recall without wincing the terrible finality and truth with which she uttered her fell judgement on her own children's looks – 'flesh without feature'. When my brother became engaged to be married we expected trouble from Mother, who was no friend to the marriages of her children and who would, we thought, be particularly hostile to that of her only son. We were quite wrong, however. Mother was reconciled by his bride's beautiful bones, which she thought would improve the family's looks, as indeed they have done.

In all things simplicity was Mother's watchword and rule of life. We admired this theoretically but not when it came to serious matters, such as our dresses. I see now, from old family pictures, that Mother was in fact far in advance of her time in the matter of children's clothes. Those worn by other children were far more elaborate than ours. Simple clothes for us were of course cheaper and involved less starching and ironing, but Mother also liked them because they were more distinguished. Poor Lorna and I did not care a rap for being distinguished, we just wanted to be in the fashion and wear what other girls wore. That, said Mother, was sheer vulgarity; did we want to look like the daughters of a linen-draper? We would have liked nothing better, as we pictured such girls as enviably free to command from the stock all manner of lovely silks, foamy lace, crisp muslin and endless ribbon bows. We yearned for starched petticoats, frills and lace 'insertion' on our best dresses; but what we got were short, straight, plain little garments with raglan sleeves, with a cord round the waist instead of a sash, and the only trimming permitted was some small buttons down the front. We even had black velveteen dresses made like this, when black was an unheard-of colour for children, and in summer we wore the same model in poplin or undyed tussore silk.

In one way Mother was quite unlike any of her family at 'Hughenden'. She was restless and hated any kind of routine, and would say, 'Why do we have to have dinner again today? We had it yesterday'. She began life anew every day, as if she had just been born and every problem was presenting itself for the first time, and she said this was because she had never had time to form any habits. In those days the butcher used to come to the house for orders. When he was expected poor Mother would get quite frantic; she would say, 'That awful man will be standing on the doormat and asking me what I want and I haven't the slightest idea'. Mother was profoundly undomestic and nothing ever reconciled her to the fate of being a housewife. She would have liked to have been a gypsy and live in a caravan, staying nowhere for long. She hated all the paraphernalia of a household, all the sofas and armchairs and tables and carpets and curtains, and she used to say what sensible people the Japanese must be to dispense with them and just sit on the floor on nice clean matting, with lots of lovely space about them, contemplating a single picture or a bough of cherry blossom. When we bought some object and brought it home and displayed it proudly, Mother would cast a cold eye on it, sigh and say, 'Another link in the chain'. She lacked the acquisitive impulse, and in a world full of people who seem to want more and more things, it is refreshing to remember a mother who disliked possessions.

It was not easy to live with Mother, but all the same it was a privilege. She had great gifts of which she never made full use. When she was a girl at school her English teachers had been excited about her future because they thought she was a born writer. But, alas, she just would not write and they found that the only way to get a composition out of Gertrude Buxton was to lock her up, with no resources at hand save pen and paper and no window to look out of. Left to herself she would read or dream or just stand and stare at the spectacle of the world. She had a naturally pure and elegant style of writing and an artist's feeling for the sounds and meanings of words. But as for writing anything except a letter, that she simply would not do. She had studied at the Conservatorium of Music and could play the piano and the organ, but she did so very rarely. She read a good deal, and never rubbish, but there was no order or method in her reading and she never really studied or mastered any subject or author. I have sometimes thought there was a kind of sleeping-sickness, a fatal lethargy, in the blood of the Buxtons which tended to bring their talents to naught. In Mother's case this tendency was strengthened by her highly critical turn of mind. She felt that unless you could do a thing superlatively well there was no point in adding to the ugliness of the world by doing it imperfectly. She saw the faults before the promise in any attempts made by her children, and I think this was damaging to any initiative we had and to the very small measure of self-confidence that was ours by nature.

The third of the Buxton daughters, aunty Kit, was married before my memory of 'Hughenden' begins and I was her godchild as well as her namesake. She was, perhaps, the prettiest of the Buxton sisters, although less striking in appearance than aunty Dot, because she took after the Buckhurst side of Grandpa's family in being short, a characteristic which appears in the family from time to time. Aunty Kit was intelligent and gifted. She was a constant and discriminating reader, the best read member of her family, and she was also musical. She loved plants and was an excellent gardener, so that she could turn an ordinary suburban garden into a thing of beauty by placing a willow tree or a group of shrubs exactly where they would have the most aesthetic value. She was also a first-rate cook, a real artist at pastry and she used to bring to family picnics lamingtons that melted in the mouth, with no gluey raspberry jam in them, just perfect sponge with the maximum amount of chocolate and coconut coating. Her mind, like Mother's, was highly critical; she tended to be struck by the unsatisfactory aspects of things and to take their better sides for granted. Aunty Kit was always interesting and instructive, but also rather disturbing because she struck me as profoundly dissatisfied with her lot and as bearing a grudge against life because it had not made her more prosperous.

Fate was really malign to Grandpa in designing, as a husband for Mother, Henry Arthur Pitt, the son of an Irish Catholic from County Wexford. The scene of the meeting of Mother and Father was in itself ominous because it was the Carmelite Church in Middle Park, where Mother played the organ and Father sang in the choir. From Grandpa's point of view the whole affair reeked of Popery from the first and also practically of treason, because Father was as keen on Gladstone and Home Rule for Ireland as Grandpa was on Disraeli and the Empire. Worse still, Father was not merely an Irish patriot but a liberal by conviction and practice, who was later to earn the stigma of 'pro-Boer'. As well, Father was plain, a cause of great offence, because Grandpa, like all the Buxtons, set great store on good looks. Finally, Father was poor, so poor indeed that when Mother invited him to

'Hughenden' for the first time, to a tennis party, he had to refuse for lack of enough money to buy a new pair of tennis shoes for the occasion. Grandpa was not altogether to be blamed for regarding Henry Pitt as a most undesirable suitor for his beloved eldest child Gertrude, who was always known by the nickname of 'Plum' which he had given her.

Although Father had all the negative virtues, being temperate, honest and hard-working, the only positive attraction he had to offer at this stage of his life was that he was highly intelligent. This was no recommendation to Grandpa, who distrusted brainy people and would have delighted in the term 'egg-head' if only it had been invented in time for his use. Grandpa was emotional and irrational, and Father's cast of mind, cool and eminently rational, must have been utterly alien and very provoking to him. Worst of all, from Grandpa's point of view, was Father's command of the spoken word, his enjoyment of verbal play and his dry, stinging Irish wit, based on a strong sense of the incongruous and a delight in puncturing pretensions.

Father's wit can best be illustrated by examples. One of them is from a public banquet at which Sir Robert Menzies, then in the midst of an election campaign, was the main speaker. In his address he likened himself to a bull in the ring, deliberately maddened by the provocations of his adversaries. Father moved the vote of thanks and spoke appreciatively of the brilliant speech, and particularly of the vivid figure of the bull-ring, but added that there seemed to him a point at which the analogy broke down, because the bull was trying to get *out* of the ring. My other example is an incident of family life. My brother John and his wife and Father and I were making a motor tour in northern Victoria. It had been a long, hot day and as we covered the last few miles along a dusty country road my sister-in-law fell into a doze. Just then Father exclaimed, 'We've just passed a big black snake!' Sheila, half asleep but always agreeable, managed to respond, pleasantly but not quite sensibly, 'Oh really, what was it doing?' to which Father replied, 'Reading the *Herald*'.

The encounter of J.R. Buxton and H.A. Pitt was foredoomed to failure. Grandpa thought Father thoroughly unsound and Father thought Grandpa an ass. Between the two of them Mother's situation must have been decidedly uneasy, but she was as strong-willed as Grandpa himself and announced her engagement. During the engagement it chanced that one day Grandpa thought fit to deliver himself of some political sentiments of a reactionary kind in a letter to a newspaper. When Father saw it he could not resist the lark of replying, under a pseudonym, and a controversy developed. Poor Grandpa sat up late at night painfully shaping his thoughts, or rather feelings, into further ill-advised words, while his nimble adversary danced round him, twitching his nose and making a laughing-stock of him. Grandpa went on doggedly, swinging his cudgel at the agile fencing-master in vain until someone took pity on him and put an end to the unfair contest by letting him know that it was only young Harry Pitt who was causing him to lose his sleep. Grandpa's rages were generally shortlived, but not on this occasion. It was poor Mother who paid for all the tomfoolery because Grandpa gave her twenty pounds for her marriage portion and then washed his hands of the whole affair and refused to be present at the wedding, which must have been a rather depressing occasion.

Luckily for Mother, not long after her marriage Father was removed from the Melbourne scene when he was sent to be Clerk of Courts at Omeo, where my parents lived for ten years and where both Lorna and I were born. Meanwhile fate had played a second knavish trick on Grandpa when his daughter Kit chose as her future husband, of all the young men in creation, another Pitt, Father's youngest brother, Ernest. By that time the breach with Father had been healed, or at least covered over, by the birth of Lorna, for what grandparent, and particularly a patriarch like Grandpa, could resist a first grandchild? Grandpa behaved himself on the occasion of aunty Kit's wedding and a photograph shows him in the wedding group, in which that little olive branch, Lorna, is well to the fore. In due course the marriage of uncle Ernest and aunty Kit was to be a source of great satisfaction to me, too, because when great-grandfather Buxton died and I could no longer brag about him, I was able to replace him with an almost equally *recherché* relationship with my 'double first cousins', Mark, Mary and David Pitt. As the

Pitt family played an important part on the 'Hughenden' scene by providing two sons-in-law, it is time to introduce it properly.

X

Despite industrious reseach by my cousin David, the mystery of how an Irish Catholic family came to have the uncharacteristic name of Pitt has never been solved. A legend of descent from the great Earl of Chatham used to circulate in the family, based in part on a quite striking facial resemblance in some members and in part, no doubt, on a hankering for grand beginnings. Regretfully, this splendid origin has had to be foregone, for the simple reason that all three sons of the elder Pitt died without issue, though diehards cling to the hope of a progenitor higher up the family tree than the first William Pitt. Cousin David has traced the Irish family back to a great-great-grandfather, Thomas Pitt, of whom nothing is known except that his son Mark was baptised in 1796 in County Wexford in southern Ireland. It is possible that Thomas was a son of one Mark Pitt, a Cornish soldier known to have married in 1744, who may have come to Ireland on duty and, after serving out his time in the Wexford garrison, settled in Ireland. 'Mark' is not a very common Christian name but it has been very persistent in our family, where we know of five Mark Pitts. In any case, it seems probable that the Pitt family in Ireland was originally English: both the family name and the habitually used given names point in that direction. There is not a single Irish name, not a Patrick nor a Michael nor a Brian among our Pitt forebears. My grandfather, Mark Augustine Pitt, named his sons Charles, Frederick, Henry, Edwin, Herbert and Ernest. It seems probable that the Pitts became Irish by settling in Ireland and Catholic through marriage with what Macaulay (who must have been rather like Grandpa) called the aboriginal Irish.

Like other tenant farmers in the 1850s, great-grandfather Mark Pitt was evicted from his small farm at Kerlogue, County Wexford, following the great potato famine of

1845-1849. After that he kept a pub and three of his sons, Richard, Mark and Robert (who were twins) migrated to Australia.

All that is known of Richard Pitt is that he was a witness at the wedding of my grandfather, Mark Augustine Pitt. Nor do we know for certain why the twin brothers, Mark and Robert, left Ireland, nor even when they left, though it was either in 1848 or 1858. If it was 1848 the potato famine, which drove millions of Irishmen from their homes, may be the simple explanation. Family legend supplies a more romantic one, to the effect that Mark and Robert were journalists, working on an Irish nationalist paper considered seditious by the English government of Ireland, and that they had to leave in haste, with the police not far behind them. In favour of their being political refugees is the extremely strong liberal tradition in which Father and his brothers were nurtured and in which I, too, was brought up. Also in favour of it was Mark Augustine's marked literacy and articulateness and my memory of Father's singing to us, when I was a child, the *Shan Van Vocht,* the once banned Irish revolutionary song, which he must have learnt from his father. The Pitts were orthodox nominal Catholics. They went to Mass on Sunday and did not eat meat on Friday, but they were not pious; indeed, they tended to be anti-clerical. The origin of the family of grandmother Pitt is known. Her maiden name was Kate Gibson and she was descended from a Captain Gibson of the seventeenth century, of whom Father used to say, with a rare lapse into the locution he must have heard from his Irish parents, that he fought in the army of Dutch William at the battle of Boyne Water.

We never knew our Pitt grandparents as Mark Augustine died in 1888, and although his wife Kate long survived him she too died before my time. I wish I had known my Pitt grandfather because he seems to have been, in his way, as much of a character as Grandpa Buxton but more congenial to me because of our common interest as teachers and scribblers. On his marriage certificate he described his occupation as 'literary'. In his early days in Melbourne, Mark Augustine seems to have been a journalist, and on at least one occasion he essayed the role of a public lecturer, his subject being Napoleon, but this proved an unprofitable enterprise because the dress suit he bought for the occasion cost as much as the takings.

It was, I suppose, the responsibilities of marriage that put an end to Mark Augustine's more precarious occupations and caused him to enter the public service as a State School teacher, and, as he had eight children (of whom seven survived) in thirteen years, kept him there till the day he died. His family led a wandering life in the various country towns to which he was posted – Colac, Koroit, Port Fairy and finally Timor, near Maryborough, now a ghost town but once, when it was known as Chinaman's Flat, a booming gold-rush town with forty thousand inhabitants. If the illuminated addresses and the inscribed marble clock are any form of measure, Mark Pitt was highly regarded wherever he went, both as teacher and citizen. Perhaps my Father, one of the products of his schools, was more reliable evidence of his father's competence as a teacher. Father wrote a beautiful hand, his grammar was perfect and his spelling faultless, and his brothers and sisters were equally literate and well-spoken.

As well as being thorough, Grandfather Pitt must have been a very kindly and jolly teacher who understood children. In those days the Education Department demanded an enormous amount of rote learning from pupils, especially in Geography, where they were required to know by heart all the straits, islands, capes, rivers and cities of the five continents. To help the hapless wights grandfather Pitt wrote (and published in 1882, price sixpence) his *Geography in Rhyme.* The verses were written to be sung and the appropriate tune for each was suggested. My favorite is 'Rivers of Europe'. It must have been fun to sing, to the tune of 'Yankee Doodle', such rhymes as:

> Weser then through Prussia flows
> With splendid fish up-springing;
> Rhine through Prussia, Holland goes,
> German war-songs singing.
> Meuse through Belgium, Holland flee,

Scheldt through France and Belgium,
All these rivers daily see
Every North Sea beldame.

My imagination responds vividly to that North Sea beldame. I picture her as a robust old party, well-nourished on soused herrings, down on her knees, her ample skirts hitched up, her sabots kicked off, and her poor red hands rubbing the family wash to death on a scrubbing board in the chilly waters of the Meuse or Scheldt.

Mark Pitt was a ready penman and wrote a play, a novel and verses as well as his helpful mnemonics. Although known as an Irish patriot, he was an enthusiast for his adopted country, including its Queen, and for her Jubilee composed (according to the *Maryborough and Dunolly Advertiser,* which published it) 'a beautiful ode', which was sung by his pupils on the occasion of the local Jubilee celebrations. His status as a public servant prevented his participation in contentious issues, but he was active in all that were open to him, particularly every forward movement on the educational front. At one time he was a member of the municipal council of Colac, where he was charged with the delicate function of executing a decision to erect a public lavatory in the park. Here his lively imagination led him astray, as he caused the convenience to be made of cast iron, in the form of an Indian temple, and his fellow councillors, while conceding that as a public building grandfather's fantasy was very tasteful, were of the opinion that considered in the utilitarian light of a public lavatory, it was unduly expensive.

One day in 1888 Mark Pitt had a heart attack in his classroom at Timor. He never recovered consciousness and died soon after. Only three of his seven surviving children were then grown up. The eldest, Charles, aged twenty-four, was a clerk in the Post Office; and then came two daughters, May, aged twenty-two and Kate, twenty-one, who were State School teachers. Next came Father, who was fifteen, his brother Edwin, only one year younger, and lastly Herbert and Ernest, identical twins, who were only eleven. The death of Mark Pitt left his wife in dire financial straits. For my father it was sheer tragedy and inflicted on him an injury from which, in a sense, he never recovered, by depriving him of the higher education on which he had counted.

He was an extremely clever boy and, I think, ambitious – not for money, for which he never cared, nor for possessions, of which he had fewer than anyone I have ever known – but for personal achievement and distinction. He had already been awarded one of the few scholarships which existed in those days to the University of Melbourne and was only waiting to be old enough to begin his chosen study of law, in which he would have excelled. But after the death of his father his duty was clear: he must leave school and earn some money to support himself and contribute to the stricken household. So he entered the Public Service, in the capacity of an office boy, and this experience was to him what the blacking factory was to Charles Dickens, one of grief and humiliation so profound that the wound never healed. Father never spoke of it and when I was a child Mother told me that I was never to ask him questions about when he was a boy. Father remained in the Public Service for exactly half a century and, in a way, the brilliant career did eventuate, because he rose to be the head of the State Treasury; and I once heard Sir Robert Menzies, who knew him well in the days when Menzies was in State politics, say that Henry Arthur Pitt was the best public servant Victoria ever had. In a sense, though, his success was dust and ashes, because he had been deprived of higher education and the career of his choice.

It was inevitable that the next brother, Edwin, should soon follow Father into the Public Service: he went into the State Savings Bank. With five of the children now earning, at however junior a level, the Pitt family kept afloat, and Charles and Father, the eldest males, put their heads together to devise a better future for their little brothers, the twins. The family had moved to Melbourne and Herbert and Ernest attended St Patrick's College, which was the Catholic public school before it was replaced by Xavier. They were clever boys, and an old press cutting shows Herbert as Dux of the school and Ernest as first in every subject in which Herbert was not, and second when Herbert was first.

The grand design was that they were to proceed to the university and they chose medicine as their profession. This long course entailed ferocious economy for the wage-earners of the family but they were, in a sense, happy to make the sacrifice and the twins justified it by sailing ahead most prosperously until they reached their fourth year and began to frequent the hospitals. There Herbert contracted tuberculosis, then an incurable disease, and died soon after. The trauma of the loss of his other half brought Ernest to the verge of a nervous breakdown and he had to confess to his elder brothers that he simply could not continue his medical course alone. So the great effort had been all in vain, or nearly so. Ernest completed the degrees of Bachelor of Science and Bachelor of Arts, but then, like the rest of the family, he had to enter the Public Service, by way of the Public Library, of which he ultimately became the Chief Librarian. For entrance to the professions the Pitt family had to wait another generation. It is pleasant to record that the medical degree, twice *manqué,* was achieved by Ernest's younger son, David.

XI

Mother's sister, my aunty Doone, was the second of the children of John Robert Buxton and Mary O'Brien, whose marriage was first blessed by four daughters and then (when Grandpa was giving up hope and resigning himself to a life spent among females) five sons. One writes 'poor aunty Doone' as unconsciously as one writes 'poor uncle Jack', for these were the unhappiest members of the family. Alone among the Buxtons aunty Doone was red-haired, perhaps an inheritance from some O'Brien forebear, and although she had rather aristocratic bones, she was the plainest of the Buxton sisters. As well, she was very deaf, as a result of severe influenza when she was a child. I always felt that her intelligence, too, had received a check when deafness fell upon her, but I do not really know what she had been like before that. Aunty Doone had a grudge against life. She was a moaner and the combination of her deafness and her plaintiveness tended to keep the world at arm's length, so that loneliness increased her isolation and resentment.

There was never, as far as I know, any question of marriage for aunty Doone, and I do not think it would have done at all, for she was immature and decidedly prudish. She was the only member of the family who was really pious, much given to early Mass, the making of missions and novenas and decorating the altar at the Carmelite Church. I think she would have been happiest as a nun, because she was very good and simple and quite unfitted to cope with life in the world. The question, however, never arose, for aunty Doone was a perennial daughter. She was her Mother's right hand and she revered 'the Boss'. She worried about Grandpa's not being a Catholic: what if he should be excluded from Heaven and unable to preside over the re-united family there? To avert this, long years after his death she was still, out of very slender means, paying for Masses to be said for the repose of his soul. The Boss would have been furious had he known that even by death he had not escaped from Popery.

Poor aunty Doone was a trial. Never have I known anyone in whom the habit of repeating the same complaint in the same words was so highly developed: her repetitiveness really drove one mad. Her low-spirited outlook on life was not wholly, I am sure, caused by her affliction, but in part by a strain of melancholy in the family, evident in lesser degree in some of its other members, such as aunty Kit. That was not, however, by any means all that was to be said about aunty Doone. Although her mind was not very active, her body was immensely so. Never was there a harder or a quicker worker, or one more self-sacrificing and faithful, always the first person to be sent for when a family crisis demanded a helpful pair of hands. She had a great love for nature, was green-fingered in the garden and adored the bush. She had a special affection for my brother John and while he was still a very little boy used to take him for long bush walks: I am sure it was from her that John gained his lifelong love of wild bush country and of growing plants.

Aunty Doone never forgot the important part which re-freshments play in any outing for children. A letter from John to Mother, written when he and his cousin Mark Pitt were little boys on holiday with aunty Doone at Macedon, relates the story of a twelve-mile walk they took, with midday dinner at a boarding-house – 'soup, roast lamb, roast potatoes, cabbage, plums, cherries, vermicelli and rice, and cream, all for 1/6d each' – followed by afternoon tea at a hotel, where 'Mark and I had a glass of bonzer raspberry cordial and aunty Doone had a cup of tea and there was two piles of cakes and scones and the whole lot was only a shilling'.

Aunty Doone was the Martha of 'Hughenden' and aunty Dot, the youngest of the sisters, was the Mary. She was as unlike aunty Doone in temperament as possible: sunny, sociable and gay, the life of every party. Aunty Dot was a beauty, with finely cut, regular features, blue eyes and a fair complexion. She was not pious like aunty Doone, really more like a Protestant, I used to feel, by which I suppose I meant that she was more of a Buxton that an O'Brien, more English that Irish. She had a fine singing voice but it was said in the family that her voice had been ruined by a showy teacher, who had forced it too soon. Perhaps it had been ruined for grand opera or concert performance but it sounded lovely in the 'Hughenden' drawing-room. In her young days, when I first knew her, aunty Dot was rather frivolous and given to extravagance in dress. She was always buying new hats, but they never pleased her. They were hardly home from the shop before she was taking them apart, re-trimming and invariably ruining them. Then she did not have a thing to wear and had to buy a new hat.

I loved rummaging in the walk-in closet where her clothes hung. Mother never had one garment more than was necessary but aunty Dot had lots of lovely dresses which she hardly ever wore, many of them made of impractical materials on which Mother would not have wasted money. In the closet, too, there were endless bandboxes, some containing the wrecks and others the spoils of hats – ribbon bows and streamers, squashed silk and muslin roses and even ostrich feathers. There were lots of dance programmes, too, with their little pastel-coloured pencils dangling from silk cords, with scrawled names that I could not read; pretty, broken fans, hair decorations for balls, and the programmes of all the theatres and concerts aunty Dot had ever attended. Her dressing-table was very different from Mother's austere one, with endless little jars of sweet-smelling creams, big bottles of eau de cologne and little ones of more precious perfumes.

Aunty Dot amassed and hoarded possessions, but the most perfect order prevailed in her closet, on her dressing-table and in her chest of drawers. I have never seen a bed more exquisitely made than hers. She took her time and when it seemed that the effect could not be improved, she gave the final touch, fetching from the closet a walking stick kept there for the purpose. This was run hard over the quilt until it looked as if it had just been ironed and the surface of the bed was as smooth and compact as a sculpture in stone. But aunty Dot was rather a lily of the field in regard to household tasks. She did some of the lighter ones, such as polishing the banisters with a chamois leather and dusting the drawing-room, but she never worked like a slave, after the fashion of aunty Doone. Her role was decorative and social and she spared no pains to play it well. It was aunty Doone who made the tea and carried the heavy tray from the distant kitchen, but it was aunty Dot who went to the drawing-room and entertained the unexpected guests until tea was ready. She loved to give pleasure and exerted herself as much for the dreariest of bores as for the most glamorous of guests. We could always relax in company when aunty Dot was present, knowing that she would take the social responsibility. She was tactful and saw to it that everyone had a lovely time, transforming the most ordinary social occasion into a delightful party. Like any virtuoso, she enjoyed practising her art, but I see now that it must have cost her a great deal. We always expected a fine performance and she always gave it, but I think we all helped to drain the fount of her limited vitality.

The eldest son, uncle Ray, was the head of the Firm in my time, and was said to be a good man of business. His nick-name was 'Mose', short for Moses, because he had inherited Grandma's dark hair, creamy skin and aquiline nose and was thought to have that resemblance to a Jew which is not uncommon among Irish people. Also in the Firm was the next son, my uncle Tom, whom I remember as gentle and rather dreamy and physically not robust. Ray and Tom were great friends and so were the youngest sons, Astley and Len, which left uncle Jack as the middle one of the five and rather isolated. It was poor uncle Jack's fate never to feel really at home in the world. Somehow he always tended to be overlooked and put upon. He worked for the firm like the others, but at the South Melbourne office and not in Collins Street like his more important brothers. I always had the impression that his education had been neglected and that, somehow or other, he belonged to a rather lower social class than the other boys.

Physically, too, uncle Jack was the odd man out, because his brothers were tall and handsome but he was slightly built and short. Although he was not ugly, he was not good-looking, and was the only one of the brothers who always had to wear glasses. He was extremely shy and sensitive and never brought friends home to 'Hughenden' for meals or billiards or a game of cards like the other brothers. Perhaps he thought that his friends would have been subject to criticism at 'Hughenden', and probably he was right, for his lack of self-confidence made him feel more at ease with chaps encountered in pubs and pool rooms than with the middle-class young men suitable for introducing to his mother and sisters. Uncle Jack was devoted to Grandma and because he considered her ill-used, he tended to be at loggerheads with Grandpa.

When I first knew 'Hughenden' Astley and Len were still schoolboys, Astley at Melbourne Grammar School and Len at Xavier; I never knew why they were sent to different schools. Astley, our beloved, everyone's beloved 'Ack', was an utterly charming person. In looks he combined the regularity of Grandpa's features with the O'Brien colouring, being slender and dark, with Grandma's violet eyes. Ack was born at home in the world, a genius of sociability, as outgoing as uncle Jack was introverted. His vitality and mirth overflowed and warmed everyone in his company and he had only to come into the room to make you feel that life was a lark and that champagne was about to be served. It was partly his beauty and partly his grace and largely his clear, infectious laugh that put heart into everyone. He had not a trace of self-importance and took life lightly, as a good joke.

He was a dare-devil was uncle Ack, absolutely unafraid of anyone or anything, but he was not in the least brutal. He was no respecter of persons but he had a profound respect for life, was amiable to the core and nothing human was repugnant to him. Lame ducks of every kind found in him a ready-made friend who did not want to see their credentials. I remember his arriving once at our house with a dirty, drunken old woman he had picked up out of the gutter. He explained that he had brought her to us to put up for the night because Grandma, who was conventional, might not understand. Mother was not madly enthusiastic about his find either, for that matter; still, she gave the disreputable old party shelter and succour because no one, really, ever had the heart to refuse Ack anything. Naturally, he was much pursued by girls and, according to Grandma, fast young women were always telephoning him at 'Hughenden', but he was equally beloved by his male friends.

The uncle I knew least was Len, the youngest and nearest to me in age. Len always seemed to have a chip on his shoulder and to be rather unfriendly. I wish I had understood his situation then as I do now. Not only must he have been the subject of eternal and unfavourable comparison with the matchless Ack, but he was deprived of his place as the baby of the family by the appearance on the scene of another deadly rival, his niece Lorna, who was only three years his junior. The birth of five boys in succession at 'Hughenden' had rather depreciated the male currency and there was great excitement when Mother's first child was a girl. Grandma, so rarely absent from 'Hughenden', made the long journey to Omeo to support Mother, and Len, who was only three, must have felt deserted. It was no doubt at the moment when he found he was no longer his mother's chief concern that Len's jealousy of Lorna began.

There is a charming letter from Grandma to her own two little children, Ack and Len, describing her trip to Omeo, first by train to Bairnsdale and thence by a coach, drawn by relays of four splendid horses, all the eighty miles of the uphill bush road to Omeo. 'Harry and Plum's house is such a nice little one, roses growing all over it and everywhere you look you can see big hills,' she told the boys. Plum's baby, she said, was a darling little girl, but the boys would not enjoy visiting her yet because she was too small to play with them, Poor Len! He was too young for babies or rose-garlanded cottages or even coach-horses, all he knew was that his mother had deserted him and gone away for ages to some other child. Relations were not improved when Lorna, who was a charmer, actually made her appearance on the 'Hughenden' scene as a veritable little Queen of the May, putting even Ack in the shade for the time being. Lorna tells me that Len did not like either of us, and positively disliked her. I did not know this at the time but merely felt that, like most boys, he was bored by little girls.

While I was still a very young child the family at 'Hughenden' dwindled from nine to seven when Ray, the eldest son, and then Tom the next one, got married and went to live only one street apart, in Brighton. Uncle Ray became engaged to a Protestant girl, which caused a stir at 'Hughenden' and lowered tones among Mother and the aunts as they discussed the difficulties caused by mixed marriages, of which they had had so much painful experience. However, this trouble blew over as the bride simplified everything by turning Catholic and the wedding took place in a Catholic church in Brighton. My family's means were very modest in those days, and so were our preparations for the wedding. I daresay that Lorna, being a little older, realised that new dresses would have been correct for such an important occasion, but I had never been to a wedding before and was very pleased by the ingenious way in which Mother made us seem to have new hats when we really did not, by painting our old mushroom straws with shiny black paint, and, after hanging them on the rose bushes in the back garden to dry, trimming them with lovely new ruches, pink ribbon for Lorna and blue for me.

All went well until the wedding breakfast – which seemed to me such an odd way of referring to a splendid luncheon. The bride's parents courteously invited the Irish priest who had celebrated the marriage to say grace. In their Protestant benightedness they had selected for the wedding what in Catholic parlance is called 'a day of abstinence', which meant one on which you must not eat meat, even though it was not

Friday. As very few of our family were either pious or observant Catholics, not many of us knew that it was a day of abstinence and those who did would have kept quiet, but before saying grace the priest saw fit to remind all Catholics present that they must not eat meat on a day of abstinence. We were all embarrassed by the shame brought on our hosts and exasperated, too, by the abstinence from turkey and ham forced upon us; but the fatal word had been spoken and we could not defy the authority of the Church, and so were forced to content ourselves with sardine sandwiches, horrid soggy things from which I still have an aversion. This incident made a deep impression on me. Although I was so young I minded the mortification of those who were giving the party even more than the deprivation of turkey and ham, bitter disappointment though that was, too, to a child who had never heard of such fare except for Christmas dinner. I brooded endlessly over this matter and arrived at a dangerous distinction between God and the Church because God, being good, could not, I opined, approve of the bad manners and unkindness which had been forced upon us, and therefore it must have been the Church that was in error.

Uncle Tom's wedding, however, was an occasion of un-alloyed bliss. I was a child who enjoyed the limelight and was delighted to hear that Lorna and I were to be flower girls. I do not remember whether we had new dresses, but we were supplied with little baskets full of rose petals and brought great credit on our family by managing, as the bridal pair were leaving the church, to walk down the aisle backwards, strewing the petals for our pretty new aunt to walk on, without any undignified mishap, though not without a wobble or two. The reception was held at the Bank – what bank I do not know because I was not then aware that there was more than one – the bank where the bride's father was the manager and the family lived upstairs. The breakfast was, in my eyes, simply dazzling. No doubt a caterer had been employed, but I had never heard of such a person and could not understand how jellies and *charlotte russes* could be so elaborate and come out of their moulds without a flaw instead of being a bit lopsided like even our best puddings at home, or by what magic cream could be induced to take on the colour and form of roses with leaves adorning the pudding itself, instead of merely being white and served in a bowl with a spoon.

Aunty Dot was engaged to be married for years, but it all came to nothing. The young man was poor and had a widowed mother and dependent sisters, who seem to have acquiesced in the notion that he should provide for them indefinitely. The date of the wedding was fixed several times but always had to be postponed. Our elders used to lower their voices maddeningly when they discussed this fascinating topic. By pricking up one's ears one heard certain words often repeated, such as 'sisters', 'selfish', 'no money', and 'weak'. It was not much to go on and Lorna and I entertained various hypotheses, of which the most probable were that the young man either had an exaggerated sense of duty towards those millstones, his sisters, or was too weak to insist that he had a right to a life and a wife of his own and that they must bestir themselves to find husbands or earn their own livings. We never knew for sure why aunty Dot's engagement was finally broken off, but it was and there was never another one. Perhaps she never loved any man but that shilly-shallier; perhaps she was too disillusioned for further entanglements; perhaps she just never met any other man both suitable and willing – who can say now?

Frustrated in marriage, aunty Dot was also defeated in her alternative ambition, which was to go on the stage. She was a born entertainer, had a good figure, danced well and even if her voice had been ruined for grand opera it was more than good enough for musical comedy, to which she aspired. She could have been, we all felt, another Nellie Stewart – not that I ever saw Nellie Stewart on the stage but she seemed to represent to the adults the *ne plus ultra* of musical comedy. When aunty Dot announced her intention of going on the stage there was, of course, an uproar from Grandpa, who fulminated, just as if he had been on it himself playing in old-fashioned melodrama, in soliloquies to the effect that he would prefer to see his youngest daughter dead at this feet and that if she disobeyed him and went, she need never darken the doors of 'Hughenden' again. She did go, however, and went on tour in the chorus of a musical comedy

72

called *Madame Angot* and also *The Chocolate Soldier*. She had to live hard and in rougher company than she had ever known, but she throve on it and loved it. Then something happened that put a stop to it all. I never knew what it was, but it was somehow associated with the outbreak of the First World War. Did the theatre fall on evil days, or was it something to do with the uncles going to the war? Whatever the reason was, aunty Dot came home to 'Hughenden' and stayed there for good.

For the good of her parents and sister and brothers and of us, the grandchildren, but not, certainly, for her own. She was brave and bright and never complained, but somehow the spring of life had been broken in aunty Dot. She just did not seem to have anything to live for. Sometimes she made an effort, like trying to learn French, but she never stuck at it, I suppose because she had no real incentive. She bore with her difficult sister Doone, whose life she was to share till the end, with heavenly sweetness and patience and ruined her voice by perpetually raising it to repeat everything that was said, so that aunty Doone's deafness would not exclude her from the conversation.

Aunty Dot's fate has always angered me. She would have made a lovely wife and mother, a wonderful hostess or a gifted actress, but she just petered out and went to waste. Almost to the end she gave unstintingly of what she was allowed to give – the charm of her society; and the very last time I saw her, as a dying old woman in a nursing home, I wept not because she was dying, for I think she wanted her long, empty life to end, but because of the effort she made to entertain me, and the weariness with which she at last closed her eyes and sank back on her pillow, saying, 'So sorry, can't do the honours'.

XII

The year 1914 brought great changes at 'Hughenden'. When the war broke out uncle Jack rushed off to enlist as soon as the recruiting depots opened, and in consequence was a private in the Fifth Battalion when it landed at Gallipoli on the first Anzac Day. His dash to arms was not in the least demonstrative of a belligerent temperament, for uncle Jack was the least military of men and always looked as if he had borrowed his uniform from a taller, fatter man, and he never mastered the art of winding his puttees in a smart, soldierly fashion. Uncle Jack never felt he counted in the scheme of things and his idea in springing to arms was to save his younger and better loved brothers from doing so. His sight was poor but he proved quite artful, because, having worn glasses all his life, he was familiar with the procedure in oculists' rooms and managed to learn the chart off by heart before presenting himself for examination and, with his glasses in his pocket, he passed the test with flying colours.

Poor uncle Jack, his luck was out, as usual, in the war. He never rose from the ranks, he was never wounded or invalided, he just had to sweat it out. The whole dreadful promiscuousness and sordidness of life as a private in the infantry of the tough AIF, all through the Gallipoli campaign and later, year after year, in the trenches in France, was sheer torture to a terribly thin-skinned man. When he came home, at last, we thought he would enjoy sleeping in a proper bed, but for months he could sleep only on the floor, and when he began to use the bed it was only after he had nailed boards over the spring mattress. Physically uncle Jack was unscathed, but the ordeal had been too much for him. He went back to 'Hughenden' and he went back to the Firm and he did his best, but he could never join in the life and as the years went on he drank to shut out his memories of the horrors and the carnage he had been unlucky enough to live through.

Jack's sacrifice was, inevitably, ineffective, because Ack enlisted too, and he also was at Gallipoli, but not in time for the Anzac landing. Ack's entrance into the war was quite another affair from Jack's – nonchalant and gay. He was a born participant and wanted to be in everything that was afoot and his gregariousness, tolerance, and love of life (which included a complete disdain of death) made army life, however unpleasant, quite bearable for him. He looked smashing in the private's uniform in which uncle Jack looked so badly dressed and self-conscious. Ack had only one problem, an invincible repugnance from killing anyone. Turks and 'Huns' (as they were called) were simply human beings to him, just like Aussies, and he could not hate, much less shoot them. This problem was solved by his joining the Army Medical Corps. He served as a stretcher-bearer both at Gallipoli and in France and his loving kindness and irrepressible courage and gaiety must have brought comfort to the suffering men he carried. Like Jack, Ack should probably never have been accepted by the army, because he had nearly died of rheumatic fever as a lad and was never really strong after it. When the youngest brother, Len, turned eighteen he too enlisted, but was rejected on medical grounds, being told that he had a weak heart. Actually, he was probably the only one of the three brothers completely fit for military service, because no more was heard of the weak heart and he did not die until 1977, having been for many years the sole survivor of the nine children of Grandpa and Grandma.

After the war, the number of Hughendens sank to six when Ack married. I was not at the wedding, and as I was certainly in Melbourne at the time, I think there cannot have been any festivity on the occasion. Ack married a Protestant girl who did not 'turn', and since he was a cheerful pagan, as incapable of distinguishing between Protestants and Catholics as between Turks and Aussies, the wedding may have been in a Protestant church, which we, according to the rigorous rules of the Catholic Church in those unecumenical times, would not have been permitted to attend. Ack's wedding may even, for all I know, have been in a registry office, a practically unmentionable institution in the bourgeois society in which we moved. Ack had two children but died suddenly in his forties. I was at his funeral and never saw, for a private citizen, such throngs of men and women overflowing the church. No one knew who most of them were but, according to their own accounts, Ack had been the best friend of each and every one of them.

By the time that uncle Len married, Lorna was a university student and I was quite a senior schoolgirl. Len's marriage was plain sailing because he married a Catholic girl. Len was the only Hughenden to 'marry well', as used to be said, meaning prosperously. After his marriage he really passed out of our lives into a rich circle which remained unknown to us. Alone of the five brothers he left the Firm and entered the business of his father-in-law. But before Len faded from our sight there was his wedding, a splendid occasion on quite a different level from the other family weddings, and the first sophisticated social occasion I ever attended. I had supposed it to be a law of Nature, or at least of the Church, that a bride must wear white, but Len's bride wore a marvellous apricot-coloured gown, from Paris, it was rumoured. The other weddings had been in the morning, followed by a breakfast which was a luncheon, but Len's wedding was at night, with everyone in evening dress, followed by a dinner party and dance at Carlyon's Hotel at St Kilda, then the height of fashion. It was a wondrous experience, to be relished most by talking it over at home afterwards, for, being at the awkward age, neither a child nor an adult, I felt self-conscious and out of place and did not really enjoy myself. There was one episode during which I should have liked to hide under the table, when Grandpa, I felt, brought shame on our side by a simply awful speech of the robust sort, in which he did not fail to express the hope that all the young couple's troubles would be little ones.

XIII

After Len's marriage the household at 'Hughenden' shrank to five, and so it long remained, while aunty Doone and aunty Dot and uncle Jack became middle-aged and Grandpa and Grandma grew old. Still the routine of life at 'Hughenden' continued just as it always had. Much younger grandchildren than Lorna and I now collected their morning chocolate and Saturday money from Grandpa, foraged in the larder for loaf sugar and ginger beer, fed Grandma's canaries, dressed up in the schoolroom from the big box, and went down the cellar to see the wax temple from Ceylon. Lorna and I even helped to decorate the Christmas tree while a new generation of children sat in the hall, wishing the grown-ups would finish their tea and the door into the morning-room would open. Everything went on just as it always had at 'Hughenden' for years and years. Grandpa lived to be over eighty and to make friends with his first great-grandchild, Lorna's elder son. And then, one day, he died.

I could hardly believe the news. 'Hughenden' had fallen, the solid bluestone foundations had betrayed us, we were a homeless, scattered people. 'Hughenden', as an institution, really came to an end when Grandpa died. One might have thought there would have been a season of autumnal calm for Grandma, but it was not so. With Grandpa's death, her *raison d'être* was gone. There was serenity now, without any need to create it, for of what use is a balance without a strain to which to act as counterpoise? Although the physical house stood as firmly as ever, its meaning had gone and it crumbled away spiritually. Grandma, poor dear, was so tired, and I think she no longer tried to keep going but, her work done, simply turned her face to the wall. Suddenly she looked like an old woman and did not seem to care any more. She just gave up and died soon after Grandpa. Then only aunty Doone and aunty Dot and uncle Jack were left and 'Hughenden' was unthinkable to them without Grandma. The aunts bought a cottage at Macedon and furnished it with some of the smaller pieces from 'Hughenden', and made it a cosy little nest and a very charming one when aunty Doone had reformed the garden by hard work and good taste. Uncle Jack's history was ill-starred right to the end. He was still working for the Firm, and had to live in town in a boarding-house among strangers. He probably felt the loss of his home and his mother even more than the aunts, and he was very unhappy; he had his only stroke of luck when he died before the aunts, who both lived into their eighties.

So 'Hughenden' was sold and the three remaining Hughendens went away and it was all over. We were glad that the Danes bought 'Hughenden' and brought the sad, empty house back to vigorous life. 'Hughenden' stands there still, and long may it stand on its solid bluestone foundations. But its real foundations now are in the minds and hearts of the grandchildren, many of whom are now grandparents themselves. When we are all dead there will be only a Danish Club or perhaps a block of flats in its place, and 'Hughenden' will have ceased to exist, except in this record of the impressions of a child who, more than sixty years ago, was taking notes.

Only once before I was twenty was our family cut off from 'Hughenden' for long, for the whole of the year 1914 in fact. When we were suddenly uprooted we had been living at 68 Harold Street, Middle Park for five years, during which time my brothers, John and Kevin, had been born. Then that mysterious entity on which all our lives depended, the Treasury, decided that Father was to work for a year in London instead of at Treasury Place in town. By the time this astounding news reached us it had also been arranged that Mother was to go to London with Father and that all of us children were to be sent to boarding-school, to a convent at Portland for girls and boys. It was kept by the nuns of the Loreto Order, whose convent in Albert Park Lorna and I had been attending.

Although throughout my childhood the words 'boarding-school' (always uttered as a threat in consequence of naughtiness) struck chill into my soul and produced an instant and craven change of behaviour, I do not remember any alarm on hearing that we were really going to boarding-school. On other occasions the words had portended the absolute terror of being sent away to live among strangers, but going to Portland convent was not the same at all because Lorna would be there to protect me, and John and Kevin would be there too, just as at home. Mother's married sister, aunty Kit, caught the infection of change and decided that her eldest child, John's contemporary and bosom friend Mark Pitt, was to go to Portland Convent with us. Five Pitts together, I felt, would create a zone of safety in a strange world, and even that would not be quite strange for Lorna and me as we were used to Loreto ways. The parting from our parents caused me no real distress because, like most children, I had often speculated on the orphaned state and thought it might be quite a lark to try it as long as Mother and Father were really safe and Lorna was there to hold my hand.

There was much to be done before our exodus from Harold Street. Mary O. was sent for and was at her machine for weeks, making our outfits for Portland and Mother's for the ship. Everything else that Mother would need was to be bought in London, where it was an article of colonial faith in those days to believe that divine dresses could be bought for a song. We learnt with astonishment that in London Father was to buy a top hat and wear it instead of the old, familiar, battered felt that was good enough in Melbourne. His position in London, it seemed, was to be more exalted than at home, and in fact he did serve for part of his time away as acting Agent-General for Victoria.

The nuns at Portland had supplied a list of the clothes we must bring. Mother, whose unhappy nature it was to quarrel with the inevitable, regarded the nuns' demands as preposterous and did her best to circumvent them. She particularly resented being asked for bathing gowns, because the whole concept of sport was alien to her; in fact she thought it plain silly. So the demand for bathing gowns was met, but in a manner which exposed us to dreadful humiliation, because Mary O. had run them up out of an old summer dress of Mother's, made of cotton voile, and when later we emerged from our bracing dip in the ocean we might as well have been naked in our clinging, transparent garments. We were also equipped with mortifying spencers made of scarlet 'Doctor' flannel in which we furnished another astounding spectacle when making our winter toilets at the communal wash-basins.

But filled with well-based misgiving as Lorna and I were about our own equipment, we were entranced with Mother's. The ukase of the Treasury was that Father and Mother were to travel first-class to England by the P & O line, and they would have to wear evening dress every night for weeks on end. We knew what evening dress was from watching aunty Dot dressing for balls, but the idea of evening dress for Mother was sensational. She never went to parties and did not own an evening dress and did not want one either, because among her many idiosyncrasies was her scorn for women's mania for dress, which she dismissed with one of her favourite words – 'vulgarity'. Mother was particular about the cleanliness and neatness of her own and our clothes, would not tolerate holes in stockings or fingers sticking out of gloves or unpolished shoes, but she cared nothing for fashion or multiplicity of garments. Clothes, at our place, were for decency and keeping out the cold, and they were to be washed (or, if unwashable, cleaned with ammonia and hung on the line to air), ironed, kept well brushed, turned or dyed when they got shabby and when holes ultimately appeared they were to be darned or patched with patient care and sent back into the line to fight on a bit longer.

But with all her frugality and utter indifference to other people's opinions, Mother was capable of rising above her accustomed ways on special occasions. The trip to England was an occasion of the first magnitude, a great golden apple of fortune suddenly fallen from heaven into her lap. For a whole year she and Father were to live at the Strand Palace Hotel in London, and Mother would escape from housekeeping, which she detested, and from the demands of her four children, whom she loved but who were, all the same, a terrible burden and anxiety to her. Besides, she was going 'Home', to England, to that better home which she had never seen but knew from legend, as all her generation did, as so much better in every way than 'the colonies' in which their unfortunate lot had been cast. With fortune smiling on her, Mother did not lack magnanimity in response, and if wearing evening dress every night for a month was part of the price of going 'Home', she was ready to pay it. Not of course with mad recklessness, such as would have been constituted by going to Hicks, Atkinson's or Buckley & Nunn's and ordering evening dress after evening dress, but by an artful dodge for stretching the wardrobe Mary O. was making for her shipboard life. A black lace overdress was the key to this manoeuvre. Mary O. made slips of three different colours to be worn under this. I suppose dear Mother naively believed that everyone would be deceived into thinking she had three evening dresses of rather similar style and the slips could be made of quite cheap material, 'sateen' probably, as it was only the colour and not the quality that could be seen through the black lace. We were amazed by the ingenuity of this contrivance and I was sure Mother would be a credit to our family and the Treasury, especially in my favourite of the three, the emerald green which looked so rich under the black lace.

I think that we children must have been carried off to 'Hughenden' before our parents left, for no scenes of harrowing parting come back to me. Father and Mother had already sailed away when our contingent set out for Portland, under the charge of aunty Dot, by train from Spencer Street, with the Hughendens *en masse* to see us off. Lorna, the eldest, was eleven; I was eight; Mark was five, John four and little Kevin only two. We were to be in the train all day, a great adventure for children whose only acquaintance with trains so far was the one from Middle Park station which took us just a short distance, whether we went in one direction, to town, or in the other, to St Kilda. But I felt no alarm at this great adventure, because the protecting wing of 'Hughenden', represented by aunty Dot, stretched safely over us and there was also Lorna, who was already what she has remained to me for life, more of a mother than my real mother, who took maternity so hard.

I recall the journey to Portland as sheer bliss, with much larking about in corridors and frequenting of the fascinating moving lavatories. The climax of ecstasy was our main meal in a station restaurant. It was a proper dinner with white tablecloths and pleated white linen napkins arranged like fans, and waitresses in caps and aprons, all very unlike the railway stations of nowadays. I probably did not get much to eat because I have always been a slow eater and the three courses came and went at lightning speed, but what did that matter to a child in wonderland? I had never eaten in a restaurant before and our family menu was restricted and repetitive, but here there were unheard-of novelties and choices. The greatest success with us all was Canary Pudding, a bright yellow steamed pudding swimming in even brighter yellow custard. We knew all about canaries from Grandma's aviary at 'Hughenden', but we thought it irresistibly funny to call a pudding after a bird. We were seized with one of those paroxysms of giggles that visit children who have had too much excitement, and aunty Dot and Lorna had their work cut out to get us back to the train as one or other began crying 'Canary Pudding! Canary Pudding!' while the rest went into fresh attacks of the giggles at the joke which must have seemed singularly unfunny to poor tired aunty Dot.

I remember our arrival at the front door of Portland Convent, which was opened by a lay sister. Aunty Dot was standing in front, holding Kevin by the hand, with the rest of us, very sober now that boarding-school had suddenly become a reality, huddled shyly behind her. Aunty Dot explained who we were and that Reverend Mother was expecting us, but the lay sister, instead of saying 'Good evening' or 'Come in, please', just stood silent and transfixed, gazing not at aunty Dot but at Kevin. Thinking she must be deaf or a bit wanting, aunty Dot made her speech all over again, but in a higher key and more imperative manner. The lay sister came out of her trance and apologised, saying in a confused way: 'It was the little boy – so beautiful – I thought he must be the Child Jesus'. Our baby brother was, indeed, a beautiful child, blue-eyed with an irrepressible aureole of bright golden curls and, after his long day of travelling, his normally rosy cheeks must have been pale, giving him a spiritual air which was not really characteristic of him. It was not surprising that the lay sister, a simple soul living in daily expectation of miracles, should have mistaken Kevin for a heavenly visitant, but somehow the incident was disturbing and stuck in my mind.

Memory fails after our arrival at the convent and comes to life again only with us all established at Portland and aunty Dot gone back to town. We had arrived for the beginning of the school year in February but in my memory Portland is a perpetually cold place, even (or especially) during enforced summer dips in the Southern Ocean in our shame-inducing voile garments. It probably really was cold most of the year because the convent occupies a stark position on a cliff facing the ocean and is swept, many days of the year, by the prevailing south-westerly wind. In those days convents were very bleak places, with bare, gleaming, terribly clean linoleum-covered floors, a great deal of empty space, minimal furnishing and, even on the most bitter winter days, no heating whatever – indeed, in my childhood, I believed it to be part of the lax discipline of Protestants that, as I had heard, they provided fires for pupils in their schools. We had to make do with mittens, which were obligatory in winter, but they did not make much difference. All of us suffered agonies from chilblains and, as I write, my eye falls ruefully on the forefinger of my right hand, still lumpish and misshapen from the worst of the chilblains of more than sixty years ago.

There was nothing in the whole of Portland Convent on which the eye could rest with pleasure. The only non-utilitarian objects we ever saw were the customary plaster casts of the Blessed Virgin, dressed in sky-blue and white, and St Joseph in what looked like a brown dressing-gown, with a lily in his hand. We had already learnt from Mother that while these casts must be treated with respect as religious reminders, they were not to be considered as works of art, because they were manufactured objects, poured into a mould and baked, just like a caramel custard. A real statue, we had learnt, was made out of real stone by a sculptor, who imposed order on chaos, just as the first Creator did, but with the important difference that he could not transform brute matter by mere fiat, but could only realise his vision laboriously, with a chisel and the sweat of his brow.

Convents and convent life were not strange to Lorna and me: indeed, at eight years old, I was already a veteran with five years of convent experience behind me. But boarding-school was different in that rule by nuns went on for seven days of the week, without the relief of the daily escape to the secular regime of our parents or the joys of 'Hughenden' at the weekend. As individuals, the nuns at Portland were kindness itself to the more or less orphaned children under their care, but nuns are (or were) individuals only to a very limited extent. They were like soldiers: they had taken God's shilling and their prime duty was to serve Him, as it were, in the Loreto regiment. Portland Convent was a small community but it had its hierarchy of lay sisters, Sisters, Mothers and Reverend Mother. We were vaguely aware that even Reverend Mother herself was a person under discipline, that there existed somewhere far away, perhaps in Sydney, a

Mother Superior and that even Mother Superior was subject to the Head of the Order, who lived we knew not where, perhaps in Rome, subject to the Pope, who, of course, received his instructions direct from God. I never remember a time when the conception of a hierarchy, which I later found difficult to explain to predominantly Protestant Australian university students, was not completely familiar to me. On the whole it seemed a satisfactory arrangement since those at each stratum had someone to boss as well as someone to obey, but like all systems it has its defects. At the top God could boss everyone but had no one to advise Him or to take responsibility; but His position was decidedly better than ours, the pupils at the base of the pyramid.

Respect for authority is (or was) a *sine que non* of convent life. The highest form of authority known to us was Reverend Mother, and at Portland Convent her presence was the more awe-inspiring because, as far as the children were concerned, she dwelt apart and invisible, as secluded from daily life as the Dalai Lama himself. We saw her only when she made a rare public appearance in the school for a state occasion, or when summoned to her presence for some very special reason, usually reproof for a grave offence. For an encounter with Reverend Mother we were prepared as for presentation at Court, that is in the same spirit, although our resources did not permit splendour of attire. Our already clean faces and hands were further honed down by a thorough scrubbing and neat though we always were, we had to be neater still for Reverend Mother, with our dresses well brushed, our shoes gleaming, plaits freshly done and tied with ribbon just ironed and, as the final touch, the nun responsible for our correct appearance took a spotless pair of white cotton gloves from their tissue paper wrapping and supervised the straightness of the seams because – I know not why – the eye of Reverend Mother must never be allowed to fall on the ungloved hand of a little girl.

I recollect only one *tête-à-tête* with Reverend Mother. I failed to profit by her discourse on the dangers of worldliness because she illustrated it by tracing with her fingernail, on the sparkling mahogany surface of the round table in her parlour in which the audience was held, the direct route to the everlasting bonfire to which the practice of worldliness inevitably conduced. I suppose I must have been worldly, really, though not in the sense Reverend Mother had in mind, because I thought the mahogany table simply beautiful and was more worried about the immediate danger of her scratching it with her fingernail than the remote one of my eternal punishment. Besides, when she spoke of the terrible dangers lying in wait for girls when they left convents and went out into the world, I was fascinated by the Irish way in which she pronounced 'world' as 'wurrld'. The wurrld, when I ultimately encountered it, was to prove a disappointment in the way of the temptations so frequently referred to but never specified by the nuns: it did not seem much interested, still less hell-bent on seducing me.

Convents, in my day, were not child-oriented institutions: they were dedicated *Ad Majorum Dei Gloriam*. This was no mere form of words as in the Latin mottoes of many private schools, but quite literally true. AMDG was the heading I inscribed on every page of every exercise-book I used during my twelve years in convents. I write neatly and legibly to this day because the nuns insisted that blots and scratchings-out and 'm' that could be mistaken for 'n' were not for the greater but the lesser glory of God, and unsatisfactory writing had to be transcribed again and again until perfection was achieved. The same held good for the evenness of stitches in hemming and smooth invisibility in darning, even though it was not possible to inscribe AMDG all over our garments. Perfection was the standard and it was immutable. But young children, engaged in the discovery of the world, are not perfectionists but empiricists, taking up this and casting that aside, leaving a trail of deformed or maimed objects in their wake. Therefore, according to the convent ethic of my time, they had to be forced to be perfect, just as Rousseau held that men must be forced to be free. The two principal methods used in the effort to make us perfect were routine, which acts like a soporific on individuality, forming habits strong enough to last a lifetime, and fear, which paralyses self-will and induces obedience.

The routine of life at Portland Convent was absolute and at first bore rather heavily on children such as us, who had always had a good deal of freedom and came from a home in which the element of unpredictability was a strongly marked feature of life. At Portland every minute of the day was planned and no time at all was allowed for that solitary, introspective mooching around to which I was then and still am prone. At first light we made our beds under supervision by a nun who applied the AMDG method to bed-making, pointing out that every valley must be exalted and the mountains and hills made plain. When we had undressed at night and folded our underclothés neatly on a chair, we were required to arrange our black stockings in a cross on top of the pile, thus dedicating our last action of the day to God.

At first there was a certain interest, soon dulled by repetition, in the novelty of the times at which we ate and some of the dishes. Breakfast was normal but there was no luncheon proper, only 'refection' served when classes ended at midday. Refection amazed us, as it consisted of thick chunks of dry bread and a glass of 'jam-water', a concoction made by adding a great deal of water to a very little plum jam. After refection we were taken for a walk or a swim or sometimes just told to play in the convent grounds. We were never for one minute unsupervised, but we were not taught how to play any games nor did we, as far as I remember, show much invention ourselves. All there was to do when told to play was to throw a ball about aimlessly and as I could neither throw nor catch I used to try to sneak off and hide, a manoeuvre always quickly detected and stopped, because nuns, unlike our absent-minded mother, had eyes in the backs of their heads. I remember on a bitter winter day begging, through my chattering teeth, to be allowed to go indoors and being told that children's health required fresh air and that as I was cold I must run about and run I had to, just to and fro, nowhere in particular, until the ringing of the school bell, at a quarter to three, put an end to the ordeal of outdoors recreation.

Hand-washing, stocking-straightening and hair-tidying followed, a joyous rush of preparation for the great event of the day – dinner, which, strangely, was served at three o'clock. Why we had dinner at three I never discovered. It was simply the rule of the school, like everything else. Perfect silence now as we filed into the refectory, where there were long tables, girls to the left, boys to the right. It was only at meal times that we caught a glimpse of our brothers and our cousin Mark, who did not live in the main convent building but apart, in the Boys' Cottage. I hardly ever saw John and Kevin and Mark because my allotted place at table was with my back to the boys and turning round was bad manners and not allowed. No children can ever have had their table manners more perfectly manicured than the pupils of Portland Convent in my days, or at least the girls, for we had the impression that a double standard was used and that more laxity prevailed at the boys' table. The only decoration I recall in that bleak refectory was a framed notice in ecclesiastical lettering, which read – 'Do Not Eat With Your Eyes', an essay in wit which delighted me once I had grasped its import. We did not eat with our eyes and we did not grab, but pressed everything assiduously on others, and if offered something nice ourselves, did not take the largest or most succulent portion unless it happened to be the nearest one. It was considered unspeakably vulgar to eat dessert with a spoon and so that we should never succumb to this temptation only forks were provided. Once a nun gave us a lesson in how to eat jelly with a fork, but it was not very helpful because as the rules of the order did not permit her to eat with lay persons her jelly was imaginary and therefore much easier to manage than the genuine slithery article. We became adepts by necessity, learning that even stewed fruit with custard can be eaten with a fork if you hold fast to the correct technique of rationing the solid part and steeping each mouthful of it in all the liquid it will absorb. All round, indeed, we became elegant performers at the table under the constant surveillance of the nun on duty. Lay sisters, poor sainted maids-of-all-work, served the meal, while the nun proper circulated round the tables, watching, teaching and admonishing.

Dinner was a hearty meal, which began with what was called 'first meat', a kind of *entrée*, consisting of some savoury kind of meat, such as sausage or black pudding, served alone. Then came 'second meat', which was the conventional roast with vegetables, and we ended with some kind of pudding or other dessert. It was, of course, required that we should eat whatever was set before us without comment or face-pulling. This rule was hard on my brother John who had what would now be called an allergy to eggs, but was forced to eat them all the same and was always sick afterwards. It was hard on Lorna, too, who would good-naturedly and in furtive haste stuff down several plates of lemon-sago to save girls who hated it from being forced to eat it. Porridge was – and is – nauseating to me, but at the convent it was served every morning. This led to the one and only challenge to authority I ever dared to attempt at Portland. I said that I could not eat porridge, that it made me sick and that, in short, I would not. The nun in charge received this ultimatum calmly, merely stating that I would not leave the table until I had eaten my porridge. So there I sat with the plate before me, while everyone else ate theirs and finished breakfast and said grace and went away, leaving me solitary in what seemed the enormous, empty refectory. And there I sat and sat on my bench of desolation before the plate of now revoltingly congealed porridge for what seemed to me like an eternity. After a discreet interval a nun appeared and opened negotiations. I would be released from the refectory if I ate my porridge, which would be re-heated to make it more palatable. I was not made of the stuff of martyrs and to my eternal shame gave in and ate my beastly portion.

I was never forced to eat porridge again, but if you suppose that I had won a partial victory you are mistaken. I knew then, just as well as I know now, that I had suffered a major defeat. My being excused from porridge thereafter was merely an act of grace, an added humiliation of the conquered by the all-powerful conqueror, Authority. To authority the porridge itself was neither here nor there, as was demonstrated by my exemption from it. What was important was a conventual principle called Breaking the Will, familiar to all convent girls of my generation. The nuns thought it right to break wills in order to produce humble and contrite hearts: they most sincerely believed (and their whole lives bore witness to their belief) that it was to the greater glory of God that wills should be broken to perfect obedience to authority. After sixty years of brooding on the day my will was broken, my heart is neither humble nor contrite: I think it was a degrading experience and I resent it bitterly.

Hardly any memories of the formal class-room instruction we received at Portland remain. We did a great deal of learning by heart and I can still spout yards of *The Lady of the Lake* and *The Prisoner of Chillon.* Now that I come to think of it, *The Prisoner of Chillon* was rather a macabre study for a child of eight. I still feel a slight *frisson* when declaiming (as I was later to do, in the very Castle of the poem) —

> My hair is grey, though not with years;
>   Nor grew it white in a single night,
> As men's have grown from sudden fears:
>   My limbs are bow'd, though not with toil,
> But rusted with a vile repose.
>   For they have been a dungeon's spoil,
> And mine has been the fate of those
>   To whom the goodly earth and air
> Are bann'd and barr'd – forbidden fare – . . .

I am sure, however, that the sensation of the first encounter with those lines did no harm at all, for children relish horrors provided they are only in a story, with no personal application. And I applaud the nuns for beginning us with Scott and Byron instead of rubbishy rhymes.

Many of the pupils found the long hours we devoted to the copy-book very wearisome but I did not mind at all because, being both lazy and neat-handed, I have always liked monotonous manual tasks that can be classed as work but permit the mind to rove freely. My favourite text in the copy-book was 'Coconuts grow in Zanzibar', which conjured up delightful sensations and visions. I had never seen or tasted a fresh coconut (though familiar with and approving of the desiccated sort embedded in the chocolate icing of lamingtons) but I felt sure they were delicious and, being native and plentiful in Zanzibar, freely and frequently distributed to children there. As for Zanzibar itself, I knew it to be a dream of beauty for how, with a name like the sound of a violoncello, could it possibly be otherwise?

After dinner we had a bit more enforced 'recreation' and

then came our private study period. This was usually supervised by a nun called Mother Francis de Sales and (as we pronounced the name exactly as written) I have always associated her with a noble ship under full sail, rather like the Fighting Temeraire. She sailed up and down the aisle separating the desks, a fine presence with billowing skirts and soft shoes, gliding over the linoleum as silently as a painted ship upon a painted ocean. She never seemed to see us (and indeed was probably saying her Office to herself while making her patrol) but she was fitted with some fine antenna of awareness, which advised her of the faintest whisper or even of fidgeting. Then, and only then, did she utter and it was always the same sentence, spoken very quietly but with indescribable menace – 'Be careful, girls, be careful.' That was all, but it was more than enough: what would have happened had we not been careful we did not wish to know, and once that sentence had been spoken we were as quiet as if we had been at Mass. Mother Francis de Sales terrified me but she was the most gifted disciplinarian I have ever seen in action and her technique made such a deep impression that I was able to adapt it for my own use when later I was to face the problem of how one person is to keep order among many.

After private study came indoor recreation, which was rather pleasant, because we could talk (a rare treat in convent life) or even read, and at Portland Convent I made my first acquaintance with Dickens by reading *Oliver Twist*. It strikes me now as rather an advanced work for nuns to let little girls read in the full, unexpurgated edition. After indoor recreation we had supper, which was like morning refection, except that there was hot cocoa instead of cold jam-water. Then evening prayers and ablutions, carefully supervised, and the evening ended with a strenuous bout of hairbrushing, one hundred strokes of the brush and not one less being the required number. I felt it hardly fair of the nuns, who had solved the hair problem once and for all by shaving it off, to insist on meticulous hair-culture for us and, indeed, a dangerous thought weakly fluttered across my awakening mind, a question as to whether there might not be some inconsistency between shining hair and the renunciation of worldliness so constantly urged on us as an ideal.

In all seasons we washed in cold water but once a week we had a hot bath on whatever night we were rostered for. I imagine that the convent had no hot water system and that the water for the hot baths was heated nightly in coppers. 'Utterly ridiculous' Mother had said, on finding on the list of items Lorna and I must bring to the convent, the words 'bath robes'. From the specifications it was clear that these were not what we called dressing-gowns, for putting on before and after the bath, but just what the words said, bath robes, long-sleeved ample dresses right down to the ground, for wearing in the bath. At home we had long bathed ourselves, Mother attending only briefly to make sure we had not skipped the harder bits, but at Portland even the oldest girls, like Lorna, were bathed by one of the lay sisters. Each bath took a long time, because not only did the lay sister do a perfect, AMDG job, but in order not to offend against modesty, she folded back only a few inches of the bath robe at a time, washed and re-clothed the bare bit and began on another area. The same regard for modesty was shown in the dormitory where, although we had curtained cubicles, we were taught how to undress and dress without seeing any of our own flesh by making a kind of tent of night-dress or dress.

Protestant friends, when regaled with these details of convent life, have asked whether such attitudes towards our bodies did not make us prurient little beasts. No, I do not think so. Our view of the matter was that all adults were mad and nuns the maddest. We did not ask the nuns their reasons for giving us a bath in so laborious and inefficient a manner because, being children and therefore not mad ourselves, we knew that it was a waste of time to ask mad people reasonable questions. The same principle held good for the ban on what were called 'particular friendships', a curious term since friendship is, *per se*, particular: what was meant was making a favourite playmate or companion of any particular girl. No doubt it is necessary for nuns, in their sexually segregated communities, to guard against lesbianism. We, of course, had not the faintest idea of what they were guarding us from, nor did we have any curiosity about it: the rule against particular friendships was, in our opinion, only another instance of the madness of nuns.

What I remember as chiefly being stressed in our Portland curriculum was the correct way of doing things. Training was all, education (in the literal sense of bringing to light and developing individual character or talent) was nothing. What was in us, the nuns believed, was original sin and their duty was to drill it out of us by insisting that there was one and only one right way of doing everything and tolerating only that way. Sitting, for example, required the head to be up, shoulders back and down, feet side by side, heels and knees together, hands (unless usefully occupied) perfectly still and never engaged in hair-smoothing, ear-exploring or any other activity pertaining to the person. I can recognise a convent girl of my generation still by her posture and deportment. Slumping and sprawling were unladylike and anyway, impossible, because the only arm-chairs and sofas in the convent were in the parlour for visitors; for us there were only backless benches and stiff wooden chairs. An upright posture was further encouraged by a daily exercise of walking briskly round a room with blocks of wood balanced on our heads. Our speech had to be clear and our vowels correctly pronounced, and in the course of a year (for we did not return to Melbourne for the holidays) this became habitual, so that when Lorna and I at last re-appeared at 'Hughenden' our young uncles, Ack and Len, pretended to be unable to understand a word we said because, they averred, our lingo was so lah-di-dah.

The writing of home letters, a weekly task, was just the same as class-work, indeed it was done in class-room conditions. First, the nun in charge wrote a handy summary of the events of the week on the blackboard, to provide us with material. We then composed our letters on scribbling-paper and handed them to the nun for inspection, just like our Saturday morning darning. If there were spelling mistakes or any fault in the setting out or content, the draft suffered the same fate as cobbled darning and had to be done again from the beginning. If it passed the test we were given good writing paper on which to make a fair copy. This went for inspection and if there were the slightest flaw it must be written again, and again and again if need be. This discipline may have added *Ad Majorum Dei Gloriam* but it did not conduce to ease or naturalness of composition. Left to myself I would probably have informed my parents that we had had lemon sago for pudding again today and that it was beastly stuff and I hated it, and my parents, receiving this, would have known that their younger daughter was still herself, alive and kicking against the pricks. Such a communication would never have been allowed: our letters had to be absolutely bland, like the lemon sago itself. So I wrote the same letter every week, as I know, having seen several examples which Mother kept. My handwriting was excellent, the spelling faultless, and the contents succinct, both because I could not say anything that I naturally would have said and because even the best-trained child of eight, now rising nine, cannot sustain perfection of performance for more than a few lines. Therefore I wrote –

Dear Mother and Father,
I hope you are both well. We are all quite well. On Saturday we went to Government Paddock for a picnic. It was nice. I must close now.
> Your loving daughter,
>> Kathleen.

My name was indeed Kathleen, but I had never been called by it at home. That, however, was my baptismal name and that was how I had to sign my letter. How dismal it must have been for my parents in London to receive this stiff little missive, more like a tax than a gift, week after week and month after month, from their child who wrote like a stranger. Lorna, being older and much nicer, probably made more effort and wrote at greater length, but, subject as she was to the same censorship, her letters too probably had all the spontaneity and frankness filtered out of them before they were considered fit to send to London, where Mother and Father were dwelling in palatial bliss without a domestic care in the world.

Other cares, indeed, they were to know. The first was the outbreak of the First World War. We had no notion, of course, what war might mean and the chief difference it made to me was an increase in self-importance because the good nuns, always in search, I suppose, of something to pray for, began to feature 'Mr and Mrs Pitt, far off in London and exposed to the terrible dangers of war' in school prayers. I brushed the terrible dangers off very lightly – how could anything happen to Mother and Father? – but I distinctly remember feeling very superior to the other children whose insignificant parents, not being in far-off London and exposed to the terrible dangers of war, did not rate public mention at prayers.

I do not remember formal religious education as playing a greater part at Portland Convent than at the other convents I attended. Morning and evening prayers, of course; Mass and Benediction on Sundays and specially holy days, and lessons in Christian Doctrine which, at my elementary stage, meant chiefly learning by heart the Green Catechism. There was, however, one religious experience, very harmful in its effects, I have always thought, to which I would not have been subjected had I been living at home. This was attendance at one of those crash courses known as a Mission, which the Redemptorist Fathers were conducting in the parish church, which was not a special mission for children but the regular one for adults. The Redemptorist Fathers were – and perhaps still are, but I do not know for sure, having given them a wide berth ever since – a special order, trained as commandos or shock troops for their task of plucking brands from the burning by making eternal punishment so real to sinners that they could feel the heat from the fires of Hell burning their cheeks and repent while there was still time. Hardened sinners, who were the main concern of the Redemptorists, are apt to be insensitive persons and in order to get the message of their danger through to them it is necessary to describe in vivid, concrete and pitiless detail what the life of eternal torment they are heading for is actually going to be like. This technique may work well for those for whom it is devised (though one wonders why such people should be frequenting a Mission at all) but its effects on an imaginative child can be dire.

The sermons of the Redemptorist Fathers did not make me a better child, but they terrified me out of my wits. I did not, of course, know just what the sins were with which the Redemptorists were charging the congregation, but I did know, having heard it mentioned frequently, that we are all miserable sinners, and 'all' included me. Were mine mortal sins or only the venial ones for which the Redemptorist God of wrath would be sufficiently appeased by my detention in Purgatory? Better be on the safe side. If one died while in a state of mortal sin, I knew, there was no question of the soft option of Purgatory. Better not die then, and the effort to avoid the danger of death helped to make a physically timid child into a coward.

I had heard, however, that people sometimes died in their sleep, and how was that danger to be avoided? By not going to sleep. And so, for night after night and year after year I struggled to avoid falling asleep and though, of course, I did not succeed, by dint of recalling the most grisly parts of the sermons at the Mission I learnt how to postpone the onset of sleep; and not since I was eight have I ever succeeded in going to sleep until some hours after going to bed. Lorna seemed to be completely unaffected by the Mission and I think it likely that she did not listen spellbound to the Redemptorist Fathers as I did, but preserved herself by allowing her thoughts to stray to less alarming topics than eternal punishment.

Horrors make a deep impression which is not commensurate with the time they actually occupy. The general tenor of life at Portland Convent was not at all horrific. Provided one submitted, in general, to the system – and all children must submit, more or less, to some system imposed on them by adults – one could be, and we were, happy, so happy, indeed, that when, in the Christmas holidays, I learnt that we were not to return to Portland, I had a good cry. The nuns strove to break the monotony of boarding-school life by giving us little treats from time to time. On our birthdays, of which they were mysteriously apprised, we were made much of and allowed the enormous privilege of feeling, for once, like spoilt children. One's place at table was decorated, there were beautifully wrapped little gifts encircling it and special things to eat, a party in fact.

John, who had his fifth birthday at Portland, still remembers the marvellous orange he was given, on which the name JOHN seemed to grow because the nuns had cut out part of the rind to form it; and sixty years later he said that this magic orange was the most wonderful present he ever received in his life. Sad to say, however, John's birthday was nearly ruined by a scene in the refectory, an occasion of dreadful mortification to us as it was caused by our cousin Mark. John and Mark were inseparable in those days, being much of an age although Mark was a few months older. A few months give formidable seniority in early childhood and they made Mark the leader, and besides, he had a more assertive personality than our little brother. Mark could not stand the sudden reversal of relation constituted by John's becoming the centre of attention at his birthday party. All this fuss about John and none at all about him! Clearly, Mark's will had not been broken, and he lay down on the floor and kicked and screamed himself blue in the face. Little prig that I was, I strongly disapproved of Reverend Mother's handling of this moral crisis, which was by issuing a decree that Mark's birthday was to be celebrated the following week, which was dishonest because it was not really his birthday at all, and as well, it was immoral to reward him for his bad behaviour. No girl who had made a disgraceful scene in the refectory would have been rewarded, I was sure. Girls had to be ladylike, but boys, it seemed, did not have to be gentlemanly, and it was not fair.

Another of our treats, when the weather was good, was the picnic to Government Paddock so frequently mentioned in my letters to Mother and Father. It really was a treat; just not eating as usual in the refectory was a blessed relief from the routine and so was escaping from the convent grounds to the kind of place where running about seemed natural and not just another duty to be performed. There was also something thrilling about the place, because it was explained that Government Paddock was not so called merely because it was the property of the Government, but because it had been cleared, long, long ago, in the days of the Hentys (whom we believed to have been the patron saints of Portland, because of the tone of respect employed when they were referred to), by 'Government men', which was what people had then called the convicts. As well, Government Paddock was a pretty place, and had garden flowers growing wild, huge bushes of marguerites, the seed of which had, no doubt, been wind-borne from the garden of some early settler, perhaps even a Henty.

Sometimes, when summer bathing was over and Government Paddock was beginning to pall, we were taken for rambles along the beach, which we loved, especially when we came on the enormous snow-white bones of whales and the nuns told us about the old whaling days. We collected shells and picked up cuttlefish, which were ground up and used in the convent as tooth-power, to the considerable detriment of the enamel on our teeth, I now suppose. John remembers a glorious excursion to the town, to view the decorations put up to celebrate the sinking of the wicked German battleship *Emden* by our own heroic *Sydney*. I have no recollection of this occasion and surely it was too remarkable to have been forgotten. I expect it was another example of the double standard, a treat for the boys only, as the nuns may have feared that the celebrations might be marred by the rough, beery behaviour of the local males, unsuitable for ladylike convent girls to witness. But which of the nuns can have sallied out, risking the Bacchanalian scenes, in charge of a group of excited little boys, which included two real limbs of Satan, Roy Grounds, the eminent architect-to-be, and his even naughtier elder brother? I think the parish priest must have been asked to escort the boys and could hardly refuse, seeing what a tremendous fuss the nuns always made of him when he visited the convent. A pot of tea and a whole tray of delicious-looking cakes and biscuits were carried to the parlour where Reverend Mother and the senior nuns gave him their company but did not, of course, share the refreshments.

So the days and weeks and months went by quietly, peacefully, and on the whole happily. We were lucky in our fellow-pupils at Portland: I do not remember one that I disliked or feared, as at other convents I attended. And although Reverend Mother and Mother Francis de Sales were awe-inspiring they were not unkind, and the other nuns were quite jolly. For children whose home-life had always been troubled by Mother's wayward temperament and her incapacity to measure time, the firm routine and unvarying reliability of every element of our lives at Portland, though disconcerting at first, relaxed our tensions and rested our nerves and we all flourished. It was as well we did, for we were about to face an ordeal – the first break in our family circle, the sudden and tragic death of our baby brother, Kevin.

Kevin was killed in an extraordinary accident, by the falling of a great weight attached to a pulley, part of a contrivance used for generating gas for the convent. The contrivance was protected by a railing and access to it was strictly prohibited to all the children in the school. But Kevin, the baby of the convent, was a law unto himself, a high-spirited, wilful and extremely active child. The nuns were saintly in their care of him, but no one could keep him under observation every moment of the day. The enclosure round the gas plant probably had a special attraction for him because it was a forbidden and therefore unexplored place, and so one day when the vigilance of the nun in charge of him was relaxed for a moment, he made a bee-line for it and climbed through the enclosing fence. At that very moment the wire rope holding the weight gave way and it crashed down on Kevin. We were told afterwards that he was not actually crushed by it or indeed injured at all, but died from shock. I do not know if that was true but certainly there was not so much as a bruise on his head when we – only Lorna and I, I think – were taken to see him before they put him in his coffin. I see him as clearly now as I did then, an exquisite little effigy with his golden curls and his cheeks, that used to be so pink, now waxen, lying under the nuns' best embroidered linen and strewed with white violets their loving hands had plucked from the convent garden. It is as well for me that white violets are rather rare, for I have never seen one since except through a veil of sudden, blinding, uncontrollable tears.

'Hughenden' sent aunty Doone to comfort us and the kind nuns offered us little treats, such as special things to eat at unheard-of hours, and we were excused from school during the days when aunty Doone was at Portland. Hitherto our knowledge of the place we were living in had been confined to the beach and Government Paddock, but now, with aunty Doone, we explored the town and discovered, to our surprise, that it was quite attractive. The one and only time during our year at Portland when we went right away from the convent for a whole day was on an enthralling excursion in a horse-drawn vehicle, which aunty Doone must have hired from a livery stables, for the convent had no transport of its own. We boiled a billy and had a picnic lunch and went all the way to Cape Nelson, miles from Portland, to see the lighthouse, an object that seemed as remote and exciting to us cloistered children as if it had been the Golden Pagoda of Rangoon. Then aunty Doone went back to 'Hughenden' and we went back to the convent and the soothing discipline of a life governed by routine.

So our year at Portland moved towards its close and in December aunty Dot arrived to attend the break-up and take us back to 'Hughenden' for the Christmas holidays, after which our parents would be arriving home. Aunty Dot stayed at the Richmond Hotel, said once to have been the home of one of the Hentys, and Lorna and I were permitted to visit her there. Dear aunty Dot, remembering the eager interest we had always taken in her pretty dresses at 'Hughenden', thought to give us a treat by letting us have a preview of the new dress she had bought to wear at our break-up. But, alas, we were no longer quite the children we had been in pre-Portland days. When aunty Dot lifted the dress from its tissue-paper wrappings and held it up for us to admire, Lorna and I were aghast and exchanged glances of mingled horror and embarrassment. Politeness required that we should admire a new dress, any new dress, and so did regard for the feelings of aunty Dot whose new dress it was and who was so innocently delighted with it. But such a dress, cut a bit low and of so vivid a cherry-red that it nearly burnt the eyeballs to look at it! An *unsuitable* dress, as the nuns would have said, with a world of unvocalized but clearly enough expressed meaning. A dress, in short, which only a worldly woman would wear, and worldliness, as we had heard so often, led one into temptation, and temptation into mortal sin. And mortal sin, of course, led to burning in hell for all eternity.

Could it be that our aunty Dot was actually a wicked woman? All our experience of her pointed to her being kind and good and, after mulling over the situation, Lorna and I were inclined to the view that although aunty Dot was a bit worldly she was probably not really wicked but only terribly ignorant, and that it was not really her fault as she knew no better, having attended a State School and then South Melbourne College, thus being deprived of a proper Catholic education. All the same, we blushed for her at the break-up where she not only made herself (and us, of course, by guilt of association) terribly conspicuous in that shameless cherry-red dress, but also laughed right out loud in her clear, ringing voice, just as if Reverend Mother had not been present. We thought it just as well that we were leaving on the next day.

IN THE PARENTAL TENT

I

'The parental tent' is Henry James's term for the many homes of his childhood and once lodged in my mind no other term could displace it to convey the transitional character of home as understood in my family. I do not remember the Golden Age Hotel at Omeo where my parents were living when I was born, nor the house we subsequently lived in until I was three. When my memory begins, we had moved to Melbourne and were living at the Bleak House Hotel, on the sea-front at Albert Park, where Grandma's brother, Jeremiah O'Brien, was the licensee. I suppose that being a relation he gave us good terms and that the proximity of 'Hughenden', an easy walk along Beaconsfield Parade, was an attraction to Mother. Bleak House was well-named in relation to its situation in the teeth of the wind but owed its name, I think, more to the memory of Charles Dickens than to its location. I thought it a delightful place to live. Uncle Jer and his wife, aunty Alice, were very kind to children and ready to supply us with as many beautifully fresh, crisp Thin Captain biscuits as we fancied, to sustain us in the intervals between the excellent and well-served meals, in the spotless and dainty traditions of the Limerick Arms. There was only one thing I disliked about Bleak House – a queer, sweetish smell that seemed to pervade every part of the establishment, except the bedrooms, which were upstairs. The smell was of beer and to this day I have an aversion from our national drink.

After we had been at Bleak House for a while, our parents rented a house in Middle Park. It was in Harold Street, not far from 'Hughenden', which must have been why we lived there, for it had no other charms. The house was called 'Verona', but evoked no association with the city of the Montagues and the Capulets. It just happened to be named

'Verona' and not 'Cardiff' or 'Madrid' or any of the other names sold by the gross to affix to the mean little houses which speculative builders dotted all over Melbourne early this century. House-agents nowadays describe them as 'Edwardian cottages' in a vain effort to make them seem quaint and old world, but ugly they were and ugly they remain. 'Verona' has not been pulled down but it is no longer Edwardian because a massive new front of exotic character has been slapped on it and painted a dazzling white, so that it now suggests a small fort in Algeria in an economical production of *Beau Geste*.

Middle Park is perfectly flat and therefore ideally suited to the unimaginative grid pattern of streets imposed on so much of Melbourne. Harold Street is one of the many streets which run at right angles from Beaconsfield Parade, straight as a dart to the railway line from the city to St Kilda, an arrangement which ensures that no obstruction is presented to the winds raging for an outlet from Beaconsfield Parade. In our day the roads had not yet been sealed and the wind perpetually whirled sand and dust along Harold Street. There were no nature strips and no trees, and the one attempt at beautification that had been made served only to enhance the harsh aspect of the street as it consisted of very large, solidly constructed tree-guards, each containing a small dead tree. The only point of interest in Harold Street was a small industry, Mardell's Hat Factory, where, when the big gates were occasionally opened for the horse-drawn transport, we could catch a glimpse of a courtyard in which there were racks holding strips of straw in all kinds of wonderful colours, which were being dried after dyeing.

Inside the picket fence of our house there was a golden privet hedge with a weak spot in it, where a new bush should have been planted but never was in our time, because Father's activity in the garden stopped short at reluctant lawn-mowing and Mother, in the 'Verona' days, lacked time and strength for improvements. Behind the hedge was a small plot of grass and an asphalt path which led to a porch entrance, adorned with wooden curlicues, and a sliver of verandah, which served only to darken the room behind it. The house was of very red brick and as we entered there was a lobby with a tiled

Hughenden in the early twentieth century

The author as a child

Gertrude Buxton, the author's mother, as a child at a fancy-dress party

J. R. Buxton (Grandpa) on the front steps of 'Hughenden'

Mary Buxton (nee O'Brien) – Grandma

The billiard-room at 'Hughenden'

The drawing-room at 'Hughenden'

The Buxton offices in Collins Street, Melbourne, from which we watched the march of the first Anzacs to return from the First World War

The Buxton sisters

Gertrude (Mother)

Lorna (aunty Doone)

Kathleen (aunty Kit)

Mary Dorothea (aunty Dot)

Great-grandfather and great-grandmother O'Brien and some of their grandchildren at Nar Nar Goon

The second Pitt-Buxton marriage. *Left to right:* Aunty Dot, Grandma Buxton, Prior Kindelan, the bride (Kathleen Buxton), the groom (Ernest Pitt), Edwin Pitt, Lorna Pitt, Grandpa Buxton

Mark Pitt, our other grandfather

Astley Buxton (uncle Ack) at the time of his enlistment

John Buxton (uncle Jack) training in Egypt before the Gallipoli campaign

Mother and Father in London, 1914

John, Lorna and Kathleen Pitt (the author), 1915

Kathleen, Lorna and John Pitt, 1918

'The Ritz', East Melbourne

'Bonleigh' in 1924 – the last family home

John in the morning-room at 'Bonleigh'

Kathleen dressed for a theatrical performance, 1922

Lorna in the garden at 'Bonleigh'

Lorna and Kathleen in Durban, 1926

Lorna, John and Kathleen on the *Nestor*, 1926

Kathleen as an undergraduate at Oxford, 1927

floor, called the vestibule. A door to the left led to the dark little dining-room and another, to the right, to what we grandly called the drawing-room, which was the best room in the house. It had nothing much to commend it, being rather poky, with a skimped bay-window to give it *ton*, as the principle of an Edwardian cottage was that it should contain everything that could be found in a proper house, but in a sketchy, weakened or vestigial form. Between the doors on the left and right of the vestibule a third door led to a dark, narrow passage giving access to the bedrooms, bathroom and kitchen.

At the back of the house there was a lawn and an asphalt path, which led to a very primitive wash-house, with a corrugated iron roof, and the back gate, which opened on to the back lane, a useless amenity since nobody in Harold Street kept a vehicle of any kind; it was, I suppose, just another example of the pointless pretentiousness of speculative building. In the backyard some previous tenants must have had ambitions, because they had planted a neat circle of standard roses in the lawn, but either it was not a good situation for roses or they had lost heart owing to a lack of pruning and fertilising, for they never bore a flower in my recollection. The only flowers at 'Verona' were the mauve pea-flowers of the virgilia which hung over the side fence from the garden of our next-door neighbour, an alarming, child-detesting widow. Although we would not have thought of stealing, Lorna and I believed that flowers which grew on our side of the fence were ours and as we loved flowers and had none of our own we would place a ladder on our side and climb up and help ourselves when the virgilia was in bloom. If Mrs Steele discovered us, she went into eldritch shrieks and rushed in and started abusing Mother, which led to trouble for us.

Our new neighbourhood was a lower middle-class district, chiefly inhabited by youngish couples like our parents, and it swarmed with children. This did not mean, however, that we were entering a vivid social life, but quite the contrary, as the children were pronounced 'rough' both by Mother and Lorna and there were only a few of them with whom I could make friends and entertain at dolls' tea-parties in the wash-house, where I served mud pies for refreshment. The children of Harold Street and thereabouts really were rough and sometimes a bit frightening. They used to roam the streets in packs, formed on a denominational basis, according to whether they went to State schools or Catholic primaries. When the packs met the State School children would chant:

> Catholic dogs
> Jump like frogs
> In and out the water

to which the correct but not very original rejoinder was:

> Proddy dogs
> Jump like frogs
> In and out the water

This exchange of courtesies, which I would have relished, was strictly forbidden to the children of our house.

All the same, we were contaminated by one of the rough ways of the neighbourhood children, which was writing on the pavements in coloured chalks. Lorna and I saved up our pocket money to buy chalk, and one Saturday morning had a glorious time inscribing on the pavement outside 'Verona' the statement that 'this bit of the street belongs to us', decorating it prettily and signing our names. Just before one o'clock Father arrived home for lunch and discovered the abomination we had committed, for in his opinion the defacement of public property was nothing less. No man ever had a higher regard for *res publica* than Father, who always uttered such terms as 'public property', 'public money' and 'the public good' in the tone of one speaking of sacred matters. Father told us very sternly that we were never again, as long as we lived, to deface public property, much less to write our silly names on it, and that meanwhile we were to fetch two buckets of water and two scrubbing brushes and get down on our knees and scrub the pavement until it was spotless and this, to our infinite mortification, we did. Naturally word of the spectacle outside 'Verona' got round quickly and there was no lack of jeering witnesses of our peer group. This was the most effective punishment ever administered to us: henceforth public property was as safe from Lorna and me as from Father himself.

In fairness to the bad old days, it could be argued that there were some ways in which Melbourne housewives, even of modest means, lived more comfortably sixty years ago than even the mothers of properous families do now. They did not have to take the younger children to school and bring them home again, because they usually sent them to schools that were fairly close to home and as there was still very little motor traffic in the suburbs it was safe to let even very young children walk to school, alone or with a sibling. Parents, as well as children, had rights in the days before the permissive society, and mothers did not live in dread of destroying their children's creativity by forbidding finger-painting on the sitting-room wall. The (often literal) burden of shopping was much lighter then than now. At 'Verona' the milk and bread arrived on the doormat every day except Sunday, the butter-and-eggs man called twice a week, the grocer delivered his orders and the butcher not only delivered his but called three times a week to receive them. John Chinaman's covered cart made a stately progress along Harold Street as he stopped the horse outside the gate of each of his customers and came to the back door with his wickerwork basket, wide and shallow, divided into small sections, in each of which, attractively lined with fresh leaves, lay a sample of his wares, such as a couple of perfect tomatoes, a handful of peas and beans, fruit in season, of which the prettiest in the summer were the cherries, both light and dark, and the muscatels in a nest of vine-leaves in autumn. More bulky, boring items, such as potatoes, pumpkins and cabbages, beetroot and rhubarb, remained in the cart. They would be bought anyway, and carefully weighed on the scales in the back of the cart, which was a kind of travelling shop, but the basket was the dangling of temptation before the housewife's eye. Mother defended herself by adopting a rather grand, lady-of-the-house manner and took liberties no one would dare to nowadays, such as opening pea-pods to see if the contents were as succulent as the pods promised, nonchalantly snapping the beans in half to find if they broke cleanly and with a loud pop, as fresh

French beans should, or helping herself to a grape and eating it in a slow, considering way, as if the flavour were open to question. There followed a long pause while John did his weighing and calculating in the cart, brought the goods in and was paid. All this took time, but John Chinaman was always serene and never bustled his customers. On his last visit before Christmas he always came in beaming, bearing his Christmas present, a jar of ginger. I thought the ginger dreadful, the grown-ups were welcome to it, but I dearly loved the exotic little jars that had come all the way from China and could never decide whether I preferred the blue and white of the last or the lovely, splotchy green glaze of this year's present.

Despite all this help in provisioning there were sometimes oversights or emergencies which caused shortages, or Mother thought she would like to bake an unscheduled cake for which some ingredient was lacking. The solution then was to bid one of us, home from school and sustained with bread and jam, to run a message to the shop. 'To run a message' seems now an odd locution as messages are passive and cannot run, but it was literally exact. The message was the piece of paper for the man in the shop, on which Mother had written 'two ounces of mixed peel' or 'six penny worth of cream of tartar' or 'three eggs', and Mother wrapped the message round the money and told us to wrap the change in it for the homeward journey. As for the running, what child walks when running free is possible? Sometimes we muttered a bit about homework when told to run a message, but we really rather liked it. Shops were never too far off in those carless days and we knew every inch of our neighbourhood from constantly seeing it on foot. Being entrusted with the conduct of family commercial negotiations gave us a sense of independence and responsibility. Certain light tasks were considered the domain of children at 'Verona', such as setting the table, shelling the peas, and (heaviest and most disliked of our duties) cleaning the knives, a frequent task from which we were ultimately delivered by the blessed invention of stainless steel blades.

But even when all the vanished benefits have been recalled it remains true, I think, that for women who could not afford to employ servants they were more than counterbalanced by the sheer difficulty of housekeeping in the early years of this century. The only help that Mother had was a washerwoman, the irreducible minimum for middle-class housewives in those days, and, from time to time, what was called 'a girl', in contradistinction to a properly trained servant. The girl was usually a thirteen-year old waif from an orphanage, whose chief duty was to relieve Mother of the care of our little brothers for a few hours each day.

We had gas for lighting and cooking, but the bath-heater and the copper for the washing had to be lighted with newspapers and stoked with wood-chips. Ironing was done with relays of flat-irons, heated on the stove, and was very burdensome as there were no materials which could be worn unironed and in any family with pretensions to decency, petticoats, aprons, blouses, summer dresses and men's shirts had to be starched. As dry-cleaning had yet to be invented heavy woollen clothing was also cleaned at home: Mother scrubbed men's suits, everyone's overcoats, the boys' trousers and jackets and her woollen dresses and ours with a nailbrush dipped into warm water and ammonia, after which they had to be dried and aired on the clothes-line and finally pressed under damp cloths to prevent them from shining. Without refrigeration the preservation of food was a constant worry. Some people had ice-chests but we did not and there was no cellar at 'Verona'. Meat was kept in a meat-safe hung in an airy, shady place out-of-doors, but if the weather were really hot there was always a danger that the meat would 'go off' and something else would have to be improvised for the family dinner, no easy task when food in cans was a luxury and people with small incomes did not have cupboards full of it. Butter was kept in a butter-cooler and milk in a Coolgardie safe, but if these devices ran short of moisture the butter would liquefy and the milk would 'turn'.

In the absence both of flywire and of sealed and adequately cleaned roads, Melbourne swarmed with insects and the summer was one long fight against flies and mosquitoes. 'Fly-papers' were an effective form of warfare against house-flies but were hazardous, as they consisted of sheets of stout paper with a gluey surface, on which little children delighted to sit. We defended ourselves against mosquitoes, more or less, by burning incense sticks and sprinkling citronella on our pillows at night. Once a week Mother swept the carpets with a straw broom, having first sprinkled them with wet tea-leaves saved for the purpose of keeping down the dust and in between these radical treatments the carpets were kept looking fairly decent with the carpet-sweeper, which we regarded as the last word in modern technology. Ready-made clothes were expensive and as a sewing-bout by Mary O. was only an occasional event, Mother made our simplest clothes herself on a hand-machine and made our old ones last a long time by patching and renovation. Socks and stockings were made of wool in winter and lisle thread in summer and there was always plenty of darning awaiting the mother of a family when the rest of the work was done and the children were at last in bed.

Life at 'Verona' must have been very hard for Mother, indeed the hardest and unhappiest time of her life. Lorna was six and I was three when we moved in, John was born shortly after and Kevin two years after John. The house was too small for us and it must have been impossible to keep it in that good order which was always necessary for Mother's peace of mind. I suppose we could not have afforded a better house. Father had a steady job but despite his outstanding ability and devotion to duty he was only inching along in the public service, where promotion was slow. Ours had to be a very frugal house and Father did his share of going without; the sandwiches he put into his Gladstone bag to take to the Treasury for lunch every weekday had, for filling, tomato sauce and nothing else. We always had enough to eat, but our order to the butcher was much more frequently for a pig's cheek, rabbits, sheep's head or lamb's fry than for expensive steak or chops. When we had a joint it was usually roast seasoned veal, which was very good but in those days veal was a despised meat and much cheaper than lamb or beef. Mother was a good cook but making cheap cuts appetising is much more laborious than grilling or roasting prime cuts. Besides, Mother kept up civilised standards in the serving of meals; not even in the 'Verona' time was there the indiscriminate serving on plates in the kitchen. Our meat came to the table on a meat-dish and the vegetables in covered, heated dishes and we could specify what we would or would not like on our plates.

I recall the 'Verona' days as a time when there was nearly always sickness in the house. Mother suffered from painful throat complaints, such as quinsy, and prostrating headaches and John was a delicate child with a poor digestion. But Lorna was the star performer. She caught everything that could be caught, always had it very badly and, in the congested conditions of 'Verona', soon passed on anything contagious to the rest of us. Lorna began her career of sickness with a real *coup de theâtre* when, soon after our arrival from Omeo, she was found to have hydatids, the result, it was said, of drinking unboiled water from streams on the sheep-walks surrounding Omeo. She had to be operated on by the celebrated Dr Bird, who had his own private hospital in Spring Street in the city, and a pretty penny all that must have cost poor Father. Dr Bird, it was said, saved Lorna's life by skilful removal of a morbid formation from her inside, a horror which became larger at every telling, until I pictured it as the size of a football.

Having begun, as it were, at the top, Lorna could never again quite equal the hydatids drama, but she gave a very strong performance when she nearly died of scarlet fever. Mother nursed her at 'Verona' while the rest of the children were cared for at 'Hughenden'. When Lorna was convalescent we came home to find our sister almost unrecognisable because all her beautiful golden hair, which used to fall in loose waves, had been shaved off and she was as bald as an egg. So that her sister and brothers should not be too shocked Mother had made her a little cap to wear, but as soon as Mother went out of the room she whipped it off. I was terrified and screamed so hysterically that poor Mother came racing back, expecting to find that Lorna had died after all. She was forbidden to frighten us like that again but I suppose she had became rather spoilt during her illness because she was disobedient and for weeks I shunned her like a leper for fear of seeing that dreadful sight again. Lorna's hair continued to cause trouble for a long time because when it grew again the new lot was quite unlike the old, being dark brown, dense and fuzzy, so that she looked like a Fijian. It took Mother a whole hour to comb it thoroughly, and as a whole hour could not be found on weekdays it was just brushed before she went to school and only properly combed on Saturday mornings, to the accompaniment of shrieks from Lorna when Mother lost patience and attacked the tangles too vigorously.

Mother's work was incessant and she did not suffer in silence, so that our home life was sometimes rather depressing. Mother could never reconcile herself to the inevitable and every day of her life bruised herself anew in protest against it. For example, when Lorna and I began to attend the Loreto Convent in Albert Park we were required to wear a uniform. Mother had never worn a uniform herself, thought it ridiculous and never ceased to complain. 'And what a uniform!' she added. This referred particularly to the rather dowdy length of skirt insisted upon by the nuns ('silly women', said Mother, whose ideas were more advanced) and to the starched white piqué collars and cuffs, which had to be fresh every day. This was a legitimate grievance for Mother, who had to iron the collars and cuffs and affix them with pins, but Lorna and I were made to suffer for a rule of the school for which we were not responsible.

Mother's discontents reached their weekly climax on Saturdays. Father went to the office on Saturday mornings but came home to lunch, and expected it to be ready on his return, sharp on one o'clock because he was going out again straight afterwards to engage in some sporting activity for, although he had little aptitude for sport, except rowing, he loved to participate in games, either in person or as a spectator at cricket and football matches. He liked routine as much as Mother hated it and he was as punctual as she was the reverse, and his view of the matter was that his Saturday afternoon was for sport and he meant to be on time. Mother was totally out of sympathy with the concept of sport: I never remember her playing with us, even when we were very young, and she thought it ridiculous for a grown man to concern himself with games. Also, she not unnaturally resented the fact that Father was going off to disport himself while she, just as on week-days, would have to stay home and mind the children, and I suspect that the lateness of lunch on Saturday was not solely the result of her deficiency in a time sense but to some extent deliberate, a form of protest. My parents never abused each other in front of the children but their suppressed hostility created thunder in the air over the dining-table, an atmosphere for which I had been waiting, half sick with dread, ever since I woke in the morning to realise that this was Saturday, the day of awfulness, as I always called it to myself. After lunch Mother often had a headache and Lorna and I had a rather dreary afternoon of baby-minding, first John and then Kevin.

Sunday, however, was a day of sweetness and light at 'Verona'. Perhaps this was because we all went to Mass at the nearby Carmelite church and were spiritually the better for it. In any case, peace broke out in our house on Sunday mornings, especially when we were all invited to 'Hughenden' for midday dinner and Mother had a holiday from the kitchen. Father was off again on Sunday afternoon, when he always played tennis, but Mother, in her Sunday serenity, never seemed to mind this at all and family harmony prevailed. It was even rather festive, because we always had a special afternoon tea on Sundays, when we consumed the shillingsworth of cakes that Lorna and I had carefully selected on Saturday morning at the bakery in Armstrong Street, cream slices with icing on top and abundant real cream inside, Napoleons made of pastry and sponge cake and raspberry jam, and luscious vanilla slices, each cake costing a penny. As far as domestic work was concerned, Father was as free as air. He carried the rubbish tin in and out twice a week and he cut the lawn and that was all. I never saw him make a cup of tea or help Mother with the drying-up. This will sound callous to the present generation and indeed it was hard on Mother, but Father, like the uncles at 'Hughenden', had been brought up by an Irish mother in a household where there was a strict division of labour. The work of men was to provide for their families and the work of women was to manage the household and attend to the children. In any case Father, like many men of Irish descent, was useless with his hands. I never saw him use a hammer and nails or take a spanner to a blocked sink. Left to him our house would have become like one belonging to some relations of ours in Ireland which I visited long afterwards, where, if a blind would not go up or a floor-board caved in, nothing whatever was done about it. When domestic disaster struck in our house, even in so minor a form as a dripping tap, Father would say – 'We'll have to get a man in'. A man, in this context, was made to sound quite unlike a fellow-creature, a being of another species (all hands, no doubt) and by 'we' Father meant Mother, whose duty it was to track the strange animal to its lair and induce it to come to our house and perform its odd tricks.

In his own field as a provider no reproach could be brought against Father. He had entered on that career at fifteen and continued until a week before he died at the age of eighty-three, having changed his occupation to that of stockbroker when he retired from the public service. Father was a very conscientious worker and in his fifty years as a public servant never had a day's sick leave and rarely took more than a week of his statutory holidays. He was always cheerful and never complained of the drudgery, which most of his work, in those early years, must have been. Although we knew, of course, that we were not rich, I never thought of us, as poor, even in the 'Verona' time, because we knew that Father would provide for us and he never permitted discussion of family finance in the presence of the children. When we lived at 'Verona' Father used to work at home at night, at what or why I did not know then but have found out since. At Omeo he had been Clerk of Courts but in Melbourne his post was at the Treasury and he had set out on an intensive course of studies and examinations in accountancy to improve his qualifications and prospects. Father was intensely reserved in all personal matters and never mentioned that what he was doing when he was working at night was trying to winkle us out of 'Verona' and give us a better time.

Although as children we suffered no real hardship or unkindness life at 'Verona' was not very gay and had it not been for the blessed haven of 'Hughenden' we would not have had much fun. In those days we did not go away for summer holidays and the only treat I remember as originating from 'Verona' was our yearly visit to the pantomime at Christmas time. We were not, like the children of nowadays, taken to ballet class or sporting events and we learnt no arts or crafts at school. We did not have many toys or books, we never had birthday parties and, in consequence, were rarely invited to those of other children. 'Out of school' we had few friends. Perhaps that is why Lorna and John and I have always seemed to me closer to each other than many brothers and sisters I know; we probably depended on each other to an unusual degree for society and affection. Mother was too busy keeping us clothed and fed and healthy to get to know us and in a sense we had more mothering from Father than from her. Father was always the first person up in our house and he used to wake us by singing little rhymes which he made up, always different from the one of the day before, which put us in a good humour for parting with our warm beds, and at night he sometimes sang us a lullaby to help us get to sleep. On hot summer evenings we occasionally had real fun, running and laughing in the back garden, while Father sluiced us down with the hose. The only reading aloud I ever heard was done by Father, but my memories of that are chiefly of a later, happier stage of childhood, when he used to read us poems by Tennyson, of which my favourites were his spirited rendering of *The Charge of the Light Brigade* and the splendid sonority of 'O mother Ida, Many-fountained Ida, Dear mother Ida, harken ere I die.' But on the whole amusing us was not a parental responsibility and we had to manage that ourselves as best we could.

During the 'Verona' years I became a very difficult child, subject to rages, kicking and screaming, disobedience, impertinence and general unruliness. I received fairly frequent corporal punishment, the back of the hairbrush being the instrument of my correction. I say of my correction because Lorna and John, blessed with sweet natures, neither required nor received corporal punishment. As I shared the general opinion that I was simply a bad child I did not resent the hair brush and was even sorry for Father who had to administer it and hated the duty. But in view of the fairly rapid subsidence of my violent temper after the 'Verona' time I am now inclined to think that original sin was not the sole cause of my stormy period but that a temperamental factor, for which I was not responsible, was exacerbated by the conditions of life at 'Verona'. I was born with a thin skin, with exposed nerve-ends one might almost say, which registered and felt as pain every abnormality of atmosphere. At 'Verona' the atmosphere was often highly charged and I was becoming a little nervous wreck. I did not then know what was wrong but I knew that something was, and lashed out in protest. What was really going on was an irretrievable breakdown of my parents' marriage, which, in the sense of a union, did not survive 'Verona. There was never to be a scandal nor an overt separation; Mother and Father reached a *modus vivendi*, going their own ways, civil but strange, under the same roof. As time went on and our living conditions improved, we children became less dependent on our parents and more absorbed in our own affairs, accepted the situation and did not mind it much, but at 'Verona' I was still too young and vulnerable for such adaptation.

II

The time we lived at 'Verona' seemed very long and was in fact five years. When Mother and Father came back from London early in 1915 we returned to 'Verona', which I suppose had been sub-let in our absence. This would have been a dismal anti-climax after our initiation into a wider world but in fact we were cheerful because we had been told that it would not be for long. Mother was going to look for a nicer house and when she found it Father would buy it and it would be our very own, with no landlord lurking in the background. The Treasury, it seemed, had been very pleased with Father's work in London: he had been promoted and our family was entering what seemed to us an age of affluence.

We could hardly believe our eyes when we saw our new house, which was in East St Kilda, in Alma Road and was called 'Cluny'. It might have been in France itself, so different was it from old 'Verona'. East St Kilda was a long-settled district, not new and raw like Middle Park. Alma Road was not bleak and bare like Harold Street, but a leafy place, with a double row of well-grown trees, and instead of being lined with mean little cottages with the smallest front-ages allowed by the building regulations there were solid Victorian houses, some of them two-storeyed and many with large gardens, so that it was almost like living in the country. Our new garden was not large, but its dimensions were park-like compared with the 'Verona' garden and the front verandah was smothered in climbing roses, one with dainty little white flowers and the other, a Banksia, with innumerable clusters of golden blooms.

'Cluny' was a solid, well-proportioned, spacious one-storey villa with big rooms and high ceilings. Instead of the vestibule and dark, narrow passage of 'Verona' there was a fine, wide hall with an arch, real architectural form. There was a proper drawing-room and dining-room, five bedrooms and a service wing at the back with a maid's bedroom, a box-room and the laundry. As owners of this treasure of a house we could take liberties unheard of at 'Verona' and Mother, whose ideal for a house was sun and air all round, instantly took one by causing a new window to be made in the drawing-room, which was rather dark because it was lighted only by a bow-window at one end. A previous owner had ill-advisedly modernised the fireplace with an ugly wooden over-mantel but Mother had it plucked forth and replaced by a really beautiful white marble mantelpiece, with chaste and elegant carving representing heads of wheat, bought from an old mansion in St Kilda Road, which was being pulled down. Fresh from a year's rest from domestic responsibilities in London, and overjoyed by our escape from ugly, poky 'Verona' to a house that was a joy to the eye, Mother embarked on what seemed to us, reared as we had been in strict economy, reckless expenditure on furniture and carpets and curtains, and Lorna and I were even allowed to have a say in how our bedrooms were to be furnished. Woodwork and the fine old ceilings, with cornices and plaster rosettes in the middle, were painted and walls were papered. The drawing-room was lovely, with a frieze of wistaria without a border to its lower edge, so that the long mauve racemes flowed freely down to the plain wall-paper, which had just a hint of pink in it. I was not quite happy about the carpet, though, because although new and splendid I thought it should have been green, as at 'Hughenden'.

When all was in order, there came the most amazing change of all, when we learnt that henceforth we were to have a maid. In due course Lottie arrived, a short, thickset woman of indeterminate age and rather dour expression, who proved to be hard-working, clean and competent. Our family life was really transformed by the move to 'Cluny'. The mere space at our disposal relieved the tension we had all suffered from being too close together at 'Verona'. Each of us children had a room to ourselves although John, in accordance with the Spartan mores of the time which decreed that boys must be 'hardened', had to sleep outdoors, in all seasons, on the side verandah. We even had a whole room which was never furnished, known only as 'the big room', where we could make nearly as much mess as we liked and John could occupy most of the floor space with the encampments and battles of the toy soldiers so dear to his heart at that time. Lorna and John were now safely through the stage of childish ailments and the doctor no longer frequented our house. We were no longer really little children (even John now going to school at the Christian Brothers) and as Lottie was there when we came home from school, Mother could get out more often and her health and spirits improved. As Lottie served our meals on time one of the great causes of dissension in our house ceased to operate and even Saturday morning was no longer awful. I became less nervy and began to behave better and I have no recollections of the use of the hairbrush at 'Cluny' for any other purpose than that for which it was invented.

We lived at 'Cluny' for six years, and the first five of them were the happiest of my childhood. 'Cluny' was at the corner of Alma Road and Westbury Street, and a hill led up Westbury Street to Dandenong Road. How I loved that gentle rise, a veritable alp after the flatness of Middle Park, and I spent many hours under the pepper tree that commanded a view of Westbury Street, just to revel in the sight of the hill. Mother had some time for gardening now and we had flowers of our own, so many that I was allowed to pluck some and take them to school for the adornment of the chapel. The element of play entered our lives for the first time. We all practised tennis against the back wall of the house and John and I played cricket in the garden, with frequent interuptions for accusations of cheating from both of us. We made some friends among the local children, no longer banned as rough, and sometimes we visited their houses and they ours. Life was more sociable than at 'Verona' and I even had a party once, the only party ever held at our house in my childhood. I think it was a birthday party but Mother would not permit it to be called so, not wanting the guests to have to bring me presents, so I had a 'pink party', which I had read about in *Home Notes,* the magazine to which Lottie was addicted, with pink roses from the garden on the table and pink things to eat, such as ham sandwiches and cakes with pink icing and raspberry vinegar to drink. Mother had more money to spend than in 'Verona' days and sometimes would buy amazing things for us. Once it was a pair of party shoes for me, Clark's black patent leather, each adorned with what I took to be a tiny diamond: they were so beautiful that for weeks I put them on the end of my bed before going to sleep at night, so that I would see them again first thing in the morning. There was also my Confirmation dress, the prettiest I had in all my life, which was not made by Mary O, but bought in a shop, white muslin with a skirt made of three scalloped tiers, just like an inverted white rosebud.

It was in our 'Cluny' days that Father, who was a great believer in exercise, decided to train his children in walking, and even forwent some of his week-end outings for this purpose. We used to take a train to Ferntree Gully, and walk to Nathania Springs and back, and so home again by train. The walk was not a difficult one for children, and the way was enchanting, through bird-haunted fern glades, but it was definitely a training walk. Father worked out how long we should take and divided the route into stages, interspersed with rest-pauses of three minutes, timed by his watch. Even if every muscle screamed for further repose we had to be on our feet and on our way when the three minutes were over. At times I rebelled in my heart but was grateful to Father later because we all became capable walkers and as a young adult I could thoroughly enjoy walking-tours on which we walked from fifteen to eighteen miles a day, carrying packs. On our training walks we arrived at Nathania Springs with a real sense of achievement and were richly rewarded, because at the end of our journey there was a delightful boarding-house, where the refreshments were first-class in quality and abundant in quantity; there was also a glorious garden, full of European trees of the kinds that grow better in the Dandenongs than in the coastal area of Melbourne, and there was also a fish-pond with water-lilies, in which there lived fish so tame that they would come and eat out of our hands.

It was from 'Cluny' that we first went forth, as a family, for holidays away from town. Sometimes we went to Macedon, where we rented a cottage from some distant relations. This was a fascinating place, 'old-world' even in the second decade of the twentieth century. It was a log-cabin with a lovely garden in which laburnums bloomed and where we could gather cherries from the trees. Formidable little walkers as we were becoming, we could range at large, climbing Mount Macedon and the Camel's Hump, walking to Woodend and back, and even catching a glimpse of the mysterious Hanging Rock. Mother and the aunts loved Macedon because it was, they said, 'so English', with many grand country houses with huge gardens in which English trees grew to perfection because of the cool mountain air. A generation further removed from 'Home', we children loved the fern gullies, channels of coolness on hot days, aromatic with musk, springy to walk on because of the fallen trunks of tree ferns and very quiet except for the gentle babble of shallow streams, fringed with maiden-hair fern, where we balanced on rocks to fill the billy for afternoon tea. We loved the cottage too, because it was so romantic, isolated in the forest like a house in a fairy-tale by the brothers Grimm. The appointments were extremely primitive and there was no bathroom, so we made our ablutions in an ice-cold spring and did not mind a bit because that was a part of being at Macedon. That spring nearly wrecked one of our holidays, when aunty Doone was with us and also some of our friends from Westbury Street, one of whom was a boy. One fine morning aunty Doone woke early and went to the spring to take her bath and was doing so when young Douglas, who no doubt had it in mind to have his bath in peace before the females began competing for it, walked down the path to the spring. Aunty Doone, surprised in the nude, screamed, and

Douglas bolted back to the house. A great to-do followed, because aunty Doone, who was prudish, nearly died of shame, was angry and tearful and declared her intention of returning to town immediately and that we had better keep that dreadful man out of her sight until she made her escape. We had great difficulty in calming her down and inducing her to stay, with arguments to the effect that Douglas was not an awful man but a harmless schoolboy and that he had not really seen her but only heard her scream, which had frightened him. She gave in, but retired to her room and wept for hours and went on and on about her dreadful experience, as if it had been rape.

Once we went for our Christmas holidays to a boarding-house at Toolangi. For some reason that now escapes me, this venture was a total failure. We did not like our rooms, we did not like the children staying there, we did not like the food and everything went wrong, including an episode when John fell into a pigsty and smelt simply dreadful afterwards. The only thing we enjoyed was our visit to the first literary man we had ever met, C.J. Dennis, the famous author of *The Sentimental Bloke*, who lived nearby and whom I remember with affection, because he was charming to children. Despite the lovely forest all about us, and an abundance of tracks for bush walks, Lorna and I detested Toolangi, to the point of writing to Father, still in town at the Treasury, begging him to take steps to deliver us from the body of this death, which he obligingly did and arranged for us to move to 'Gracedale House' at Healesville. Lorna and I enjoyed Healesville but the highlight of our holiday experience was when we all went to Lorne for the first time, to stay at what was then called the Grand Pacific Hotel. We all fell in love with Lorne at first sight and it was to prove a lifelong affair.

The journey to Lorne was a thrilling experience in those days, long before the Ocean Road was built. At dawn the cab was at the door to take us to Spencer Street to catch the early train to Geelong. Despite preparations for days before it was always hard to be ready in time and there were terrible moments when it seemed we might miss the train because something vital had been mislaid. But we never did miss it and in due course we arrived at Geelong, where we changed onto the Colac line for Birregurra and then changed again and proceeded by branch line to Dean's Marsh. There we transferred to a coach with four horses, in which we set off for Benwerrin, where a wonderful spread awaited us, including scones just out of the oven, with jam and unlimited thick country cream. Then came the best part of all, the crossing of the Otway Ranges, through virgin forest, and every now and then, when we came to a steep stretch of the road, we all had to scramble out of the coach and walk, to save the horses. Somewhat after three o'clock in the summer afternoon the sharpest-sighted would call out – 'The sea, the sea!', and there, ahead of us was the blue, sparkling Southern ocean, the glorious curve of Loutit Bay and our journey's end, the little township of Lorne.

We knew the bush from Macedon and the Dandenongs, and the Bay from occasional picnics and excursions by ship on the old *Edina,* but Lorne was magical, both bush and beach, and ever so much better than Port Phillip Bay: this sea was the mighty ocean and instead of having only scrubby, marine vegetation such as tea-tree distorted into strange shapes by the prevailing wind, the foreshore at Lorne was sheltered and huge blue gums grew right down to where the sand of the beach began. We could choose between bathing and going for bush walks, and sometimes there were longer excursions in a coach with a picnic lunch. The Grand Pacific Hotel was a delightful place in those days. It still exists but nowadays has a scruffy look, with garish signs proclaiming the service of Counter Lunch and lots of unkempt, rowdy people drinking beer out of cans, but in our day, when it was managed by the legendary Miss Leyden, it was quite an elegant establishment. For Lorna and me there was only one fly in the ointment, our clothes. Mother still held rigidly to her concept of simplicity for children and although we had proper bathing gowns by then, she considered that a clean summer dress was all we needed for dinner in a sea-side hotel. Lorna and I knew better, from looking about us, particularly at a girl of Lorna's age whose shell-pink *crêpe-de-chine* with accordeon-pleated skirt was the most enviable garment I had ever seen. On another visit to Lorne we stayed at 'Erskine House', at the other end of the town from the Pacific Hotel, and it turned out to be a very 'dressy' establishment, where the dressing was competitive and some girls wore a different evening dress every single night of their stay, with high-heeled satin shoes to match. The 'Erskine House' experience was really marred for both of us, but especially for Lorna, by mortification about our clothes.

Five happy years in Alma road induced in the children of our house a false sense of security, a belief that 'Cluny' was a minor 'Hughenden' and that we would go on living there happily ever after. From this delusion we awoke when the whole thing collapsed on us, a catastrophe precipitated by the departure of Lottie, which came about rather strangely. Lottie won fifty pounds in a lottery, a dazzling sum for a domestic servant in those days, and it put ideas into her head. Poor Lottie, although excellent in her sphere of housekeeping, was terribly ignorant and Mother had great difficulty in convincing her that fifty pounds, although a splendid windfall, was not enough to pay for the trip to England she had decided on. Something dashing, however, she had to do, and she finally decided to go to Queensland, because, as she alarmingly said, she would be near her sister in Adelaide. So off she went, with her few possessions in a straw dress-basket, fastened with a leather strap, and we never heard from her again nor knew what became of her.

Another maid was sought and found but did not stay, nor did her successors and in between these comings and goings we relapsed into the old 'Verona' awfulness, with Mother overworked and discontented, meals at all hours and Father on edge. This unhappy state of affairs went on for a year and then we were told that we were going to leave 'Cluny'. I wept and wailed and carried on like aunty Doone at Macedon, but to no avail. The news grew worse and worse. Mother, it seemed, simply could not stand housekeeping any longer, 'Cluny' was to be sold and our furniture was to be stored and we were not going to have a house at all, but to live in a boarding-house called 'Cloyne', a fine old house with a garden, in Alma Road near Chapel Street. This was bad, but not too bad, because we would still be in the same locality and not cut off from the people and places we knew. But really a boarding-house was not a suitable place for us because Lorna and I had to share a bedroom and study in it too, at a time when our studies were of some consequence as Lorna was by now at the university and I was preparing for my Leaving Certificate. So, after a while, we moved on again, this time crossing the Yarra into the unknown terrain of East Melbourne.

III

Our new dwelling (of which we disliked only the absurdly pretentious name, 'The Ritz') was in Clarendon Street, next door to 'Cliveden' which occupied the corner of Clarendon Street and Wellington Parade. 'Cliveden' has gone now, replaced by the Hilton Hotel, but 'The Ritz' is still standing, though hardly recognizable as it has become an institution. It faced the Fitzroy Gardens and was one of the well-built old mansions of East Melbourne, to which extensive and rather ugly additions had been made. 'The Ritz' was a superior guest-house because it included some flats for families, of which we had one. Our quarters were minute, compared with 'Cluny'. Lorna and I shared a very small room and John's domain was a sliver of back verandah, but we had a sitting-room of sorts and being so near to town Lorna and I had easy access to the Public Library when we needed solitude for our studies. John and I had rather a long way to go to school, but we were no longer little children and in those days no one thought there was any hardship for children in long journeys on foot and by public transport. We all loved the Fitzroy Gardens, which were not as well kept then as they are now, but were more romantic because they included plaster casts of Greek statues, which looked beautiful among the great elms. At 'The Ritz' we had our own table in the dining-room, where the meals were abundant and delicious; there was no housework for Mother because the flat was cleaned by the management, so her tense nerves relaxed and the sun shone again on our family life for two years.

For young people whose home, even in the 'Cluny' days, had never been very sociable, life at 'The Ritz' was a broadening process. A variety of transient guests came and went and some of the 'permanents' were very congenial. The star boarder was Dr Archibald Strong, of the English department of the University of Melbourne, whose presence lent great *ton* to 'The Ritz'. He was a middle-aged Englishman, portly and of dignified mien. He was very courteous, and always dispensed little bows and 'Good evenings' as he made his way to his single table in the corner, where he read a book. I never saw Dr Strong speak to any of the inmates, but no one censured him for this; we were a humble-minded lot and it did not surprise, much less affront us, that so learned a man should have no time to waste on commerce with ordinary people like us. We all venerated him, I in particular, because he was the first representative of Academia I had ever encountered. Not permanent, but making frequent visits for longish periods were the actor Allan Wilkie and his wife, an elegant, haggard lady with a deep contralto voice and the formidable name of Friedeswyde Hunter-Watts. To the Wilkies, as they were always called, all the Australian children of my generation owed their acquaintance with Shakespeare in actual performance, as against Shakespeare in a printed text with numbered lines and notes at the end which explained the not very funny jokes and the archaisms. The Wilkies were people with a mission; they performed nothing but Shakespeare and were forever at work in the cities of Australia and New Zealand, bringing the Bard to the people. One year we might see Allan Wilkie as the aged Lear and the next year had to perform an act of faith to discern in his rather plump, middle-aged form the youthful, lyric Romeo. As Lady Macbeth Miss Hunter-Watts made our hair stand on end as she demanded to be unsexed there and then, and wrung her blood-stained hands, but the same sepulchral tones, emerging from the mouth of poor, childish Ophelia, strained credulity as far as it would go.

Because of the nearness of 'The Ritz' to town (only twopence in the tram) it was a favourite resort of members of the theatrical profession, and their constant presence made it as good as a play to live there. When there was a Gilbert and Sullivan season most of the parts were taken by local talent, but from the very source, the D'Oyly Carte Company in London, there would arrive at 'The Ritz' Mr Charles

Walenn, to play parts such as that of the Lord Chancellor in *Iolanthe;* roles which required perfect enunciation, not to be looked for in the Australian born. Woe betide the poor man if he once stumbled or spoke fuzzily, for in those days the theatre was filled with Gilbert and Sullivan *afficionados,* like our family, who knew every word of the text by heart and exacted a correct rendering. Sometimes there came to 'The Ritz' a daughter of the famous Nellie Stewart, herself an actress but regarded by us with awe because of our parents' accounts of her legendary mother. There was also Madge Elliot, a golden, gay, dancing girl, and her more serious and reserved partner (not yet her husband) Cyril Ritchard, who, between them, were to dominate the musical comedy stage of Australia and later of New York. Madge and Cyril were always accompanied at 'The Ritz' by some other members of their company, girls who danced or were in the chorus. I could never take my eyes off the chorus girls as they crossed the dining-room, because they had been trained never to turn their backs on the audience and had developed a remarkable technique, a gliding kind of walk so contrived that they always faced whoever they were passing. I practised it for hours before the looking-glass in my bedroom, and can do it still.

IV

After two years at 'The Ritz' we gave up our flat to have a long summer holiday in Tasmania, a very special occasion because Father came too. I suppose it would have been too expensive for us to have retained the flat during our month in Tasmania and that Mother gambled on getting it back on our return. If so, she lost, because some intruder snapped it up in our absence and on our return we found ourselves homeless. We went, for a while, to a guest-house called 'Hadley Hall' in South Yarra. It was a beautiful old house, with a garden and a tennis court and we loved staying there, but it was a boarding-house pure and simple, and quite unsuitable for our studies. After several years of freedom from domestic chains, Mother was quite unwilling to take another house and compromised by renting a flat in Toorak Road, South Yarra. This was the most unattractive site on which the parental tent was ever pitched, worse even than 'Verona', and we all hated it. The flat was right onto the noisy street, over a shop, and the rooms were small and eternally darkened by the shop next door. Moreover, our living in such a place caused quite a scandal because at that time a flat was considered not merely socially inferior to a house but as a dwelling with positively improper overtones, the kind of place lived in by people of irregular morals or dishonest habits, fly-by-nights who disappeared without paying the rent. It was mortifying to find ourselves in this category.

The flat episode was dismal, but it lasted for only a few months, during which Mother had quite enough of house-keeping and managed to get us all back to 'The Ritz' again. But the nemesis of domesticity was lying in wait for poor Mother and, bitterest pill of all for her, she did not recognise her enemy, gave it encouragement and thus was the architect of her own doom. The tragedy occurred because one Saturday afternoon she decided to go to one of The Firm's auction sales. One of the uncles was conducting the sale, that of an old house in Elwood called 'Bonleigh'. Mother, who still thought of him as her little brother, wanted to help him, and having heard the reserve mentioned began to bid and ran the price up briskly. As Mother had not confided her plan to her brother he did not know that her bids were not serious, and as Mother did not know that the reserve had been lowered just before the auction started she went on bidding up to what she believed to be just under the reserve and was thunderstruck when the house was knocked down to her for three thousand pounds.

Well, there it was. Mother had bought 'Bonleigh' in Father's absence and without his knowledge or consent and now he had to pay what was a large sum in 1924. It must have been rather difficult for Mother to break the news to Father, but he took it like a man and never reproached her. This heroic conduct must have made Mother feel more guilty than ever and she tried hard to sell or let her unlucky purchase but in vain, as 'Bonleigh' was a white elephant and no one wanted it. A three-thousand pound house could not be left empty indefinitely and Mother, as the guilty party, had to propose that we should live in it ourselves. No one, she least of all, wanted to. For a family such as ours 'The Ritz' was the perfect solution to the domestic problem and we had all enjoyed its almost urban situation and the interesting and varied society it provided. It was with sinking hearts and vivid recollections of our last year at 'Cluny' that we returned to suburbia and the nuclear household, and our spirits were not raised when on arrival at our new home we found that vandals had been before us and removed everything detachable: there was not a tap or plug or electric light fitting left in the house. A man, several men, would have to be got in.

During the years since we had left 'Cluny' we had been living in extremely cramped quarters in our three boarding houses and the South Yarra flat. 'Bonleigh', as an alternative, was staggering, with twelve rooms, some huge and none small and instead of sharing a bedroom with Lorna and going to the Public Library to write my essays I now had a study as well as a bedroom of my own. Even the well-beloved 'Cluny' was undistinguished in comparison with 'Bonleigh' which was a truly beautiful house, older and of much greater architectural merit than 'Hughenden' itself. In early colonial days 'Bonleigh' had been the manor-house of its neighbourhood and the street in which it stood, constructed much later, had taken its name from it. It had already been shorn of the extensive grounds in which it had once stood but this did not matter much because as no houses had yet been built between 'Bonleigh' and the sea only hardy shrubs could have survived the wind. There was a small, sheltered garden at the back, very pleasant, with a fine persimmon tree which I shall forever associate with Shelley because it was in its shade, on a long summer afternoon, that I first read, enthralled, *Prometheus Unbound*. 'Bonleigh', now well into its second century, is still standing, beautifully cared for by its present owners and looking still more handsome than it did in our day.

Life at 'Bonleigh' had its ups and downs. I was a university student by now, and this involved two hours travelling every day; the journey to Xavier College was too long for John, who was not very strong, and he had to become a boarder. The domestic problem was, from time to time, very harassing, because maids came and went and frequently did both on the same day, arriving for an interview, surveying the size of the house, and departing without knocking on the door. No maid with the staying power of Lottie was ever found again and even when we had one we used to live in dread of the anouncement that she had given notice. Maids, in fact, were beginning to disappear from the homes of the middle sort, like us; for a time they would be the prerogative of the rich until they too, would have to face the era of do-it-yourself. Still, things were not too bad at 'Bonleigh'; Lorna had finished her university course and helped Mother a lot, even I helped a little, and there were no longer any young children needing attention. We all loved 'Bonleigh' because the house was so beautiful. Mother was pleased because her brother Tom and his family were just round the corner and uncle Ray and his lived in the next street, North Road. Father loved swimming and liked having the sea just across the road and hospitable neighbours with tennis courts abounded. With our settlement at 'Bonleigh' the wanderings of our Melbourne youth ended, but we lived there for only two years because when I completed my university course and John left school Mother, Lorna, John and I set out on our travels to Europe. The whole five of us were never to share the parental tent again.

SOWTHISTLES AND BRAMBLES

I

I began school at the age of three, not because I was an infant
prodigy but because I was a nuisance. When we moved to
Melbourne from Omeo and stayed at the Bleak House Hotel I
was the baby of the establishment and a great fuss was made
of me. I began to get above myself, the parents exchanged
glances and *sotto voce* remarks in which the word 'spoilt'
recurred. My brief and glorious reign as the little queen of
Bleak House came to an abrupt end when, like many mon-
archs before me, I overstepped the boundaries of my prerogative. Among the guests at the hotel there were some
permanent residents and these included one of the pests
found in such places, a self-important woman who was
always complaining to the management. One day she took
umbrage at some dish served in the dining-room, abused the
waitress and got up from the table, preparatory to stalking
out. But I, too, had risen, and in the good, strong voice I had
inherited from Father, admonished her, saying – 'Don't you
know, Mrs So-and-So, that it's very rude to leave the table in
the middle of the meal?' I was hastily removed from the room
and reprimanded for my pertness. The parents held a council
of war and it was decided that I must stop queening it at
Bleak House and go to school.

Thus it came about that I was plunged into the world of
real school, not kindergarten, so early in life. The school was
at hand, in Beaconsfield Parade, between Bleak House and
'Hughenden', and Lorna was already a pupil there. The
Convent of the Good Shepherd was a strange institution,
which combined a primary school for girls with a kind of
penal establishment, the Magdalen Laundry, where first
offenders worked instead of going to prison. I soon learnt
that the workers in the laundry were called 'fallen women'
but did not know why as their legs were not cut or bruised as

mine were when I fell down. Some of them were rather frightening, though, wild looking and rough in their ways, and sometimes they shouted at the nuns in charge of them and used what I suspected were rude words. The laundry was out of bounds for the school children, but it had an irresistible fascination for us and we managed, occasionally, to elude observation and hang about the entrance, peering at the fallen women working at their washtubs in a cloud of steam and sniffing the queer smell of the hot, soapy, dirty water.

The pupils at the Good Shepherd must, I suppose, have come from very humble families. On Monday morning the first incident of the week was the collection of the 'school money' which the children brought with them, all except Lorna and me, whose father was said 'to pay by cheque', whatever that might mean. I wished we did not have to be exceptional but I expect it was necessary. Mother, who was no planner, would have been surprised, each Monday morning, by our demand for sixpence each for school money and would rarely have been provided with the correct coins. I would almost certainly have lost mine on the way to school, because I was a born loser, unlikely to arrive at a destination with all the possessions I set out with, unless they were securely fastened to me with a safety-pin, as my handkerchief always humiliatingly was in the days of the Good Shepherd Convent.

I liked school pretty well, especially when we sang 'ABC' in chorus, and I learnt the rudiments of reading and writing young, because after all there was nothing else to do, such jolly diversions as finger-painting and craft being unheard of at our school. Social life was rather lacking. Lorna, who was a fastidious child, disapproved of the Good Shepherd because the children there, she said, were rough, and I daresay they were. Some of them used to boast that they stole their school money and then pretended to the nuns and their parents that they had lost it, and I wondered whether the fallen women could have done anything more infamous than that. Lorna selected what she considered to be a relatively respectable child in my class and bade me play with her and no other. I obeyed Lorna, as I always did, but I was very bored with my sole playmate, a goody-goody child who was also plain, wore glasses and a dress of a very ugly shade of green. I am sure that it was owing to Lorna's representations that the Convent of the Good Shepherd was not a suitable setting for little ladies like us that, as soon as I was old enough for a longer walk to school, we left and were sent to the Loreto Convent in Albert Park, an establishment socially superior to the Good Shepherd and unsullied by the presence of profane laundresses.

Lorna was very happy at the Loreto Convent, where the teaching was good and her classmates congenial, but down at the bottom of the school, where I was, I sighed for the happier days of the Good Shepherd. Although I have a clear memory of learning the alphabet and how to read at the Good Shepherd, I cannot recollect learning anything at all during four years at the Loreto Convent, Albert Park. I was living under persecution and all my attention was absorbed in self-preservation. Under the unseeing eyes of the nuns I endured torture at the hands of an infant sadist in my class, a girl named Nancy, whose desk was next to mine and remained there – owing to the spelling of our surnames, which determined position – year after year as we progressed through the school. Owing to my very early start at the Good Shepherd I was the youngest and smallest girl in the class, the predestined victim of vicious young Nancy, for vicious she really was, a skilled and practised pincher to whom it gave positive pleasure to inflict pain. My sole occupation was watching her and trying to keep out of her range. If, being called on to answer a question or for any other reason, I relaxed my vigilance, she would give me a terrible nip. Then, caught off my guard, I would yelp with pain and be punished by the teacher for making uncouth noises in class, while Nancy sat looking very quiet and good, as if shocked by my ill-bred behaviour. So strong already was the influence of the school ethos against tale-bearing that I never told my woe to my parents nor even to Lorna, who might have thought it her duty to inform them.

The most exciting thing that happened when we were at the Loreto Convent was the visit to our school of the Papal Legate. It was explained to us that this dignitary was a Cardinal and a prince of the Church, and that the Pope, who had been thinking of his distant people in Australia, was sending his delegate to see how we were all getting on and to bring us the Papal blessing. From then on the school fell into a frenzy of preparation. One would hardly have thought it possible for the convent to be made cleaner than it was already, but the miracle was wrought, the windows were washed until their brightness made us blink and we walked in peril of broken legs on the linoleum, polished to a mirror finish. At home our mothers were holding reviews of our best white dresses and wondering if they would do if lengthened and let out here and there or whether new ones would be necessary. Yards and yards of yellow ribbon were bought and on the eve of the great day parents' gardens were ransacked for white and yellow flowers, so that the school could be decorated in the Papal colours of white and gold.

The pupils' part in the celebration was to be a general assembly, with singing, and the highlight was to be the presentation of addresses to the Papal Legate, one from the boarders and the other from the girls in the day school. To represent the day girls the nuns selected a pupil whose name was Mascotte Ralston, and in every way, except one, Mascotte was the right, indeed the inevitable choice. Her father was an actor and Mascotte, who was also destined for the stage, already had a fine carriage, graceful movements and more cultivated speech than the rest of us. Her primacy was self-evident and we all felt that the Papal Legate could hardly fail to be impressed by a day-school so well represented. But the appointment of Mascotte to her high office presented me with the first moral problem I had ever recognised as such, and it was to prove that for me moral problems were to have the endless fascination that some people find in chess. Mascotte was a Protestant and while, from my point of view, there was no harm in that, the problem was whether it was right for the nuns to dress up a Protestant child in the Papal colours and pass her off as the representative of Catholic children, just because she would do them more credit than we would. My vocabulary did not yet include the word 'hypocrisy', but I had a firm grasp of the concept, and called it cheating. After mulling the matter over I reached the conclusion that God, who was, as I knew from the Catechism, omniscient, would see through the nuns' disreputable exploitation of Mascotte's charms and might be expected to take a stern view of their hanky-panky.

And so, it seemed, He did. A few days before the ceremony Mascotte failed to come to school and a note arrived to say she was in bed with laryngitis and that the doctor said it would be impossible for her to appear before the Legate. Sorry as I was for Mascotte, I felt that justice had been done and was pretty pleased with myself for having read God's mind like a book. There I was in error: I had read His mind but superficially and He had not been pleased to see a forward little girl ensconcing herself on His seat of judgement. Retribution followed swiftly on the heels of hubris. Hardly had we recovered from the shock of Mascotte's withdrawal than something really amazing happened, a ukase from Reverend Mother that I was to take Mascotte's place. I was panic-stricken and guilt-ridden too, for I felt that the unwanted honour that had fallen to my lot was a punishment for my presumption. But once again I had over-simplified and underestimated God's capacity for seeing all the moves ahead, for His plan, as it revealed itself, was that I was to be punished severely but not wholly undone. My punishment was terror, for I was timid in any public situation and it was not possible for me to imagine one more public than that which now lay before me. The salvation concealed in the cannon's mouth was the discovery in myself of a capacity hitherto unsuspected, that of being able to present a brave front in public, provided I had a role to play and knew my part.

This part I knew already, because we had been rehearsing for weeks and I had seen Mascotte go through it again and again. At a signal one must step forward from the ranks and stand before the Legate, who would be seated in an armchair which would be converted into a throne by means of draperies and floral decorations. At three feet from the Legate one must stop and curtsy, an exercise very easy for me because the knees of Catholic children, at least in those days, were kept flexible by the constant practice of genuflexion. Then I must make my speech, in which I was already word-perfect and still am: 'May it please Your Excellency, in the name of the children of the day-school, I offer you a heart-felt welcome.' Then I must step forward again and present an illuminated address which, I suppose, expressed similar sentiments at greater length. Then came the hard part. Reverend Mother could not predict whether His Excellency would or would not be graciously pleased to offer me his ring to kiss. Therefore I must hold my pose calmly, await his pleasure and act accordingly. In the event he did hold out his hand and I kissed his ring, in which there was a huge amethyst. Then two paces back and curtsy again and after that step, backwards, of course, to my empty place in the ranks. Although I was almost paralysed with dread before-hand, some mysterious thing happened when the moment came. I lost all sense of personal responsibility, I was not myself but had become, in effect, the missing Mascotte and found the taste of life behind a mask exhilarating.

II

When Lorna was eleven and I was eight we left Loreto, Albert Park, to spend a year as boarders at Loreto, Portland. When we came back to town we returned to our old school but not for long, because when we left 'Verona' and went to live in East St. Kilda we were sent to a new school, nearer home. Thus Lorna and I entered our fourth Convent, the Presentation Convent, in Dandenong Road, Windsor. Lorna strongly disapproved of the Presentation Convent from the first, on comprehensive grounds, educational, ethical and social. The teaching, she said, was very inferior to that of Loreto Convent, most of the girls cheated in class and in examinations, a practice unknown at Loreto, and there was a lack of *ton*, the result of the presence of a large number of daughters of shopkeepers from nearby Chapel Street. Lorna remained for only one year at the Presentation Convent and then succeeded in her demand to be sent to a more suitable school. She went as a boarder to the Convent of the *Sacré Coeur* in Burke Road, the nearest thing to a fashionable school the Catholics had, and breathed in its refinement thankfully, her nostrils no longer curling as they had in the dust of the social rough and tumble at the Presentation Convent.

The *Sacrè Coeur* was a terribly strict school. The pupils were never allowed to go home during the term, so we used to visit Lorna on Sundays and I could not understand why she liked her school so much because it seemed to me a daft place and hopelessly old-fashioned. By then schoolgirls were wearing tunics and blazers, which, if they were lucky, were made to order at Lincoln Stewart, the tailor in Flinders Street, but all the girls at *Sacrè Coeur* looked perfect frights in dresses Mother might have worn when she went to PLC in 1890: grey poplin with high necks, constricted waists and calf-length skirts. They all spoke lah-di-dah, instead of the good broad Australian accent I had acquired at the Presentation, and they were forever dropping idiotic curtsies, as if they had been living at Versailles before the French Revolution instead of in Burke Road, Melbourne, in the twentieth century. As a matter of fact the *Sacrè Coeur* was a most reactionary establishment. The playing of the *Marseillaise* was prohibited in the school as the order had never recognised the Republic as the legitimate government of France and still adhered to the Bourbon dynasty. But while I reacted to all this with Aussie irreverence, Lorna found it fascinating and I think the whole course of her life was determined at the *Sacrè Coeur*. What she discovered there was the existence of an older and different civilisation from ours. She learnt to speak French properly from nuns who were native speakers of that tongue, and since few of the girls expected to earn their livings and therefore the school did not bother much about examinations, the curriculum allowed plenty of time for cultural subjects, such as the history of art and architecture. As well, there were the delights of the cuisine: Lorna used to make our mouths water with her tales of the delicious and unheard-of things they had to eat at Burke Road. It was there that the virus of 'Europe' entered Lorna's bloodstream and determined her destiny, which was to spend most of her life there.

Lorna tried hard to rescue me from the Presentation Convent, but I did not want to be rescued. I suspected that it was not a school of the first order but I dreaded change and encounters with strangers and thought anything better than moving on again. Being younger than Lorna I was no judge of educational standards and as I had a less refined social nostril I had no objection to the shopkeepers' daughters. I did dislike the cheating, however, because when it came to ethical standards our parental tent rested not on sand but on solid bluestone foundations, and the parents thought cheating dreadful. Most of the girls in my class cheated, which was why most of them never learnt anything at all, but I was a perfect prig about cheating and was never even tempted to practise it. I should have won a prize for Christian Doctrine once but was defeated by a girl whose marks were a hundred, because she copied all her answers from books concealed in her desk. I was outraged by this incident for it seemed to me that its perpetrator had added the sin of blasphemy to that of dishonorable conduct by cheating in an examination about religious matters. I informed God of my views (for such was my method of prayer) and expected speedy action, a thunderbolt or something of that order, against the blasphemer. When nothing happened I began to lose my faith.

The educational fare provided at the Presentation Convent in my day was of the kind described by Milton in his treatise *Of Education* as 'an asinine feast of sowthistles and brambles'. The nuns were good women who worked hard and did their best for us, but they were not highly educated themselves and lacked pedagogic skill. They insisted on good handwriting and faultless fair copies, and I am grateful for this training, but we gave far too much time to it. What could be learnt by heart, such as history, some parts of geography, French verbs and Christian doctrine we learnt by heart, and what could not be memorised we did not learn. Everything was arbitrary; the concept of discussion did not exist in our classrooms. The school purported to teach French but although I 'did' this subject for several years I was never taught by a nun acquainted with the French language in its spoken form. We learnt French grammar and vocabulary and ultimately could do simple translation: we could spell French words but had never heard one spoken and had never been required to pronounce one ourselves. When, at the age of fifteen, I discovered that French words are not pronounced as they would be if they were English, the shock and shame created a psychological block which proved insurmountable and to this day the necessity to utter a few words in a foreign language reduces me to drivelling idiocy.

None of our teachers of mathematics was able to explain anything and very few of us had the slightest idea of the purpose of the operations we were called upon to perform. I had already been properly introduced to arithmetic at Loreto and managed to grasp the notion of simple algebra but never came within cooee of the drift of geometry or trigonometry. What 'sine' and 'cosine' might signify I never found out, nor what on earth the square was doing on the hypotenuse, the name of which I could only remember by thinking of 'hippopotamus', an association which led the mind off to Africa, thus compounding the confusion. Night after night I wept over my maths homework. Father, to whom anything to do with numbers was an open book, tried to help me but to no avail as he had no gift as a teacher. He would glance at my problem, see the answer in a flash and ask where my difficulty lay. Where did it lie, for heaven's sake! Everywhere, like a thick fog over the whole ground of my mind. Perhaps I had a total incapacity for mathematics, but I maintain that this is still an open question as the experiment of teaching me was never tried. No one can 'look into the seeds of time And say which grain will grow and which will not' and therefore, although some seeds will not germinate, all should be given their chance.

Only one magic casement opened on the world for me at the Presentation Convent. The view from it was enchanting, nor did it prove delusive: that promised land was so fruitful that I have been nourished by it for the rest of my life. Let me record the name of the only teacher from whom I learnt anything, dear Mother Aloysius, teacher of English literature, to whom I owe a debt that now can never be repaid. Mother Aloysius was already old and half blind when I met her in the sub-Intermediate class. She could not see what was going on and the girls played up in English literature lessons. This angered me, both because it was mean to take advantage of her infirmity and because I wanted to hear what she was saying. Somehow I was aware that Mother Aloysius was unlike the rest of our teachers, a being of quite a different order, a scholar who loved her subject and had the capacity to communicate with those who wished to learn. I had always been sensitive to the wonder of words and the beauty of verbal rhythm and I knew a good deal of poetry by heart, but I had assumed that poets wrote it only in order to make nice sounds and images. The idea that it could have meaning had never occurred to me until Mother Aloysius gave a lesson on Shelley's *Ode to the West Wind*.

We had been told to read the poem before the lesson, and I had done so, in *The Golden Treasury*, of blessed memory, and it fulfilled, exactly, my idea of what a poem should be. I could both see the driven leaves – 'yellow, and black, and pale, and hectic red' – and hear their dry rustle as they scurried before the wind. When the time came for the lesson I was surprised to see on the blackboard a diagram in coloured chalks. Mother Aloysius began her exposition and that, at first, was still more puzzling. The diagram, she said, illustrated the paths of the prevailing winds in Europe. Surely this was Geography and not English literature? Perhaps Mother Aloysius, being so old, had got mixed up, and those beastly girls would start laughing at her for giving the wrong lesson? But no, now she was winding into English literature, because, after explaining the characteristics of the different winds, according to where they came from and the countries they had passed through on their way, she called attention to the fact that Shelley's Ode was not concerned with any old wind but a particular one, as the poet made clear by addressing it in the second person singular — 'Oh Thou!'. Then she proceeded to demonstrate, by analysis of the text, that Shelley had given a detailed and perfectly correct, indeed scientific, account of the nature of the West wind as it crosses Italy, his point of observation, in the autumn, and of its effects on foliage. He had done this in words so precisely chosen and so arranged in rhythms as to make the reader see and hear what he had seen and heard and share his experience. And so a great light dawned, in which it was revealed that poetry has meaning and that the meanings it expresses are more memorable than those in, say, a geography text-book, because of the poet's mastery of language. I was an omnivorous reader of any printed matter that came my way, such as *Home Notes* and *Home Chat* bought by our maid and *The Gem* and *The Magnet* bought by my brother John, but after Mother Aloysius's revelation I began to understand that what she said applied to prose as well as to verse and to perceive that there was a qualitative difference between what was and was not 'literature', between *The Magnet* and *David Copperfield*, for example.

The only other subject from which I learnt anything at the Presentation Convent was Christian Doctrine. I was not a pious child and it was the doctrinal rather than the religious part of the subject that appealed to me. Our study was but little on the Bible and not at all on the Old Testament. Our Bible was a booklet with a royal blue cover and it was called *The Explanatory Catechism,* a more advanced work than the ordinary Catechism with the green cover, which dealt with such primitive questions as 'What did God create on the fourth day?', 'What is my duty to my neighbour?' and so on. We were required to know by heart every word in *The Explanatory Catechism* and there never was a more detested book, because parts of it were difficult and, despite its name, it explained nothing, but laid everything down in completely arbitrary fashion. For example, Luther's revolt from the Church was attributed solely to his resentment, as an Augustinian monk, of the right to preach a plenary indulgence being given to another order, the Dominicans. 'Pride and jealousy', we used to rattle off, 'induced him to attack the ancient faith and invent a new one'.

I was secretly fond of *The Explanatory Catechism* but never told my love because my class-mates would have thought me crazy. Like the real Bible, *The Explanatory Catechism* is a miscellany and some parts of it seemed to me more like poetry than prose. There was, for example, an enumeration of the vestments worn by a priest when celebrating Mass – the amice, the alb, the girdle, the maniple, the stole and the chasuble – Byzantine raiment, silken and incense-perfumed, so much more interesting than, say, the hat, the trousers and the jacket that they slid readily into my memory. It was delightful to call over the rolls of names of the Spiritual and Corporal Works of Mercy, of the Seven Deadly Sins and the Seven Gifts of the Holy Ghost, but best of all was the glorious cadence of the hierarchy of the angels – Seraphim, Cherubim and Thrones, Dominations, Principalities and Powers, Virtues, Archangels and Angels. Being a child of the First World War, I was well versed in military rank and was astounded by the lowly status of archangels. To think that the Archangel Michael, splendid with his flaming sword, who expelled our first parents from the Garden of Eden, must have been merely a non-commissioned officer in the heavenly host, probably only a corporal! Reflection on the strangeness of this brought the first glimmer of light into my anthropomorphic darkness: the spiritual world must be essentially different from the material one.

A good deal of the contents of *The Explanatory Catechism* was historical and some of the history, I have learnt since, was not only partial and prejudiced but downright dishonest, but at the time I believed every word of it and had no objection to its dogmatism and polemics. What interested me in the little blue book was my first encounter with the history of ideas and beliefs. Hitherto I had supposed history to be concerned only with battles and treaties which to me were, and are, sowthistles and brambles at their dryest and most indigestible. Now I learnt that men could divide and even die for differences of opinion. In this light even the interminable pages of the Councils of the Church, all to be committed to memory, became interesting, because these Councils were frequently, though not always, concerned with condemning false beliefs and defining true ones.

Outside the members of the Catholic Church, believers of true doctrine, there were, I learnt from *The Explanatory Catechism*, other groups of people, known as Infidels, Schismatics and Heretics. One could only be sorry for the Infidels because, being ancient Greeks and Romans and Buddhists and Hindus and other outlandish persons, they had never had the chance to be Christians and would never be able to go to Heaven but would have to spend eternity in Limbo. Ordinary sinners would do a stretch in Purgatory and then move on to Heaven but the Infidels would just have to sit and wait for ever in Limbo. Although compassionate for

Infidels, I did not have much patience with Schismatics. They were, I though, just tiresome, silly Christians who had not appreciated their privilege of belonging to the Catholic Church and had childishly split off into similar but slightly different churches, such as the Greek Orthodox and the various Protestant Churches. Heretics, however, were a different matter. They were neither pathetic, like Infidels, nor foolish, like Schismatics, but had some smatch of greatness in them because they felt ideas to be so important that they were prepared to die for them, and some of their ideas, while doubtless terribly erroneous, were about important things and downright interesting. Starved minds find their food where they can and in all the varieties of religious experience with which *The Explanatory Catechism* dealt it provided nourishment for mine.

Apart from showing some aptitude at English and Christian Doctrine I was a poor performer at school. I recollect that when I was in sub-Intermediate there were thirty-two girls in the class and that my place was sixteenth. It was accepted at home that unfortunately I was not clever and not much could be expected of me. When I had enquired whether I should begin Latin my parents, who had both studied it themselves and thought it important, very regretfully said 'No', believing that I was incapable of learning anything difficult. I have never ceased to regret this decision, but my parents were not to blame, because apart from a measure of the gift of the gab, very common among people with Irish blood, I had given little evidence of intelligence. I was, in fact, a dull child among other dull children, all of us undernourished on our diet of sowthistles and brambles. It was boring at school and year after year I filled in time by looking out the window at the livelier doings in the State School across a side-street or by reading books under the desk, including the whole of the bulky *Count of Monte Cristo.* In my day extra-curricular activities were almost non-existent at the Presentation Convent. There was never any occasion during my five years there when we made a class or a school excursion in pursuit of either instruction or pleasure. Once, indeed, we went out as a school, but that was to grace the funeral of Archbishop Carr, dressed in our best white dresses, worn without coats although it was cold, and to this day I feel faint with fatigue when I remember the hours we spent being marshalled with children from all the other Catholic schools and standing waiting, in ranks, for the cortège to pass by. The mania for sports which swept the Protestant girls' schools in the second decade of the twentieth century hardly touched our school. The convent had a tennis-court and one for basket-ball but no one taught us how to play games and at playtime most of the girls just hung about chatting. Arts and crafts were unheard of, except for sewing, and that consisted solely of the embroidery of innumerable doilies, tray-cloths and guest-towels, bought with their ugly designs ready-stamped on them.

The only breaks in the dreary monotony of school life were one weekly period of Swedish exercises, conducted by a visiting teacher from Bjelke-Petersen's school of gymnastics and any 'extras' we might take, such as music or elocution. Music meant piano-playing, at which I had already been found to be hopeless, so, as it was unthinkable that any decently brought-up middle-class girl should be wholly devoid of accomplishments, my 'extra' was attending the elocution class conducted by Miss Charlotte Hemming. Miss Hemming was an authoritarian lady of the old school of elocution and taught us to recite rubbishy verses, with a maximum of gesture and 'expression', although there was little or nothing to express. But I had always loved the spoken word and thoroughly enjoyed elocution class. I doubted the quality of our 'pieces' and found some better ones for myself, which I was only too willing to recite when I could find an audience. My masterpiece, I thought, was my rendering of Dorothea Mackellar, with a deliberate suggestion of a sob when I came to – 'I love a sunburnt country', sheer histrionics because I knew nothing of sun-burnt country and 'I love an asphalt pavement' would have been a truer rendering of my Australian experience.

III

Lorna left the *Sacré Coeur* suddenly in 1918, owing to a

conflict with Reverend Mother concerning the return of uncle Jack from the war. All our family was to gather in Collins Street, outside the Firm's city office, which uncle Jack would be sure to look at as he came marching by with his comrades of the first Anzac Day, sent home before the Armistice on leave after four gruelling years of service. Mother applied to Reverend Mother for permission for Lorna to be present but was told that the rule of the school did not permit absence during term except for urgent medical reasons: Lorna, she said, must obey the rule or leave the school. It was unthinkable that the eldest grandchild should be absent from so great a 'Hughenden' occasion, so Lorna had to leave the school she loved. The march was memorable and moving, but not in the least the gay outing I had anticipated. The 'boys', as we used to call them, were boys no longer, but prematurely aged men, survivors of unspeakable experience. The watching crowd was very quiet. Many people were weeping and it was hard, even for children, to cheer when uncle Jack went by, still a private just as in 1914, but so much older and wearing the little brass 'A' for 'Anzac' on the red and black colour flash of the Fifth Battalion.

Lorna lasted only a year at her sixth convent, where she was a day pupil. She did not like 'Genazzano' much and her health suffered from her long journeys to and from school. So it was decided that she must change schools again and the choice of her new educational milieu was dramatic. Just across Alma Road from 'Cluny' was 'Fairelight', a Protestant girls' school which was really the rump of 'Clyde', recently departed to Woodend. So Lorna crossed Alma Road, the Rubicon dividing us Catholics from the Protestants, and the daring deed was successful as Lorna finished her schooling and prepared for the university very happily at 'Fairelight'. Lorna had a good deal of Mother's gypsy strain in her make-up. She throve on change and not being self-conscious or shy never minded, indeed rather liked, her constant immersions among strangers. But my temperament was very different and until I turned fifteen and had passed my Intermediate certificate I resisted every effort to prise me out of the Presentation Convent. Then, however, I had to move on because I wanted to follow Lorna to the

142

university and the Presentation could not provide a science subject for the Leaving Certificate, then the qualification for matriculation. The expedient of a Protestant school had answered for Lorna and my parents thought it might be even better for me, because with my narrower range of experience I needed a shake-up more, and the change to a non-Catholic school would be a good preparation for the wider world of the university. The convenient 'Fairelight' had been closed and so, equipped with a new blazer, a 'gem' hat and a sinking heart, off I went to my new school, 'Lauriston' in Malvern.

Everything was as different as possible from the convent. Instead of Reverend Mother, there was the Principal, Miss Irving, a tall, handsome woman with strong features and a personality to match, and her rather jolly sister, Miss Lillian, was Vice-Principal. Instead of an austere building in stone or R. C. red brick, 'Lauriston' was housed in a dear old two-storey family home and in winter, sure enough, there was a fire in our classroom, just as I had heard tell was the strange custom in Protestant schools. The girls were friendly and the teachers kind. So far, so good, but my first term at 'Lauriston' was an ordeal. There were so many things the others girls could do and I could not that I felt hopelessly inferior both in and out of the classroom. Everyone else could pronounce French words more or less correctly but I could not and my humiliation was deepened by the harshness of the visiting teacher, the formidable Madame Liet, whose mission in life seemed to be to make girls in the many schools she frequented detest the French language. Another trial of the classroom was caused by my many years of conditioning in convents which made me jump to my feet and stand to attention whenever addressed by a teacher. This was not the custom at 'Lauriston' and every time I did it a wave of hilarity swept the class, to my deep mortification.

Far worse than the ordeals of the classroom were those of the playground because 'Lauriston' was a crack sporting school, famous for the tougher types of games, such as hockey and baseball. Tennis was the only game I knew how to play, but that did not count at 'Lauriston' because it lacked the 'team spirit' said to be so character-forming. Team games were compulsory and I was ordered to play baseball and did so. I could neither throw nor catch, nor could I defend myself against battery from a hard ball with the aid of what they called a bat, which seemed to me a thin stick. I made such a spectacle of myself that I determined I would never play a team game again even if I were expelled from 'Lauriston' in consequence. It was fairly easy to bolt after school but harder to disappear at lunchtime because home was far away and I had nowhere else to go. I just used to run somewhere, anywhere, to escape, sometimes finding a refuge in public gardens, sometimes simply roaming the Malvern streets until it was time to run back to school again. News of my failure to appear for games reached Miss Irving and I was sent for and asked the reason why. Although Miss Irving said that I could not be a law unto myself she must have been sorry for the oddity from a convent and given orders, because my name ceased to appear on games lists and I no longer had to live the weary life of a fugitive. Such a confrontation with any of the Reverend Mothers I had known, not to mention Lorna's at *Sacré Coeur*, would have had a very different outcome.

Indeed, an attitude of sweet reasonableness prevailed at 'Lauriston', in marked contrast to the hard, cold, unyielding conventual discipline. The teachers and pupils seemed to respect and positively to like each other, a relationship I had never experienced before. The constant surveillance, so familiar to all convent girls of my day, did not exist at 'Lauriston'. The teachers trusted the pupils and with good reason, for I never knew one of them to lie or cheat. If a girl in class did not understand something in the lesson she said so and the teacher did not regard this as insolence but tried patiently to make the rough places of learning plain. If a pupil were charged with an offence of which she was guilty she owned up at once, and if she considered herself innocent she protested, and this was not regarded, as it would have been at the convent, as an added offence of 'answering back' but as a legitimate statement to be considered seriously. The teachers, although they demanded and got order in their classes, did not mind if silence were not perfect from start to finish of the period. They did not seem to care, one way or the other, about 'particular friendships' and as for the worst sin of all at the convent, being seen talking to a boy, it was not a sin at all at 'Lauriston' where both pupils and teachers seemed to take boys quite calmly, as if they were human beings and not wild beasts. There was even a school dance, to which boys were invited and which I enjoyed very much, dressed in one of Mary O's creations, sky-blue velveteen with white swansdown trimming.

The free and cheerful atmosphere of 'Lauriston' was a delightful surprise because, although I had never hated school, the concept of really enjoying it was new to me. A more pleasant lot of girls one could not have met than those in the lower and upper Sixth form at 'Lauriston' in my day. They must have thought me a queer fish but I do not recall an unkind word nor a scornful glance from any of them. I made friends and in my last year at school one of them gave a real dance, the first I had attended, her 'coming-out' party, a grand event with programmes, at 9 Darling Street. Mother rose splendidly to that occasion, giving me a real evening dress (not made by Mary 0.), of rustling lilac taffeta, and even allowed me to wear a broad ribbon bandage over my forehead, which was the last word in fashion in 1922.

A great delight at 'Lauriston' was the elocution class taken by Miss Irene Webb, a young and gifted visiting teacher. Miss Webb was an educated and cultured person and had real theatrical experience, gained as a member of the Allan Wilkie Shakespearean company. In her class I had to unlearn the exaggerated, declamatory style favoured by Miss Hemming, renounce 'expression' until there was something to express and grasp the importance for communication of understanding what you are saying. By endless exercises, which were never dull to me, our dipthongs were brought nearer to the purity of vowels and we learnt to speak the speech trippingly on the tongue. Constant in our ears was Hamlet's advice to the players, and in Miss Webb's class we were not permitted to saw the air with our hands nor to tear a passion to tatters nor, in any way, to 'o'erstep the modesty of nature'. Miss Webb taught us the elements of acting and it was sheer bliss to be given a good part in a one-act play which was 'Lauriston's' contribution to a programme given by her pupils in a real theatre, the Playhouse, which was near the present Arts Centre.

'Lauriston' was, however, a disappointment for a girl with

a vague, almost unconscious, but still real aspiration towards intellectual achievement. The teachers were better educated and more highly qualified than at the convent but their teaching was, on the whole, sowthistles and brambles all over again. At worst, in Physiology, the science subject which was the immediate cause of my presence at 'Lauriston', the teaching was truly deplorable. The only step forward was that I learnt a little Latin, just enough to give me some understanding of the structure of language.

In my last year at 'Lauriston', with my passport to the university, the Leaving Certificate, already gained, I took my own education in hand, to some extent. Not many of the girls attempted Leaving Honours and those who did were treated as privileged beings, almost like adults. Discipline, never strict, was further relaxed and as long as we turned up for our not very numerous classes, no one bothered much about us. Girls used even to go home in the middle of morning school for reasons which seemed to me fantastic, such as that they wanted to wash their hair. The old Leaving Certificate, even at Honours level, was an examination of very low standard and we simply did not have enough to do. There was a whole day each week on which I had no classes and the school library was inadequate for private study. I therefore laid before my parents the proposition that on this blank day, instead of going to school, I should retire to what was then the Public Library and is now the State Library and conduct my own education. They were rather startled, supposing 'Lauriston' would object, but as I assured them that no one would notice, unless I was absent from a class, and that I would cope with any unpleasant consequences without invoking their aid, they gave their consent.

Thus began a blissful year, when, without pressure from curriculum or examinations, I simply read at large, book after book, week after week, month after month. It seemed to me that in the Public Library there was every book in the world, and I was sixteen and nearly grown up, eager to learn but very ignorant. All knowledge lay before me, or at least all knowledge that could be acquired without the aid of mathematics or science. I remember measuring with my eye the row of books by Bernard Shaw, the guru of my youth, and resolving to begin at Volume 1 and go on till I finished Volume XX or whatever it was, and so I did, imbibing a welter of radical notions on practically everything. I was mad for the drama at that time and read innumerable plays, including the complete works of Ibsen. I have never failed to call blessed that wonderful last year of school, from which I emerged fresh and full of enthusiasm and wide open to new ideas, unlike many of the exhausted adolescents I knew later as my own students at the university, already spent by their premature, competitive athletics at Matriculation.

It seems amazing that a child could attend school from the age of three until she had turned seventeen and learn as little as I did. I was not, of course, an exceptionally gifted child but I was not impenetrably stupid and wished to learn. There were better schools than those I attended but I think mine must have been about average because I did not find myself worse equipped for the university than most of the girls I met there. The fault lay chiefly in the very low educational standards prevailing in my youth. I qualified at what was considered a respectable level at Leaving Honours, but Leaving Pass would then have sufficed for admission to university. Only four subjects were required for Leaving Pass and they need not include any mathematics, which was as well for me because I could not have entered a university had matriculation called for mathematics. It is true that some girls were taught mathematics properly, but good teachers of the subject were rare in girls' schools and my fate was the rule rather than the exception. Without mathematics no exact science can be learnt and without at least an elementary knowledge of science it is impossible to understand the intellectual conquests of the twentieth century. So I and many other nominally 'educated' girls of my generation were crippled before we started, condemned to remain virtual illiterates in the context of the time in which we were to live. For this, among other reasons, I conclude that I was schooled but not educated.

147

ALMA MATER

My love for the University of Melbourne began when I entered as a student in 1923, survived my spending most of my working life there, in two departments and every rank from part-time tutor to Associate Professor, and will end only with my life. I believe that most of my fellow-students were devoted to their university. I doubt if this is still true. Although the age of confrontation, during which students expressed militant hostility to the administration and sometimes the academic staff of universities, has come and gone, there has never, I think, been a return to the old student attitude of affection towards the university. It has become something the student can take or leave and if he decides to take it his emotions are not involved and his stance is detached and critical.

In a half-century of breakneck change it should not be surprising that student attitudes have also changed in all more or less advanced countries. The generation gap is as old as human nature, but it can hardly be denied that it has widened more rapidly than ever before since the Second World War. School and parental discipline are relaxed earlier and going to a university is no longer associated in the mind of the student with initiation into the freedom of the adult world. It is said that young people mature earlier nowadays and while this seems biologically improbable it is true that they feel and conduct themselves with more self-confidence than was usual among their contemporaries in my student days.

Although the cooling of student enthusiasm for their universities is by no means confined to Australia, some special factors here help to explain it. One is the general rise in the standard of schooling. Intellectually, university education is not now the revelation it was in my day for all except a minority of students from really good schools, but rather a continuation of school, just more of the same. Moreover, students feel now (with some justice) that, if they meet entrance requirements, they have a right to higher education, a right won by personal achievement in reaching a far higher matriculation standard than was expected in the past. This conviction has been confirmed by government abolition of university fees and the provision of living allowances which, though far from lavish, do in fact enable the determined boy or girl to enter a university, even in the teeth of poverty or parental opposition. Those who enter an institution by right feel that they have a further right to demand that it should be conducted in a manner they find satisfactory.

The concept of a right to university education did not exist in my time because it did not correspond to the facts of life as we knew it. No matter how well we matriculated, if our parents could not or would not pay our fees, meet our other expenses and support us for years, we could not attend a university. There were a few free places but they were only for the really brilliant and without the addition of living allowances they were useless to working-class boys and girls and even to middle-class ones whose parents could not afford higher education for them or were not in favour of it. The height of a privilege is determined by its power to exclude, and as a larger proportion of young people now has access to higher education they are in fact less privileged than we were. We knew we were lucky to have the chance of university education and therefore tended to value it highly and rejoice in being among the happy few. I did not know a single student who dropped out from choice, although a few had to give up owing to persistent failure, ill-health or financial stringency at home.

II

When I entered the University of Melbourne in 1923 the campus was the same size it is now, but in those days it seemed much larger because one's general impression was of a few buildings scattered through a large park. In the middle there was a rather romantic lake, fringed with reeds and pampas grass, haunted by birds and student couples engaged in flirtation or courting. Into its shallow waters the more boisterous students occasionally threw those of their fellows who gave them offence. The grounds were not well-kept in those days: indeed, until the macadamised roads were sealed and municipal services improved the whole of Melbourne was rather scruffy. The water-supply was poor and no attempt was made to water parks in the summer, when the great extent of grass in the University grounds became as dry and brown as it still does on the Western Plains in a season of drought. The only well-kept piece of ground was the grass plot in the quadrangle where the camellias grew, and where indeed they (or their descendants) still blessedly grow.

Some buildings which were there at the beginning of 1923 still stand in the University grounds – only, I think, the Conservatorium, the Zoology School, the one remaining Professor's residence (now University House) and the old cloisters, though even they look very different since the addition of the long-missing fourth side of the quadrangle. Apart from the cloisters the only building which in the least corresponded to the 'dreaming spires' image of a university which we had acquired from books was the old Gothic-style Wilson Hall, high and narrow, with stone finials on the roof and beautiful wooden angels in the ceiling. The Faculty of Arts possessed no home of its own, although one was being built and was opened during my first year, the building then known as the New and now as the Old Arts Building. Before that, Arts lectures were held wherever a theatre was available and for English we had to traverse the grounds to the Medical School near Swanston Street, running all the way and still arriving late if our previous lecturer had gone over his time.

Sporting facilities were fairly good because there was plenty of room for them, but otherwise the amenities of the University were few. There was no Students' Union but Men's and Women's Club Houses, both in the same building but segregated, with separate entrances, sitting-rooms and places to eat which could not be called dining-rooms because only pies, sandwiches, cakes and tea were served. The furniture was far from luxurious: rickety rattan chairs in the

Women' Club House – to which we quickly learnt to give the correct university pronunciation of 'Clubbus' – and battered leather chairs and sofas in the large sitting-room for men, which the women students could use at night when student societies held their meetings. Indeed, woman students were quite welcome as it was taken for granted that we would serve the supper and wash up. There also stood in the grounds a wooden hut with a tin roof, an old canteen bought from the Defence Department after the First World War, which housed a dining-room known to the students as 'the profiteeria' both because it was, from our point of view, expensive and because it was frequented by professors. Ernest Scott, in his *History of the University of Melbourne* recalls that 'on hot summer days its corrugated iron roof made it a place of torture; whilst the whitewash with which the roof was covered on the inside, flaked off and fluttered down to float in the soup'.

University thinking was not higher in those days, I imagine, than it is now, but certainly living was plainer. Despite the fact that the student population was even more predominantly middle-class than it is now student society was perhaps more egalitarian, because there were certain amenities we all lacked. One was private transport. I never knew a student who owned a car although some of the men from prosperous homes could borrow one from their fathers occasionally to take a girl to a dance. The ordinary method of getting to the university from town was by cabletram and the fare was twopence, but some students could not afford that and walked instead. We all walked along Swanston Street past the baths to the Public Library and back, and Honours History students did this almost every day, because the resources of the University Library (the upper floor of the north side of the quadrangle, where the Law Library now is) were hopelessly inadequate for our needs. For most of us the simple life was the rule. As a student I never heard the word 'sophisticated' used with approval: it still had its old meaning of 'adulterated'. Of glamour there was absolutely none. If we stayed at the university at night we had dinner at a modest café in town; the question of *filet mignon* and a nice drop of claret at a neighbouring bistro simply did not arise.

Apart from having the freshness of youth we, the students, did not look very attractive. Few girls from the fashionable and well-dressed classes went to the university in those days. We did not have many changes of costume but, having all served our apprenticeship by knitting washers and balaclava caps and socks during the War, we were great knitters of jumpers to eke out our slender wardrobes. By 1923 most of the returned soldiers had disappeared from the university and all the 'men' in my year were boys fresh from school. They wore three-piece suits, some of them carried over from school and rather shiny. A great revolution in the men's dress was, however, imminent, and its first herald was already on the scene: Bob Fraser (predestined to be Sir Robert later), an elegant young man from Trinity, a little older than other students because he had already been 'Home' to England and had returned equipped like an English undergraduate in a tweed jacket and wide-legged grey flannel trousers known as 'Oxford bags'. This new uniform was soon to sweep all the blue serge suits and waistcoats into oblivion and (with some modification as to cut of jacket and width of trousers) to stay in fashion for decades until it was at last replaced by pullovers and jeans.

Now there are 17,000 students at the University of Melbourne but there were only 2,000 in my day. Everything was on a small scale. There was no paid Vice-Chancellor, Deputy Vice-Chancellor, or Vice Principal: the administration was conducted, with the help of a few clerks, by the Registrar, an officer regarded with awe by the students. The academic staff was also scanty. An establishment consisting of a professor, one or two lecturers and tutors was considered ample for an Arts department. A lecture attended by a hundred students was regarded as huge, whereas after the Second World War many lecturers, and I among them, were to cope as best they could with classes of four hundred. There were many disadvantages in the scale of the little old university of my student days but it had its merits too. According to Cardinal Newman, a true *Alma Mater* knows her children one by one and in 1923 at least some university teachers knew their students and their students knew them. In recent times the student's ordeal on entering university has been much aggravated by the sheer massiveness of the institution and the pressure of its population. In my student days I never heard of the problem with which I was to become familiar later, of students being so desperately lonely in the crowd that they had nervous breakdowns. In a small-scale university it was easy to make friends, not only in one's own year and faculty but in other years and faculties, a broadening experience now much less common.

Never having known any other university I did not then recognise it as a defect that a very limited range of learning was available within each discipline. Courses were completely arbitrary: as in a boarding-school you ate what was put before you or went without. Only once in my three years did I have a choice and that was in my first year when, in addition to the two subjects prescribed for an Honours course, one subject at pass level might be selected. Severe rationing of the varieties of learning available was necessary, given the smallness of the academic staff, and indeed the wonder was that the resources could be stretched as far as they were. Our teachers had to spread their learning rather thin and it was inevitable that some lectures were superficial and others delivered between gritted teeth by lecturers not interested in some of the topics they were required to teach. Most of the members of the academic staff in the Faculty of Arts were so hard put to it to prepare lectures, set and read essays and examination papers in all the subjects it was necessary for them to profess that it was virtually impossible for them to carry on much serious research of their own.

The University of Melbourne was, I am inclined to think, an especially delightful place for girls in my student days when Australia was even more markedly a man's country than it is now. 'A man is in the right in being a man' Simone de Beauvoir once wrote, 'it is the woman who is in the wrong'. Accustomed as girls were to this point of view very few of those who found their way to a university really relished it and it was delightful to find ourselves in a world in which no one seemed to feel that we must be inferior simply because we were women and where this tiresome subject did not arise. It was strange but fascinating to discover that at the university there were even women who lectured to men without, as far as we could see, batting an eye. There were, in fact, very distinguished women academics in the University of Melbourne at that time, perhaps, in proportion to numbers, more than there are now. Their *doyenne*, so to speak, was Dr Georgina Sweet, the first woman in Australia to be an Associate Professor. Dr Gwyneth Buchanan was another learned biologist and in Botany there was Dr Ethel McLennan, who became an Associate Professor. In History the second in command was Miss Jessie Webb and in English the same position was held by Miss Enid Derham. At a time when most middle-class girls just stayed at home until they married the sight of these professional women going about their work, without aggression but also without apology, was very encouraging to those of us who had, with considerable misgiving, ventured into the world of work outside the home.

III

Modest as it was, the University of Melbourne was a hopeful, forward-looking institution, entering an expansive and exciting phase of its history in the early nineteen-twenties. The First World War was at last well behind us and government had some, though not much, money to spare for the university. It was an era of building. In 1923 both New Arts and the Anatomy School were opened, in 1927 the Tallis wing of the Conservatorium and the Geology building and in 1929 the Botany School. The Melbourne University Press was established in 1922, new chairs were founded in Agriculture, Commerce, Economics, Metallurgy, Obstetrics and Jurisprudence and eleven Associate Professors were appointed in the 'twenties. By 1923, when I arrived on the scene, Honours courses had been introduced into the Faculty of Arts, and I, greatly daring, embarked on one of these, in the combined school of English and History.

English literature was the subject that really interested me and I should have loved to devote myself to it, but a fairly solid study of Old English was required in the pure English school and as this was said to be difficult and I was vividly aware of my intellectual limitations, it seemed wiser to do a course combined with History, because it was my belief, encouraged by my experience at school, that History was an easy subject, requiring only literacy and a good memory. Without knowing it I had selected, in the combined school of English and History, the most laborious course in the whole Arts syllabus. It was not intellectually difficult, because in those days both English and History were studied more superficially than they are now, but the work load was extremely heavy. The combined school of English and History consisted of all the subjects in the English school except Old English and all the History school subjects except Ancient History. The amount of reading and writing required was enormous. In every Honours History subject (and in the second year two of these were required) we wrote six three-thousand word essays and one of the light-hearted prescriptions in English was 'Shakespeare – *The Complete Works*'. There never seemed to be a moment when an essay, either for English or History, was not weighing on one's mind. Honours students had the added burden of shuttling between the University and the Public Library, where we often stayed until it closed at 10 pm. It was necessary to be keen and tough to stand the pace. I realised from the first that, given my inadequate schooling, my only hope of continuing an Honours course was by hard and consistent work. Great is the power of motivation and my bewildered parents found they had a transformed younger daughter on their hands, one who positively needed to be restrained from overwork.

Much as I enjoyed English at the university, the teaching was disappointing. Our lecturer in first year literature was a former school-master and he was a dull teacher. His first text was Browning's *Men and Women*, a fortune, one would have supposed, for any lecturer, but ours just worried away at every wonderful poem, explaining it literally, so that all the poetry leaked away, as, like a Midas in reverse, his touch turned gold into lead. In sharp contrast to this prosaic person was the senior lecturer, Enid Derham, a poetic-looking woman who resembled a figure in a painting by Burne-Jones. She did in fact write poetry and was a fine scholar but her feet were not on the ground. She seemed to dwell on some spiritual cloud and to be unable to communicate with earth-bound students. She adored Shelley and gave us innumerable lectures on mysticism, which were probably learned but of which we could not see the relevance. I admired Miss Derham and liked her as a person but the romantic spirit which she embodied was uncongenial and indeed hardly intelligible to me: I felt there should be more substance and less moonshine in literature.

In the English department, I had hoped to become personally acquainted with Dr Archibald Strong, the revered star boarder of 'The Ritz', but he had left for Adelaide before my arrival at the university. The head of the department was a Scot with an Oxford training, Professor Robert Wallace. There had been a considerable stir about his appointment, ten years before, which had followed a long interregnum after the death of the previous professor, E. E. Morris. In the interim English had been taught by Walter Murdoch, who also wrote in the *Argus* under the name of 'Elzevir'. His literary column was held in high regard by the more literate citizens. When it was decided to fill the vacant chair Murdoch was an applicant, but the appointment went to Wallace. It was said that the reason for this decision was that Wallace professed both language and literature whereas literature alone was Murdoch's province. It is also very likely that the selection committee felt that a Professor with an Oxford degree would add more lustre to the chair than one of its own graduates, which Murdoch was. As the establishment of the English department was then for one person only, Murdoch had to leave when Wallace was appointed. His former students and the many admirers of his 'Elzevir' articles were hotly indignant and very vocal, but the die was cast and Walter Murdoch went away to the new University of Western Australia, where generations of students called his name blessed, for he infected many of them with his own love of literature and taught them to write our sweet English tongue as it should be written. I wish he had remained in Melbourne and that I had had the privilege of being one of his students.

Professor Wallace was an intelligent and informed man but he was not a stimulating teacher of literature. He had served in the First World War and was said to have been gassed. He had a very weak voice and in my time he did not take large classes. He always sat down to lecture, a posture inhibiting both to the lecturer's command of his situation and the use of his lungs. As well, when Professor Wallace had seated himself and arranged his lecture notes it was his habit to put his hand over his mouth and talk through it. The strain of trying to hear him was tiring and made concentration difficult: we thankfully gave up when he read us poems by Burns in Scots, because as we did not know that language we would not have understood the poems even if we could have heard them. Wordsworth was Professor Wallace's favourite poet and he lectured on him, as it seemed to us, interminably. Nature not being all in all to me, there were many poets I should have preferred to hear more of, particularly Shakespeare and Milton. Still, I did learn something of Donne and the metaphysical poets, hitherto unknown to me, and recall with pleasure Professor Wallace's lectures on the minor poets of the eighteenth century, such as Gay and Matthew Prior, whose grace and wit I found delightful.

Given the small number of students taking Honours courses in English combined with some other Honours school (fewer than ten a year if I am not mistaken), it seemed strange that Professor Wallace took no interest in us whatever. During my three years in his department he never corrected any essay I wrote, made any comment on my work (which proved, by class-list standards, quite good) or, indeed, addressed a single word to me on any subject. There was, I am sure, nothing personal about his neglect, which was shared with all the students taking combined courses: we were poor relations in the English department. Puzzling it out long afterwards I am inclined to think that Professor Wallace felt that the study of English literature, without the stiffening element of language study, is rather a feeble discipline, likely to be favoured by the weak-minded. As English departments tend to be self-sufficient, even introverted places, he did not allow for the possibility that our other branch of study might be contributing something towards our intellectual growth.

It was from the young tutors, who read our essays and discussed them with us, rather than from the Professor or lecturers, that I really learnt something in the English school. They were Muriel Berry (later Mrs Ian Maxwell) and Vera

Jennings. Miss Berry was a disdainful beauty, of autocratic temper, whose blue pencil made havoc of my carefully copied pages as she cast forth errors of syntax, dissonances and absurd purple passages from my composition. I felt rather mortified at times but did not really mind, because I knew how able Miss Berry was and how much more she knew about the writing of English than I did. Besides, like all the students, female as well as male, I simply loved to look at her, so tall and golden-haired, so queenly in demeanour. Miss Jennings made a thorough job of her correcting too, but was more encouraging than Miss Berry and made one feel less like a peasant. She was a fine scholar but so unassuming that she never alarmed us and we were not afraid to ask questions. Learning from Miss Jennings was lightened by her lack of self-importance and cheered by her infectious, rather boyish grin.

English literature studies were not profound in my day but the scope was broad. We did not spend hours in analysing a couple of selected poems by Marvell but were told to read them all and were expected, by that process, to arrive at some understanding of what manner of poet he was and in what ways he was like and unlike other poets we had read. There is something to be said for both methods because analysis strengthens the critical faculty and increases precision of expression while ranging at large leads to general knowledge and enjoyment of literature. The old-fashioned method which prevailed in the English department in my time suited my needs very well because I had no professional designs on English literature. I did not want to teach it (although in the event I was to do so for some years) or to write or to do anything whatever with it but to read, understand and enjoy it, and the general courses given in the English department, particularly the two-year course of History of Literature, provided a good framework, introduced me to writers I might otherwise never have read, and, in general, enriched my life.

IV

For me, the real delight of the University of Melbourne was

the History department, where there was no prejudice against students who were taking combined courses. As an academic discipline History seemed to me, from the first, broader and more humane than English, not hostile or defensive in its attitude to other forms of knowledge but seeking, as far as possible, to embrace them. Its whole posture was more liberal in that it allowed for differences of interest and opinion, and it seemed, in a way, more sure of itself, less prone to demand adherence to the orthodoxy of the moment and cheerfully resigned to the likelihood of having to retreat from positions that proved no longer tenable. History students were treated as individuals and all were soon known by name to our Professor, Ernest Scott, who took a lively interest in our work.

The only other full-time member of the History staff was Miss Jessie Webb. I have always regretted that I did not study Ancient History under Miss Webb because as she taught only one subject she had time to study it in depth, which was the element chiefly lacking in my university course. Miss Webb's study was full of up-to-date specialist journals and her students were kept abreast of the advancement of learning in her field, which was dramatic and exciting in the archaeological 'twenties. She took sabbatical leave during one year of my course and being passionately interested in her subject spent it partly in Athens at the British School and partly in making a long, hard, adventurous journey to the archaeological sites in Crete, with a mule for transport. As well as being a fine scholar Jessie Webb was a delightful person. She was small and quite plain, rather like a bird, with a very alert, intelligent expression. Her hair must once have been reddish, I think, but by the time I knew her it had faded and was a pale colour, between gold and silver, extremely fine hair of the sort into which it is very hard to fasten hairpins. It was always rather wild looking and sometimes tumbled down her back, a situation to which she was so accustomed that she just put it up again unconsciously, without breaking off her animated conversation. Miss Webb was wise, witty, kind and liberal in every sense of the word, wide open to new ideas and different points of view, but her mind was eminently rational and her principles firm. I was lucky, at the beginning of my university life, to encounter so fine an example of the academic woman and long after, as her colleague, to know her well, with ever-deepening respect and affection.

The junior member of the History staff in 1923 was the tutor, Stephen Henry Roberts, a young man known to students as 'Swatty Roberts', a title he had earned by his unremitting and successful industry. He was the first of the few academics I ever knew who were chiefly motivated by the ambition of rising in the world. He was extremely capable and single-minded and would probably have got to the top of any ladder he decided to climb. It might have been in business, industry or the public service: it merely chanced to be academic. The top of the academic ladder was his goal. He was to achieve it, and knighthood too, as he became the Vice-Chancellor of the University of Sydney, which was the top job in the Australian academic world until the foundation of the Australian National University. As a teacher of History, at least in my student days, his attitude was strictly practical; he did not seek to interest us in History or to develop our minds but simply dictated dull but informative notes, designed to enable us to get good marks in examinations, just as he had done.

Ernest Scott, the Professor of History, was a remarkable man. The first thing one heard about him was that he had no university degree. I suppose that at the beginning this was something of a handicap for a Professor but by my time Scott had held his chair for ten years and his lack of a degree had become a distinction. On ceremonial occasions such as the conferring of degrees, when other professors were splendid in doctoral robes of scarlet, purple or emerald, or wore, at the least, the crimson hood of an Oxford M.A., Professor Scott's plain black gown arrested attention and led to enquiries. The answer was that when he had been a boy, in England, his family could not afford to send him to a university but he had had a passion for historical study, which he pursued while earning his living as a journalist. He migrated to Australia when he was twenty-five, arriving in the late 'nineties when the colonies were emerging from depression and beginning to move, slowly and with difficulty, towards federation and nationhood. The sight of history growing under his eyes fascinated him when, in his capacity as a journalist on the

Melbourne *Herald*, he attended the various federation conventions and observed and met the founding fathers of the Commonwealth. This interest broadened out to embrace the whole historic process of the birth of a nation and led Scott back to study the very beginning of the history of white settlement, the discovery and exploration of Australia by sea. Soon he wished to write about it too, but as it is difficult to reconcile scholarship with daily journalism he changed his occupation. Like Charles Dickens before him, Scott, as a young reporter, had mastered shorthand and he decided to become a Hansard writer, a calling as remunerative as journalism but one which left a margin of time and energy for study and writing on topics less ephemeral than the events of the day. During his years as a Hansard writer, first for the Parliament of Victoria and, after Federation, for the Parliament of the Commonwealth, he made his great contribution to Australian history by writing his *Lapérouse, Terre Napoléon* and *The Life of Matthew Flinders*. It was in consequence of his scholarly work that he was appointed Professor of History in the University of Melbourne.

As well as being a Professor without a degree Ernest Scott was a Professor who had been divorced, a fact mentioned *sotto voce* in those unsophisticated days. This gave him, in the eyes of his students, most of whom, like me, had never met a divorced person before, a fascinating aura of worldliness, rather like Don Juan. In fact he had merely been unfortunate in his first marriage and was utterly devoted to his second wife, Emily Dyason. But although Scott was a person of blameless life, he gave the impression of being a man of the world rather than an academic and indeed he had lived in the busy hum of the world until he became a Professor at the age of forty-five, when his tastes and friendships had already been formed. Academic men tend to be careless or, at the least, casual in dress, but Scott looked like a prosperous businessman, very neat, indeed rather dapper. Physically he was short, stocky and undistinguished, except by his possession of a pair of very bright, alert eyes. He knew artists, writers, musicians, journalists, politicians and businessmen. He had a great love and considerable knowledge of music, was a confirmed theatregoer, liked good food and was an authority on red wine. He delighted in the landscape and plants of his adopted country and was a formidable bush walker. He was a keen gardener, especially knowledgeable about roses, which he planted and manured and pruned himself in the lovely garden of the old stone house in Brighton in which he lived. Mrs Scott was an accomplished musician and an heiress and, unlike any other woman I had ever met, she did no domestic work: she once told me that she had never made a pot of tea in her life, surely a unique achievement for an Australian born and bred. The Scotts kept servants and entertained a good deal. As Ernest Scott's idea of education extended beyond the classroom he used to invite his Honours students to dinner parties, not in groups but one by one, no doubt in order to help us gain social experiences. I was amazed, on my first visit, to learn that there was no need to pass the salt and pepper, because there was a tiny silver set for each person at the table. This seemed to me the very peak of refinement, to which I have ever since aspired, but I have never felt that the meals laboriously and rather anxiously cooked with my own hands justified such splendour.

As a young man in London Scott had moved in radical circles: his first wife was the daughter of the formidable Annie Besant. Like most journalists he probably became lukewarm about politics but his general attitudes remained very liberal. Jessie Webb, who was his right hand for over twenty years, recorded that he greatly disliked heavy punishments for student offenders and that his influence was always thrown on the side of mercy and the second chance. Scott was a firm supporter of the emancipation of women and once gave an excellent public lecture in Melbourne in support of this cause. This attitude made him very welcoming to women students even, perhaps, to the point of some positive discrimination in their favour. I realise now that he was perfectly aware that we felt inferior to the male students and knew that if we were to achieve equality our self-confidence needed building up. He was a friend and admirer of Marshall Hall, the first Ormond Professor of Music, who was dismissed from his chair for having published verses of 'a lewdness which is insulting to womanhood'. Scott, who detested cant and hypocrisy, wrote in his *History of the University of Melbourne* that the verses in question were love poems and that 'there is in them nothing lewd or insulting to anybody. They deal with themes which have been treated by innumerable poets throughout the ages, and will be treated, as long as verse is written.' During the First World War Scott was disgusted by the hysterical persecution of Germans domiciled in Australia, which was a feature of that time, and gave aid and support to Walter von Dechend, who was dismissed from his lectureship in German language and literature. Scott died in 1939 but had publicly committed himself to an anti-Nazi stance long before such a posture was acceptable to the establishment.

Ernest Scott was the most hard-working academic I was ever to know in a lifetime spent in universities. He arrived at work on the stroke of nine and never wasted a moment. Except in Ancient History, the province of Miss Webb, he lectured in every subject taught in the History school, set all the essays – a task which included the finding and listing of the relevant primary and secondary sources – heard every Honours student read his essay aloud and discussed it with him, and supervised the long theses we wrote in our final year. Even if he did not reach home until midnight he always studied before going to bed and his card index, preserved in the Archives of the University of Melbourne, shows how he kept his historical reading up to date and was able to direct his students' attention to the progress of scholarship in the subjects they were studying. He was a first-class administrator, ran his department with cool efficiency and was in great demand on committees dealing with general university affairs. Scott took a most active interest in furthering the careers of graduates, being always ready and willing to furnish a helpful introduction or to write a concise, informative and well-expressed testimonial. His concern for the teaching of History in schools was active and practical. He wrote the only readable school history textbook available in those days: his *Short History of Australia* was, for many of us, our first introduction to the history of our own country. At the University he gave a course of lectures in Australian History, the first to be given in any university in his adopted country. He lectured and wrote for the Royal Historical Society of Victoria and was, for a time, the president of the Shakespeare Society. He was frequently asked to give lectures to various bodies, which he always did if possible as he regarded service to the community as part of the duty of a university Professor. Such was his standing that he was the only historian who has ever been (or, I should imagine, is ever likely to be) the president of the Congress of the Australian and New Zealand Association for the Advancement of Science. Something had to be sacrificed to make all this activity possible, and it was Scott's own historical research, in which he had delighted. His *Life of Matthew Flinders* was in the press when he was appointed to his chair and he never wrote another major historical work although he continued to write scholarly papers and books for the general reader.

Professor R. M. Crawford, in his biography of his old master, Professor Arnold Wood of the University of Sydney (*A Bit of a Rebel*, 1975), observes how strange it was that although Wood, a graduate both of Manchester and Oxford, was professionally trained and Ernest Scott self-taught, it was Wood who was the old-fashioned historian and Scott the up-to-date one. It was true, but not perhaps strange. Wood was the heir to a great tradition, which to some extent circumscribed as well as enriched him, but Scott was free to look around and choose for himself and he chose the Cambridge school, founded by Lord Acton, who had been educated in Germany and soaked in the methodology of Leopold von Ranke. The essence of the new method of studying history was the importance attached to primary sources, documents contemporary with the historical events in question, in preference to the later reflections of historians on those events. History was to cease to be the historian's individual view and to become 'history without the historian', the record, free from subjective influences or interpretation, of what actually happened. The study of primary sources is not an 'Open Sesame!' to absolute truth about the past but it has a tonic effect on the mind of the student of history. I had arrived at the university with the notion that the study of history consisted of the mastering and memorising of a number of text-books, each stuffed as full of facts as a

Christmas cake of fruit, but far less appetising as the facts in question were extremely dull, such as the main battles of the Thirty Years' War and the provisions of the Treaty of Utrecht. The study of history from primary sources, which reveal the thoughts and feelings and ways of life of the people of the past, was a revelation to me, a source of unending wonder and delight, and as a teacher I was to observe that it had a similar effect on my students.

In my day at the university Professor Scott was considered the best lecturer in the Faculty of Arts. He had, among other gifts, that of authority, and when he entered the theatre and took his place at the lectern silence fell and remained unbroken until the end of the lecture, unless he saw fit to crack a joke or two, in which case a bit of uproar was licensed. His voice was strong and even those in the back row could hear him without strain, but he could not sound the letter 'r' and it was a measure of the force of his personality that even when he had to pronounce in succession several words containing 'r' there was never any tittering. Scott took great pains with the structure of his lectures. Every one of the hundreds he delivered each year was self-contained, with a beginning, a middle and an end, so that he never had to start with a dreary – 'As I was saying at the end of the last lecture'. Attention was gained by the announcement of a new theme and held by its coherent development. Scott gave the same care to the construction of each sentence as to the architecture of the lecture as a whole, because in learning through the spoken word the student has one chance only of grasping what is said and each sentence should therefore be short, crystalline and without subordinate clauses, and a judicious measure of repetition should be used in linking sentence to sentence, both to carry the argument of the lecture forward and to dilute the intensity of the strain of attention. As he stood on the dais lecturing, Scott seemed in complete mastery of his situation. It never crossed my mind that every one of those lectures was an act of courage. I learnt that years later when, observing my panic on the eve of beginning my first job as a lecturer in Sydney, Professor Scott told me that he had never given a lecture without feeling sick with dread beforehand.

I suppose that Scott's lectures differed in quality, according to the subject and the extent of his interest and knowledge of it but they were all so much better than any other lectures I attended that I would not have dreamed of missing one. All had the value of being based on primary sources. I still remember a first-year lecture on British colonisation in North America in which Scott told, from contemporary documents, the story of the Pilgrim Fathers and of the terrible storm which beset them, just before their landfall, by which they were 'shrewdly shaken'. Two words, still perfectly intelligible, but which no one of my own time would have chosen, brought to life those Pilgrim Fathers – and pilgrim mothers and children, too – as no words from a later century could have done. Suddenly the people of the past became real in a way in which the named persons in text-books never had been; those folk who were 'shrewdly shaken' had been made of flesh and blood.

Further revelations were ahead when we began to write essays. These were not, it seemed, to be mere compilations, arranged in one's best English as 'composition', but a kind of enquiry, in which the humblest beginner could, by studying the primary sources, participate in the joy of discovery. The sources themselves were sometimes enchanting; for example Hakluyt's *Voyages* and Shakespeare's *The Tempest* were sources for British colonisation in the Caribbean sea and Milton's *Areopagitica* and Butler's *Hudibras* for England under the Puritans. Sometimes, of course, the primary sources were less beguiling. My worst experience was an essay entitled 'An Indian View of Dupleix'. This view had to be discovered from a translation of a many-volumed diary kept by a contemporary Indian, and published without an index, so that the only way to learn what this wretched man, Ananda Ranga Pillai, thought of Dupleix, was by examining every page of his long-winded work. For some reason I have never understood, we were not allowed any choice of essays, which were allotted according to the letter of the alphabet with which our surnames began. There was no appeal against this arrangement and sometimes it was hard to bear the thought that a succulent subject had been given to an undeserving student who did not appreciate it while you were stuck with 'An Indian View of Dupleix' or the like. Ernest Scott thought all historical study delightful and expected that we would too. Were we not Honours students, children, as it were, of the inner sanctuary?

Reading essays aloud to Professor Scott was something of an ordeal. He simply could not stand poor, scamped work, and was wont to say that 'histowy should be studied sewiously'. It was unnerving, as you stood in the corridor outside the Professor's study, waiting your turn to read your essay, to see some weeping girl or angry, white-faced young man emerge from the room you were about to enter. I was far too interested and hardworking to incur reproof for inadequate preparation but my composition sometimes failed to please. Once I was the first reader for the morning and found Professor Scott opening and reading his mail, which he continued to do after I had begun to read. I thought this rather a good arrangement, as he did not appear to be attending, but suddenly he snapped at me 'We-wead that last sentence'. I re-read it, with some trepidation as it was a reflection which, at the time of writing, I had thought quite profound but as to which I now had misgivings. 'As I thought', Professor Scott observed, 'meaningless, quite meaningless. Continue.'

The worst ordeal was an advanced class, which we attended in our third year. Each of us was allotted a historical work which had recently been published. We were required to write a review and read it aloud from the dais, while Professor Scott took his place with the students. As we were aware that our reviews of books on subjects about which we knew little were very uninteresting and that our Professor disliked dullness, we tried to compensate by being smart and, if possible, amusing. One student, to whose lot it fell to review *The Squatting Age* by our not much loved tutor, Stephen Roberts, observed that the book was written in the style of a practised examinee but Professor Scott thought the remark impertinent and said so and the atmosphere became tense and ominous. I tried to brighten up my dreary review of a book about Imperial relations with a joke based on a well-known advertisement for a brand of stockings, known as Bond's Ladderproof, by remarking that the **bonds** of the British

Empire were silken but not ladderproof. The class at once recognised the allusion and laughed most loyally, but Professor Scott, whose wide reading evidently did not include advertisements for silk stockings, was mystified by the general hilarity and rather huffy at being left out in the cold. The dreadful reading aloud was supposed to be followed by questions and discussion, but as the library had only one copy of the work being reviewed and this had been monopolised by the giver of the paper, usually no one in the class, save Scott, had read it and discussion was brief, reluctant and embarrassed. There came a day when no one would utter at all. We sat in profound silence for five minutes by the clock and then the Professor arose and, uttering the Miltonic imprecation – 'All silent and all damned!' – marched out of the room, leaving us in dismay.

Nothing gave me so strongly the sense of having entered an adult world as the discovery that History students were allowed to use books in examinations. Whether this idea was original to Ernest Scott I have never known, but I have not heard of its use outside the University of Melbourne. In our annual examinations we were permitted to use specified books of documents and as these were practically useless unless thoroughly studied in advance the knowledge that one could take them into the examination was an inducement to careful study as well as a psychological support to the student. For our Final Honours examinations we were permitted to take in any books or notes: what was being tested was not our memories but our capacity to make good use of our sources. We carried this practice to ridiculous excess in our Finals, arriving with huge suitcases of material which we did not use, but the principle was sound in placing the emphasis on understanding and discouraging unnecessary learning by rote.

As time went on I realised that Professor Scott had his limitations. He was informed and intelligent but not profound. The bent of his mind was commonsensical and practical and he carried empiricism to the point of bigotry by dismissing the whole concept of a philosophy of history as 'wubbish'. Towards the end of my course I began to feel the lack of an intellectual dimension in history as we studied it and a vague desire to engage in a quest for meaning. Scott was also constitutionally unable to enter into certain types of mind, those of mystics, for example, who seemed to him merely mentally deranged people. This defect of the imagination made it impossible for him to understand that even if one is not religious oneself, one simply must accept the abundant evidence available that there are many people, as intelligent as oneself or more so, to whom religion is a fact of experience. Religious belief was 'wot' in Scott's view, and his rather crude remarks on this subject sometimes gave offence. This blind spot made it impossible for him to understand and therefore to render intelligible some of the people he lectured about, such as the Puritans of the seventeenth century who, when deprived of the religious faith and fire within them, are hard to understand. But I hold Ernest Scott's memory in such affection and respect and am so hopelessly in his debt that finding fault with him is uncongenial work.

V

The third Professor known to me when I was a student at the University of Melbourne was Alexander Boyce-Gibson the First, Professor of Philosophy, called the First to distinguish him from his son of the same name who, many years later, succeeded him in the chair of Philosophy. The additional subject I took in my first year was called Psychology, Logic and Ethics and I chose it, as many other students did, because it 'was known for a fact' (which cannot, I am sure now, have been true) that the pass mark was 33.1/3 per cent. I have a clear recollection of the first lecture in Psychology, which was given by Professor Gibson. The class in this bargain line of a subject was large, for those days, and in holiday mood, because it was also 'known for a fact' (and this one was true) that the Professor was no disciplinarian: he not only tolerated noise during his lectures but appeared to be unaware of it. He was a rather stout man, short-sighted, with glasses and a benevolent expression and his massive, bald head fairly radiated pure thought. I expect that Professor Gibson's dedicated Philosophy students learnt a great deal from him but he was unsuited to the task of lecturing to a rabble of first-year students whose aim was a pass at 33.1/3 per cent. He began his first lecture while the students were still chattering and stamping loudly as latecomers entered the theatre, and almost at once he went to the blackboard on which he drew a circle and placed a point in the middle of it. With his back to the class, he then explained this diagram but I could not hear a word he said. I always clung to the belief that if I had only grasped the significance of the circle and the point I could have understood and enjoyed Professor Gibson's course, but as it was I understood nothing and had to mug up my 33.1/3 per cent of Psychology from textbooks.

All the same, I never missed one of Professor Gibson's lectures. He fascinated me because I sensed that he was a rare spirit, a man who really lived for the things of the mind; a gentle, refined, highly civilised person, incapable of vulgarity of thought or deed. When later, on a holiday at Lorne, I met Professor Gibson socially, I formed the opinion, unchanged more than half a century later, that he was the most courteous person I had ever met. It was at a picnic and I found myself the Professor's only companion for quite a long stretch of our walk along a bush track. He did not say a word, but just walked along, no doubt thinking philosophical thoughts and, as ever, looking perfectly serene. The silence made me uneasy, however, because I had been taught that it was the woman's part, on a social occasion, to initiate conversation. Ultimately I managed to think up and make an observation which, even as it left my lips, struck me as fatuous. Professor Gibson stopped dead, brought the whole of his powerful mind to bear on my remark, gazed at me through the thick lenses of his glasses, thought a bit and then said 'How extraordinarily interesting! Do you really think that?' and went on to question me in detail about a remark not worth a straw with as much seriousness as if he had been talking with Immanuel Kant. I wished I had held my silly tongue and yet was glad I had provoked this demonstration of his exquisite manners.

Logic was the province of a young tutor named Charles Murray, who afterwards became a Bishop. Already he had an Olympian manner and lacked the gift of communicating with the primitive mind. He scared the wits out of me and formal logic, with its major and minor premises, remained as unintelligible to me as sine and cosine had been at school. Mr Murray very naturally thought me a dolt. I have never seen such surprise on a face as his showed when, a few years later, we met by chance in the street at Oxford. I was on my way to a lecture and was therefore wearing a gown and the only possible deduction from that premise was that I was studying at Oxford. This really shook Mr Murray, and for once it was he who was struck dumb, until he rallied and asked 'How on earth did *you* get here?' The third member of the Psychology, Logic and Ethics team was the fabulous W. Macmahon Ball, later Professor of Political Science, a very handsome young man, of Irish aspect, dark-eyed and dark-haired, with a fetching dimple in his chin, known to all the women students, in the slang of the day, as a 'heart-throb'. He was also an extremely gifted teacher who could make the hardest places plain and it was he who dragged most of us up to the pass mark of 33.1/3 per cent or whatever.

VI

Apart from sports, our extra-curricular activities were few in comparison with nowadays. Perhaps the lack of the sound of music is the most striking difference between the university then and now. Today the majority of students participate, if only as listeners, in some form of music, but in our time there was an almost absolute distinction between those who were 'musical' and those who were not, and being musical was understood chiefly to mean knowing how to play a musical instrument, usually the piano but occasionally the violin. A few adventurous students were beginning to play the ukelele, precursor of the now universal guitar. We were not provided, as students are now, with free concerts at lunch time and opportunities for listening to recorded music, and the days of the radio were still to come. Nor was any provision made for education in the fine arts. There was no Department of Fine Arts, no university picture galleries or exhibitions. I do not remember seeing a single painting in the University of

Melbourne during my three years there, with the exception of the portraits of university worthies on the walls of Wilson Hall when we were sitting for examinations.

Far from feeling deprived, however, my impression of university life was of an abundance of culture. I was a constant attender at the Literature Club, the Historical Society and the Public Questions Society and an occasional one at the newly founded Labor Club, chiefly because some of my friends were interested in it: I had not yet become politically conscious. Occasionally I went to the Debating Society to hear some of the more brilliant Law students in action. I enjoyed their virtuosity and conceded that debating was a useful exercise for future barristers but the activity itself, of striving for victory regardless of the truth or falsehood of propositions, always made me feel uneasy.

Drama was flourishing in the University and was a great delight to me. In my first year I was overjoyed to be given a part in the Commencement Play, the chief production each year of the University Dramatic Society. I was rather surprised by the choice of play, which did not reach my exalted concept of what befitted a university. The play chosen was *The Law Divine*, a sex-triangle drama from the commercial theatre. What the divine law in question was I do not recall, but suppose it must have been that one should not commit adultery, as the play was about a good woman, her returned soldier husband who had been restless since the war, and the other woman, a loose, cuddly little war-widow, very free with her latchkeys, a menace to the sanctity of hearth and home. I played the merry widow and must have given a spirited rendering of the part, with rather unfortunate results. Even among intelligent people the vulgar error of confounding the character depicted on a stage with that of the actor who portrays it is quite common, and I had hardly settled at the university when I found that *The Law Divine* had made me a victim of this delusion. The manner of some of the women students towards me was decidedly chilly, and that of some of the men unduly warm, because I had acquired the reputation of being 'fast', which it took some time to live down. Plays given by the men's colleges were great occasions and I was delighted to play the part of the worldly Gwendolen in *The Importance of Being Earnest*, the Trinity play for 1924, but after that I had to give up acting because it was too time-consuming. As I loved the theatre and had some talent this was intended only as a temporary retirement from the boards, but as things turned out it proved to be for life. My unkinder critics might comment that I merely ceased to perform in the theatre and thereafter made the academic dais my stage.

Sitting on the floor listening to records or going to protracted dinner-parties had no appeal to the youth of my generation. The 'twenties was the dancing decade of this century. The terrible war was over, the Jazz Age and the time of 'Dance, dance, dance little lady!' had come and a party without dancing would have been no party at all. We all knew how to dance, having been to 'ballroom dancing' classes while still at school; the youth of the whole Melbourne middle-class had been pupils of Paul Bibron, the Misses Brennan or Miss Montgomery. If a new dance came in or an old and difficult one was revived, we took refresher courses; I recall mastering the tango at one such class with my sister Lorna and two of her young men. We danced on simple occasions in private houses when the carpet was rolled up, French chalk was rubbed into the floorboards, the gramophone was turned on and there were sandwiches and cakes and claret cup for supper. We went in parties to the Palais de Danse at St Kilda, where there was a good band and a good floor and it was not expensive. For a grander version of the same outing we went to the supper dances at Bibron's in Exhibition Street. A printed invitation for a private dance was generally for 9 Darling Street, but when Lorna and I gave one it was in the newly opened club house of the Lawn Tennis Association at Kooyong, where we were rather mortified because the caterer did not provide enough food for supper. Still, nothing could dim my joy on that occasion because I was so pleased with my up-to-date appearance. I might well have sat for a painting of The Girl of the Period because I had by then cut my hair and had a ravishing dress in the 'vamp' style – slinky black velvet with a huge design in scarlet and emerald – a broad ribbon on my forehead, long earrings and a waist-length necklace of imitation jade.

University balls abounded. There was the Commencement Ball and balls for the different faculties, and the balls of the various men's colleges – being asked to those conferred great social prestige. Women students particularly delighted in their own annual ball, because for once they were in the position of picking and choosing and it gave us satisfaction to see some of the more lordly male students showing symptoms of anxiety if not speedily invited. I doubt if I would ever have gone to a ball had I not been taken there and looked after by Lorna, because at balls there were programmes and if yours was not filled you were forced to lurk in the ladies' cloakroom during the dances for which you were not booked, in order to avoid the shame of public wallflowerdom. There were always girls in retreat in the cloakroom because there was a dire shortage of young men in the years following the carnage of the First World War. Even at balls, if they were for young people, nothing more alcoholic than very weak claret-cup was ever served. Some young men brought alcohol with them and left it in the cars they had borrowed for the occasion. Generally they sneaked off in groups to consume it, thus aggravating the man shortage, but some of the more daring invited girls to go with them. Only 'fast' girls accepted and as it was by now known that my early reputation for naughty ways was without foundation I was never invited and cannot furnish a report on the dashing doings in cars.

VII

An Honours Arts course in those days lasted for only three years, not four as now, and in one sense they flew but in another they represented a very solid chunk of experience. During those years I underwent a change of personality in that the aimless drift of my childhood was arrested and I became what I was more or less to remain for the rest of my life, one of the world's workers. At first this was a matter of necessity if I were to remain an Honours student and not to have remained one would have been like eviction from Paradise. I worked so hard that to my own and my family's amazement I quite distinguished myself in my first year examinations. This led to still harder work because, for the first time in my life, I had set myself a high standard, below which I did not wish to fall. Besides, I had discovered that hard work can be a joy instead of a drudgery, provided it is work you find absorbingly interesting. When I was sitting for my final examinations in February 1926, some wag placed a large notice on my usual chair in the Public Library, saying 'Vacant this place, formerly occupied day and night by Kathleen Pitt'. I loved working in the Public Library, pausing to look up into the great dusky dome to reflect on the rich store of learning it spanned and on the generations of learners who had studied beneath it. It may seem fantastic, but I believe I was also learning to love the great domes of the world that lay ahead of me on the road of experience – Sancta Sophia, the Cathedral of Florence, St Peter's and to me the most wonderful building on earth – the Pantheon of Rome. In the evenings, emerging from the Library in search of dinner, from the noble flight of steps I loved to see the dark old brick Shot Tower against the brilliant sunset light. I used to tell myself that it reminded me of Florence, but as I had never seen Florence it must have reminded me of some Florentine tower seen in an illustrated book. The Florentine impression was to survive the actual experience of seeing Florence, because it is not only the form but the colour and texture of that modest relic which bring the Tuscan association to mind. The old Shot Tower still survives but the students of today can see only a sliver of it from the steps of the State Library.

My library-haunting was in part caused by the fact that I did not own many books apart from essential texts, and my allowance would not stretch beyond the purchase of an occasional volume in the Everyman edition. I discovered, by leafing through the University Calendar, that there existed some minor university prizes for essay-writing, for which the award was a sum of money to be spent on books to be selected by the winner. I can relate without immodesty that I won two of these prizes because as far as I could ever discover I was the only entrant. What puzzles me is how I found time to do the fairly substantial reading required, because both essays were on extra-curricular subjects, one on the *Edin-*

burgh Review and the other on the ballad revival of the eighteenth century. I was richly rewarded because those essays brought me a small fortune, fourteen volumes of the Mermaid series of British dramatists and several other desirable works which I still have. I suppose that constant practice in essay-writing gave me a more facile pen than I have had since, for I also found time to contribute to the *Melbourne University Magazine* and the student newspaper, *Farrago,* which first appeared while I was a student, having been founded by Bob Fraser and Brian Fitzpatrick, to whom I was later to be briefly and unhappily married.

My experience at the university was one of constant enrichment. There I made most of the friends I kept for life and even at this late date although some of the familiar faces are missing I still have friends among whom I lived at the university and with whom I often spent holidays too, in houses which we put our shillings together to rent, generally at the seaside. It has struck me, on looking back, that Lorna and I enjoyed a very large measure of independence. Our parents took our work seriously and did not make demands which were incompatible with it; even when, during the last two years of my course, we were living in a large house without a maid, the very minimum of household work was asked of me. From the moment we put up our plaits and went to the university we were treated at home as responsible adults and came and went at our own sweet will. We were expected to telephone if not coming home for dinner, but whether we stayed out or came home was our own affair. We were given allowances, out of which we dressed ourselves and met our expenses, but this system was not absolute as sometimes, when our needs really exceeded our means, we were given a present of an expensive item, such as an overcoat or an evening dress. Such windfalls were delightful but the underlying independence was the greatest boon of all, because the need to make choices and take responsibility for them brought us imperceptibly to maturity. When, later, I found myself among English girls at an Oxford women's college, I was impressed by the level of intellectual accomplishment, but in comparison with Australian girls of the same age they seemed, in the practical affairs of life, as inexperienced and irresponsible as children.

I have sometimes wondered whether the later extension of the Honours Arts course from three to four years was a mistake, although at the time the change was made the argument for it seemed sound. It was generally believed (and probably rightly) that the Australian matriculant was a year behind the English one in educational preparation and had not caught up by the end of his course, for which reason Arts graduates who went abroad for further studies were advised to take an undergraduate course and not to attempt a higher degree. If our degrees were to become comparable with those of Oxford or Cambridge it was necessary to make up the deficiency at the university stage. The extension of the course did, at first, have the desirable effect of reducing the Honours student's workload, which was too heavy, and of producing graduates who were intellectually more mature because they had had time to go more deeply into their subjects and reflect on them. But then Parkinson's law began to operate and academic teachers were tempted both to widen their curricula and deepen their courses, and soon their students were as hard-pressed as ever. Simultaneously, the standard of matriculation was greatly raised, so that the last year of school corresponded, both in content and stress, to the former first year of the university and the total effect of these changes was to keep the Honours Arts student at concert pitch for five years. It is probably too long: some students flag and others become impatient and bored with life in the cloister. It is true that students in some other faculties work as hard for as long or longer, but there is no other faculty in which the student's work during his course is so purely intellectual and so utterly divorced from the general life of the community.

But for me and my contemporaries our course ended too soon. In those days final Honours students took the first part of their examination at the ordinary time, in November, but then, instead of having a summer holiday, we were glued to our desks in preparation for the second and more difficult examinations, which were held in February. It was a long, hard stretch and at the end we were as spent as winded athletes. After, there was no sense of anti-climax because a wonderful festivity was ahead before the gates of the university closed on my student life. Professor Scott had invited a group of final Honours students and recent graduates to a dinner-party at Menzies Hotel, a place of legendary splendour which most of us had never entered, and afterwards we were to go to the theatre. We all wore evening dress but only one costume remains in my memory: that of our host. Professor Scott's appearance was simply stunning, because he wore an evening cloak and an opera hat, garments whose existence was known to me only from the then familiar advertisements for de Reszke cigarettes. It was a perfect outing for young people who had been virtual prisoners for so long and our cobwebs were blown away by the exhilarating whiff of the pleasures of the great, wide world.

GOING HOME

I

When I was young, 'going Home', that is to England, was the
dream of every middle-class Melbourne girl and it came true
for me when I was twenty. Ever since Mother's year in
England in 1914 it had been her ambition to take her children
'Home' to have their colonial rough edges filed and polished
and to show them the sights and ways of the old world. This
was to be the crown of the educational programme in whose
interests economy had always been practised in our house and
to which Father had contributed substantially by his steady
rise to the top of the Treasury, where he was now called the
Under-Treasurer and later the Director of Finance. It had
long been decided that 1926 was to be the year of our exodus
because Lorna had completed her Master of Arts degree and
was at leisure, I would have sat for my final examinations in
February, and John was to leave school at the end of 1925
and to have two years abroad before beginning at the
University of Melbourne. It would, I suppose, be thought
odd nowadays for two grown-up girls and their brother to be
accompanied on their trip abroad by their mother but the
generation gap was not then the chasm it has since become
and the arrangement seemed natural to us. As our absence
was to be protracted Father could not come too, except for a
short visit half-way through our stay. This was no great
hardship for him because, having no English blood, he did
not venerate 'Home' and was quite satisfied with Australia.
Being, as well, aesthetically blind, he did not share Mother's
enthusiasm for European art and architecture: his opinion of
the Louvre on their last visit had been that he could have got
through it much faster had bicycles been provided. So Father
went to stay with relations, our house was let and Mother,
Lorna, John and I set out on the *Nestor* of the Blue Funnel
line, for 'Home' via the Cape of Good Hope, in the month of

April, it being an article of faith in Melbourne that you might just as well stay home as fail to reach England in the spring.

In those days the sailing of a passenger ship for 'Home' was a great social event. Lorna and I had new dresses for the occasion and all our friends and relations were at Port Melbourne to see us off, arriving in good time to be shown all over the ship. The other passengers were similarly accompanied and as the hosts did not know their way about any better than their guests the narrow corridors were soon choked by people making off in both directions, hopeful of ultimately arriving somewhere. Finally sorted out, and having inspected the dining-room, the saloon, the bar and the various decks and sporting facilities, they all crowded, with shrieks of laughter, into the cabins and wondered how on earth we were to live in them for six weeks and how we could manage to store our clothes in the dolls' wardrobes and chests-of-drawers provided. It was all very gay until the bells began to ring and visitors were asked to go ashore as sailing time was at hand. Then there were lumps in the throat and a diminution of gaiety, which soon returned when the throng reassembled on the wharf and began to prepare for the last act of the drama by buying rolls of paper streamers which they threw up for the passengers to catch, retaining the free end themselves. This was a difficult manoeuvre and there was much hilarity as roll after roll was bought to replace those that had been badly aimed or not deftly fielded. But at last the streamers were in place, hundreds and hundreds of paper ribbons, our last tenuous link with home. We had seen this spectacle of the coloured streamers many times before, but never from the deck and as the ship began to move and then a gap appeared between the wharf and ship and one by one the streamers snapped, it was hard to keep our tears back. We did our best though, and stayed on deck until we had seen 'Hughenden' from the sea and passed Elwood where our own house was, although we could not see it. Then, rather disconsolately, we went to our cabins, feeling ourselves to be now quite literally at sea. What a loss of drama the disappearance of the ritual of the departing ship and the symbolic streamers has involved; planes have replaced ships, and those who are leaving no longer fade from sight but disappear as abruptly as coffins in a crematorium.

We were soon to learn what liars those travellers are who return from a trip abroad asserting that they enjoyed every minute of it. We had wild weather from the moment we left Port Phillip Bay and reached the open sea until we arrived in Durban. Stabilisation had not yet been invented and the *Nestor* never ceased to pitch or roll, and I can still hear, in my mind's ear, the creaking of the fabric of the ship in the cabin, well forward, where Mother, Lorna and I slept. John had to share with a stranger, a young man travelling alone. We were all extremely seasick, especially Lorna, who was ill the whole way to Durban. I recall the frustration of our arrival there, when I was up at dawn looking out for the shore. When I saw it I woke Lorna up with 'Quick, quick, come and look out the porthole!' Poor Lorna, pale and thin, just rolled over in her bunk and turned her face to the wall. I grew desperate – 'Don't you understand? Outside is *Africa*!' Lorna did not care if the kingdom of heaven was at hand, and I was left to reflect, ruefully, that illness can change personality, for Lorna had a swift appreciation of new scenes and now simply did not care that we were, for the first time in our lives, in sight of a foreign land.

The *Nestor* was old and slow and in no hurry. We had spent two days ashore in Perth and when we arrived in Durban it was announced that we would remain there for three days, during which time the ship would be coaled. The *Nestor* would continue to provide board and lodging for its passengers, but we were warned that the ship would be noisy and dirty during the coaling procedure. So far our voyage had been a disappointment because although Mother and John and I had recovered from seasickness the weather was too cold for outdoor life and the ship too unstable for games or dancing and we were all tired of our confined quarters. Then our unpredictable mother had one of those delightful impulses which, from time to time, projected our family from a regime of economy into a spree of luxury. She announced that during the coaling episode we would stay in the best hotel in Durban. For such unsophisticated young people the Marine Hotel was the ultimate in splendour, especially the dining-room where the waiters were tall, handsome, turbaned

Sikhs, so princely in bearing that we felt the roles should have been reversed, with us waiting on them. And exotic beyond description was the rank of rickshaws outside the hotel, each attended by a Kaffir in what looked like full war-paint. They seemed anxious for custom but we did not enjoy our one ride with them because, coming as we did from a society more egalitarian than that of South Africa, it seemed terrible to us that one human being should use another as horse-power. It was better to walk in the streets of Durban, lined with flowering trees many of which were new to us, and better still when we went by car to see the Valley of a Thousand Hills and to gain, briefly but for ever, some intimation of the grandeur of the African scene, so much more dramatic than that of our native land.

After Durban everything changed for the better. Lorna recovered completely and as the Cape of Storms did not live up to its bad name but offered calm, blue seas and mild weather, there was no more seasickness, only halcyon days, and we began to understand what our travelled friends had meant when they spoke of the delights of shipboard life. Mother dodged company as far as possible, but had a lovely time reading, observing and revelling in her freedom from domestic responsibilities. Lorna, John and I did not share her aversion from society and now that the *Nestor* had ceased to roll we could play games by day and dance by night to our hearts' content. Knowing no lax foreign alternatives at that time we did not mind at all the code of discipline, presumably imitated from the Royal Navy, which British ships used in those days to apply to passengers. There was no question of breakfast in bed; by ten o'clock we were required to be out of our cabins, leaving them in perfect order for what was alarmingly known as 'the Captain's inspection'. Although the *Nestor* was a one-class ship and many of the passengers must have been of modest means, dressing for dinner was obligatory and even John, who was only seventeen, had to wear a dinner jacket and stiff shirt every night.

But there was much to be said for the *Nestor*. It was less snobbish than the Orient and P & O liners which I experienced later, though not without snobbery because wherever human beings are gathered together groups of people of greater and lesser social consequence are formed. John's cabin companion was a young man who gave himself airs and one night, when John was having difficulty in getting the studs into his stiff shirt and began to rail against the absurdity of dressing for dinner, his cabin mate annihilated him by observing: 'Oh, well, old man, it's just a question of what you are used to'. But most of the people travelling in the *Nestor* were pleasant and sensible and some were very nice indeed. There were many families like ours who were able to pay their way but had no money for extravagance. In any case, there was not much chance for conspicuous consumption. The ship provided more food than we needed and although there was a bar we spent little money there because we were non-drinkers, not by principle but in practice. Some girls had more evening dresses than others but the atmosphere was not competitive and we were content with what we had, though it was certainly necessary to wear the same dress rather often. There were a few women passengers of the bold and dashing type who always emerge from the crowd after the first few days of a voyage. Some of them took to frequenting the smoking-room, where their presence was a novelty on the staid old *Nestor*. I was never inside this den of iniquity but enjoyed hearing about the notice the Captain had caused to be put up in view of the new clientele: 'Ladies who use the smoking-room are requested to behave like gentlemen'.

It seemed as if that long, dreamlike voyage in the small, self-contained world of the ship would never end, as we sailed northwards, day after day, inching along like the old Portuguese navigators returning from the Indies. Nothing seemed to change and yet there was change, because one night when we looked up at the stars from the deck the old familiar Southern Cross under which we had been born had vanished and the constellations of the Northern hemisphere, known to us through literature, were coming into view. I remember feeling a little chill, a premonition that somehow life was never going to be quite the same again, that this going 'Home' was after all a serious business, not quite the lark it had seemed when we left Melbourne.

And so we reached our last port, Las Palmas in the Canary Islands. As we came in from the high sea to the little palm-fringed bay, with square-shaped houses painted white or in the pastel colours of lemon, pink, lilac and blue, everything seemed of toylike dimensions and the sharp-peaked, steep-sided mountains that rise behind the town were not in the least like the rounded, worn-down mountains of Australia. How strange that one should have to travel to see one's own country with clear eyes, but so it is, for without comparison there can be no definition and without definition how can one recognise the salient features which form the character of any scene? At close quarters the island continued to be fascinating. I remember chiefly the rain-forest behind the town, where bright unknown birds were flitting through the trees, and the wonderful taste of the sweet, fat little bananas, of a variety we did not then have in Australia. While John and I were revelling in these childish delights Lorna was undergoing, in silence, what I have since learnt was one of the great experiences of her life, the recognition of the concept of Europe and of her natural affinity with it. It was in the cathedral of Las Palmas that she confronted this revelation. The cathedral had merely struck me as being very large for a small city and much more ornate than St Patrick's Cathedral in Melbourne. But ever since her initiation into French culture at the *Sacré Coeur* convent Lorna had been attuned to the idea of European civilisation and her five years at university had centred round it. She recognised at a glance that the cathedral of Las Palmas was centuries older than any building she had ever seen and that it was real Gothic, not a cold, deliberate nineteenth century imitation of it. The Cathedral, as it were, spoke to her, recognising her as an adoptive child of Europe, and she responded. In a sense Lorna passed out of our Australian lives, almost for ever, then and there at Las Palmas.

After our last port the little world of the *Nestor* began to disintegrate. Las Palmas had, quite literally, brought us down to earth. Overtly the ship life continued, but it no longer seemed real. Impending engagements did not come to a head, passions cooled and friendships proved fragile as everyone began to think of something else, of the reason why they had travelled, of duties and responsibilities and discoveries and pleasures totally unconnected with our voyage. Liverpool was the home port of the *Nestor* and on our last day at sea we sailed quite close to the coast of England. All the passengers spent the day on deck, gazing at the land. Homecoming Britons stared silently but the crowd of young Australians and South Africans who were going 'Home' for the first time kept up a flow of excited chatter. It was a beautiful spring day in the month of May, and the tiny fields and the hedges which enclosed them were unbelievably green to us, the denizens of arid lands. 'There's the church and there's the steeple', we would cry, when a village came in sight, looking exactly like the pictures of villages we had seen in the story books on which we had been brought up. Everything in the English countryside seemed extremely small and tidy, even the trees as symmetrical as those in boxes of imported toy farms we had had for Christmas when we were children, so unlike our own gum trees which grow in any direction they fancy and scatter their bark all over the place. It was like having double vision as the characteristics of the Australian scene, hitherto taken for granted, defined themselves by contrast as an utterly different version of Nature was revealed to us.

II

This England seemed to us as pretty as a picture, a generalisation seen to require modification when we reached our journey's end in Liverpool. It must have been a terrible disappointment for Mother to see us all so downcast on the day when, by landing her little flock on the sacred soil of 'Home', she had at last achieved the goal she had set herself for so many years; a goal which had taken so much sacrifice and contrivance to reach. To us, Liverpool seemed hideous and rather frightening, because sub-human types of people seemed to abound, people unlike any we had ever seen before, ragged, gaunt and grim. We had never encountered stark, desperate poverty before. We were seeing our first examples of the millions of unemployed who were in the United Kingdom in 1926. Mother tried to cheer us up by saying that Liverpool was a great port and that ports are always grimy, ugly places – the real 'Home' still lay ahead. We were not altogether convinced: what we had seen with our own eyes was real enough. So, too, were the various industrial cities we passed through on our diagonal railway journey across England from Liverpool to London; dreadful black towns containing thousands of identical houses in identical streets, dwellings which did not seem designed for human habitation but as cells in great chunks of black honeycomb for worker bees. In between these scenes of horror there were visions of beauty, rural England with noble trees and fields that looked like lawns to us, villages with picturesque cottages and churches, magnificent country houses, castles and cathedrals. Clearly, this 'Home' was a more complicated proposition than we had been led to believe.

London was overwhelming and left us agape as we rushed from century to century, trying to see everything at once, our impressions a mish-mash of the Middle Ages and the Renaissance, of the London of Samuel Johnson and that of Charles Dickens. We were awed by the imperial might of what was then the capital of the world and scandalised by the contrast between glimpses of luxury beyond our wildest dreams and destitution equally outside our experience. The sheer size of London and the pressure of its population alarmed us but living there was endlessly stimulating and interesting. We were delighted to find at our hotel some young South African friends from the *Nestor*, fellow-colonials with whom we could discuss frankly, though *sotto voce*, how we felt about this 'Home' so alien to us.

The first thing to be done was to buy a car. We had never owned one before because Father, the unhandiest man on earth, had wisely never contemplated driving and John had been too young. That left, of course, three able-bodied women, but no one, in those days, ever thought of us as possible drivers, nor did it occur to us. But a car was essential to our plans of extensive tourism. John was now seventeen and eligible for an international driver's licence and uncle Jack had given him driving lessons before we left home. I marvel now at the weight of responsibility we were all willing to lay on his young shoulders and his calm acceptance of it, which was no doubt aided by his burning desire to drive. So he and Mother, neither of whom knew anything about cars, went and bought one, of very modest price and aspect, a Clyno, a brand I had never heard of before, nor since for that matter. In this car, not nearly robust enough for the purpose, we were later to demand that John should drive us from Calais to Rome, via the Pyrenees, all of which he did and returned safely over the Swiss Alps, though not without a good many anxious moments.

Both Lorna and I were to pursue further studies. We had arranged for Lorna to take a course at the Sorbonne but my future was not yet determined. From Australia I had applied for a research scholarship at a Cambridge women's college and so far the auguries seemed good as I was informed that I was on a short list and was summoned for an interview. So off we all went to Cambridge in our Clyno and found the 'Home' of our dreams in the peerless little city with its string of colleges, each a jewel, laid out like a magnificent necklace on the green velvet of the 'backs'. What a marvellous place this would be to live in for two years if I were lucky enough to be awarded the scholarship! I went for the interview and was admitted to the presence of the senior History don, who was seated at a desk with the papers of my application spread out in front of her. The academic women I had known in Melbourne had been pleasant, friendly people, dressed like other women, but the person who now confronted me across the desk was unsmiling and severe of aspect, with her hair scraped tightly back, wearing a black dress with a high neck and a long chain from which hung a large, plain, silver cross. She reminded me of Reverend Mothers I had known and made me feel uneasy. I think she did not like the look of me much either. I had made the mistake of wearing my new London coat and hat and although I recall these garments as quiet and suitable they were in the latest fashion and she probably concluded, then and there, that I was a frivolous girl, not scholarship material, an impression probably aggravated by the fact that although I was twenty I looked younger, having then rather a doll-like appearance, with blue eyes and bright yellow curly hair.

The formidable lady began the interview by asking of what

university I was a graduate, which seemed an odd question as my application was under her eyes. I replied 'The University of Melbourne'. There was a silence and then, in that tone of ineffable upper-class British superiority I was to come to know so well, the don observed: 'Here in Cambridge, you know, we don't think much of the degrees of these American universities'. It was not a remark calling for a reply and I made none but was amazed. Could a Cambridge don be ignorant of the fact that Melbourne was one of the larger cities of her own British Empire? If she really thought I was American, why was she so rude? I would not have minded being mistaken for an American, I did not feel superior to Americans and at that moment I felt strongly on their side because I had just understood, for the first time, why they had felt it necessary to cut the painter with 'Home' in 1776. The don's questions were resumed and it became abundantly clear, from their hostile tenor, that for some unknown reason she wished to humiliate and hurt me. My black Irish pride and histrionic ability enabled me to get through the rest of the interview with apparent serenity. Only when I had escaped through the college gates and saw the dear family, perched in the Clyno, all agog for an account of the interview, did my control crack, relieved by the benison of tears.

I related the events of the interview and explained that if I were awarded the scholarship I would have to spend two years under the supervision of the don with the Christian emblem round her neck and that this I could not and would not do. The family was splendidly unanimous in my support and we went to buy some impeccably chaste writing paper on which I inscribed, in my best convent handwriting, a letter of extreme brevity in which I stated that I had decided to withdraw my application for the scholarship and enter the University of Oxford. Father had always been willing to pay my fees should I fail to get the scholarship, and I now applied to Somerville College, Oxford, for a place as an undergraduate reading History. I had had time to reflect that, unpleasant as she had been, the Cambridge don might have been right in her evident view that I was not fit for postgraduate work. If the degrees of English universities were the only ones that really counted then the right strategy seemed to be to equip myself with one of these but not, please God, at Cambridge.

Somerville called me for an interview and I went to Oxford by train, with sister Lorna as moral support. My first impression, received from the railway station, was dire; there was not a dreaming spire in sight, only a factory which made sausages and another which made marmalade. Still bruised from the Cambridge encounter, these ugly factories seemed presages of harsh experience to come and I was nervous and dejected. Borrowing from Mother at Liverpool, Lorna said: 'Think of this area as the port of Oxford. Ports are always beastly and we'll see the lovely part later'. I realised she was right when we reached Carfax and caught a glimpse of the glory of Christ Church on our right and saw the High unrolling before us in beauty after beauty, all the way to Magdalen bridge. I was very nervous when I went in to Somerville for my interview, fearing a repetition of the glacial reception at Cambridge, but this time the climate was genial. I was received by the Principal, Miss Emily Penrose, a stately, elderly classical scholar with beautiful manners and a kind heart. Miss Penrose knew where I came from and not only did not mind but seemed quite to like the idea of having an Australian undergraduate in the college. My native woodnote wild was still pristine and I pronounced all words ending with the letter 'a' in the manner of my country, as though spelt 'yer'. How magical was the sound of Miss Penrose's beautiful diction as she said: 'At present we have students from Indiah, South Africah and Canadah, but none from Australiah, and I should like to have an Australian'. She asked me some questions but it was evident that my application had already been fully considered and that she had made up her mind, and when I rejoined Lorna, who was lurking outside the college, it was with the joyous news that as I was already a graduate I would be admitted without examination at the beginning of the academic year, which was in October.

Now we had the whole summer before us and intended to leave for the Continent as soon as we had met our sole family duty in England by paying a visit to my grandfather's cousin, John Buckhurst. They had been boys together but had never met since Grandpa had left England for Melbourne in 1869. The connection had always been kept up, however, and members of the family visiting England, Mother and Father in 1914 and the uncles when they were on leave during the First World War, had always paid the ritual visit to cousin John and now it was our turn to spend a fortnight with him. He was a childless widower, who had been a very successful banker, and had long retired to live alone in the pretty little village of Biddenden, in Kent. His house, called 'Hendon Hall' was not, as its name had suggested to me, a grand mansion, but had probably been a small manor house in the days of James 1, when it was built. 'Hendon Hall' was indeed the 'Home' of the story books, a neat, comely, two-storeyed house of rose-red brick, with a low paling fence, built close to the road, with the garden on one side and behind it and beyond was the village church, like the backdrop of an English scene in a play. The garden, so modestly retired, was glorious with ancient trees and weedless lawns and herbaceous borders glowing with colour and without a single dead bloom.

It was now the month of June and I remember 'Hendon Hall' as full of light and sparkling with cleanliness. Inside and out, upstairs and down, everything was always in perfect order, as indeed it should have been because cousin John employed a cook and a housemaid, two gardeners and a chauffeur to drive his enormous Bentley, beside which the little Clyno in which we had arrived looked like a handcart.

Cousin John was a kind and generous host but he was also an autocrat. The routine of life at 'Hendon Hall' had been laid down once and for all and was immutable. Breakfast was at eight and poor Mother was up by half-past six to have her own bath, get us all up and see that we were bathed, dressed and irreproachable and marshalled in the dining-room before the clock struck eight when, like fate, the master of the house and the porridge arived. I daresay that in better conducted families than ours this 7.59 parade would have presented no great difficulty, but breakfast had never been a sacred rite in our parental tent, where we only had tea and toast and got our own and washed it up ourselves, so that it did not matter to anyone when we had it. But Mother had learnt about British discipline on her previous visit to England and she impressed on us that we must not disgrace her by colonial slackness in being late for breakfast. It happened only once and poor John was the culprit. He was only a few minutes late but the air was electric with cousin John's displeasure, as he kept taking out and inspecting the gold watch that he wore in the old-fashioned way on a chain tucked into his waistcoat. Enter John, who apologised and did not forget to say 'sir'. But cousin John was not appeased and made some withering observations touching the habits and manners of the younger generation and John, who was gentle and sensitive, was embarrassed. Mother and Lorna and I, in painful silence, looked at our plates. A great wave of homesickness swept over me. Of what avail this historic dining-room, this lavish choice of bacon and eggs and kidneys and kedgeree, these relays of fresh toast arriving hot from the kitchen, when your food was choking you? How wonderful it would be to wake up and find that 'Home' was all a horrid dream and have breakfast in your own kitchen, wearing your dressing-gown, in the land of the free.

When I had lived in England longer I realised that although cousin John was a martinet he was much less singular than we, so new to 'Home', had imagined. It was we who were odd because from our childhood we had enjoyed more independence than young people of our class in England, who had been brought up in boarding-schools. There had been no strong disciplinary element in our lives, but it was otherwise in England, which seemed to bristle with rules and regulations. Cousin John was hospitably bent on showing us the sights of rural England but it took a great deal of contrivance to fit these excursions into the grid which divided the day into four parts – breakfast at eight, luncheon at one, tea at quarter-to-five and dinner at eight. A long excursion could not be made in the morning because although breakfast was over by half-past-eight cousin John then took *The Times* out into the garden, where he read it in the seclusion of his gazebo until ten-thirty precisely. Could we go in the afternoon, then? Well, hardly, given that tea was at quarter-to-five. That tea might have been later or even omitted was never for one moment considered.

Still, we did make some long excursions, by dint of leaving at a quarter-to-eleven, lunching out and returning in time for tea. With bacon and eggs behind us and a splendid tea and dinner to come, we would have been content with any old snack for lunch, a sandwich or fish and chips, as the handy meat pie, solver of all such difficulties in Australia, did not seem to exist. But cousin John was not in favour of eating snacks. A hotel had to be chosen and telephoned and a precise hour stated when we would appear for luncheon, and cousin John would have his watch out a good many times and speak sharply to the chauffeur to make sure we were as punctual at the hotel as we would have been at 'Hendon Hall'. For this reason it was never possible to stop the Bentley on impulse to look at some interesting wayside sight, a hop-oast or an unknown flower, or just to gaze at the lovely views over the Weald of Kent. A few stops of this kind would have been very welcome because on these excursions we often felt a bit sick. Brought up in windy Melbourne and in hardier days than these, we were used to plenty of fresh air, but no window was ever opened in the sumptuous Bentley. In private we said to Mother that it was like travelling in a hearse and pleaded with her to make representations to cousin John for a ration of fresh air, to which she replied with spirit that she would do nothing of the kind. Cousin John, she said, was our host and a frail old man, very susceptible to draughts, whereas we were young and healthy and had better begin learning that in travel we must take the rough with the smooth. We saw she had a case and and behaved ourselves, but that did not prevent us, when cousin John was not looking, from punishing Mother by tugging at our collars and declaring in whispers that we were about to faint.

The hotels favoured by cousin John were very solid establishments of the Victorian period, with potted palms and waiters strangely attired, as it seemed to us, in evening dress at lunchtime. In a sense we enjoyed our visits to these hotels because they seemed to us such intensely British institutions, but we begrudged the time taken to eat protracted and tasteless meals when we might have been sight-seeing. Whatever was written on the menu, it always seemed to come down to a thick soup, of many names but most often Brown Windsor, of dark brown appearance with a taste of flour and Gravox, meat with watery vegetables, a heavy pudding, biscuits and rather ancient cheese, followed by an indescribable fluid, said to be coffee, served with much pomp and ceremony in the lounge.

Our complaints that we were being turned into mere chattels, deprived of all liberty and reduced to the infantile state, freely voiced when we were alone in our bedrooms, must have been very trying for Mother who felt we were having a marvellous opportunity for seeing 'Home' at its best, as indeed we were. We were living in a beautiful and historic house in a charming village, set in lovely country. We had been to Rochester and seen the great, grim Norman castle and the interesting Cathedral which began by being Romanesque and then, when the Gothic style came in, changed its mind halfway and was finished with pointed instead of rounded arches. We had been to Hastings, redolent of English Harold and Norman William, had admired the water-lilies thickly clustered in the great moat of Bodiam Castle in Sussex and the cherry trees and graceful hop-vines growing in the fields of Kent. We had visited some distant cousins who were small farmers in the flat land near the river Medway; from the farm, ships which were anchored in the river looked as though they were sailing on fields of ripening grain. Our cousins were shearing their little flock of sheep on the day we visited them and were surprised to hear that this was a rural sight we had never seen before as they had supposed you could watch the shearing very conveniently in Melbourne.

We had gained some insight into village life by meeting the Vicar, attending the church fair and visiting the Women's Institute. We had also gained, for the first time, an understanding of what is meant by the phrase 'the pleasures of the table'. At home our food had been sufficient and properly cooked but was very economical, with roast meat for a Sunday treat, poultry only at Christmas and on Friday the cheaper kinds of fresh fish, such as garfish or flathead or a chowder made with a lot of potato and onion and a little tinned salmon. But at cousin John's we had wonderful food every day, superb beef, Southdown lamb, home-raised chickens, Dover soles both tender and full of flavour and wonderful vegetables, picked from the garden that morning, and at tea there were always several kinds of cake, as well as home-made biscuits and bread and butter sliced so thinly that it was as transparent as lace. Cousin John took us to visit some of his neighbours, always in the afternoons, to see their splendid gardens and eat their elaborate teas, one of which, I remember, was crowned in what the English guests seemed to think a sensational manner by fresh peaches from the hot-house, which we thought rather tasteless compared with the sun-ripened peaches of home.

Despite our kicking against the pricks we all realised that our stay at 'Hendon Hall' was an experience to be grateful for, but we hankered for freedom and were exhilarated when we left Biddenden in our ramshackle but airy little Clyno, with the open road before us, no plans for lunch and the Continent to come for three whole months.

From the first I felt more at ease on the Continent, despite the language barrier, than I had been or ever was to be in England. That was, I suppose, largely because our status on the Continent was not anomalous: we were foreigners, pure and simple. In England we were not exactly foreigners but decidedly we were not English either but colonials, people of an inferior race. And in England we were always at a dis-advantage because there seemed to be innumerable rules, but no one ever told us what they were until we broke one, when the point was made abundantly clear. In France and Italy it was much simpler because it was stated that some actions were *défendu* or *vietato* and for the rest you could do as you pleased without worrying whether you were giving offence and about to incur reproof.

Before we left London Lorna had discovered that she and I were eligible to attend a conference to be held in Paris for graduates of British Commonwealth Universities, under the sponsorship of the League of Nations Union; the theme was to be Intellectual Co-operation. The fees were extremely low and the promised attractions seemed glittering, so we enrolled and our arrival in Paris was timed for the opening of the conference. We were rather worried about the Intellectual Co-operation aspect, as we did not know what it meant nor whether we were capable of it, but we were determined to try. Mother and John dropped us at the designated hotel, found another for themselves and remained tactfully invisible until the conference was over. At the hotel we found a number of young people like ourselves, Canadians, South Africans and one Australian and were surprised and relieved to find that none of them was clearer about Intellectual Co-operation than we were.

We never did find out, because nothing at all intellectual happened. There were no meetings, no resolutions, no speeches except of welcome and our sole duty seemed to be accepting right royal entertainment. We dined off gold plate in a Rothschild mansion, one of those great Paris houses which look so austere from the street but where wonderful gardens exist invisible behind high, blank gates, just as in the novels of Henry James. We were received by the President of the French Republic at a late afternoon party held in a mar- vellous pavilion with a glass roof, from which a rosy light, shed by the sun, filtered through hundreds of yards of pink silk festooned below the glass. Finally, glory of glories, we went to Versailles on a day when it was closed to the public and all the dazzling fountains were turned on for our sole benefit, while we ate a masterpiece of a luncheon in the Grand Trianon, as if we had been the guests of Louis XVI and Marie Antoinette in the days before the trumbrils began to roll. Our pleasure in all these delights was only faintly dimmed by our consciousness of fraudulence because we had done nothing to deserve them, but we drained our brimming cup of rare experiences and kept on saying 'Merci' and smiling, which was co-operative, though not intellectual.

IV

Coelum non animum mutant qui trans mare currunt. Was the proposition that when we cross the seas we change only our skies, not ourselves false or true? I sat meditating on this question at a café in the Piazza dell' Esedra in Rome on the golden September afternoon of my twenty-first birthday. Why I was there alone with time on my hands escapes my memory – presumably I was to meet the family and either they were late or I was early. The piazza, which is near the central railway station, was, I suppose, in its usual uproar of traffic, but the interlude comes back to me as a peaceful, hushed hour of solitude and reverie when I was free to begin sorting out the manifold, multiform impressions I had received since we had passed through the Heads of Port Phillip Bay, outward bound, six months before, and become of those who *trans mare currunt*. I had crossed more sea and changed my skies more completely than any ancient Roman, but was my *animum,* as the sage asserted, immutable? Yes, up to a point. I had already learnt that wherever one travels one must carry, strapped to one's back, the knapsack of the self, a ragbag stuffed with genes and habits, pride and prejudice, a little knowledge and a great deal of ignorance, a heavy burden which limits freedom of movement and capacity for development. Still, is there not some possibility of modifying the contents of the knapsack by jettisoning some of the prejudices, cutting down the ignorance and increasing the knowledge? When we change skies, I brooded, we become aware of alternatives and find we prefer this one to that. The bent of mind which dictates choice is in ourselves but might never have surfaced into consciousness had we never changed skies. Awareness of our values helps us to know what manner of people we are, and surely an increase in self-knowledge constitutes a change in the *animum?*

Seated as I was within a stone's throw of the church of Santa Maria degli Angeli, in which Michelangelo incorporated the esedra of the Baths of Diocletian, the example that naturally came to mind of an increase in self-knowledge was architectural. At home I had often heard people say that they did not know anything about art, but knew what they liked. Although I recognised this dictum as absurd I had to admit, ruefully, that if they really knew what they liked they were better off than I was. How could I know what I liked when I had seen so little? For months past, during which we had haunted museums and picture-galleries and been impassioned sight-seers of cathedrals and castles and palaces, of bridges and piazzas and aqueducts and fountains, we had been undergoing an intensive sensuous education. So did I now know what I liked? The answer came loud and clear in the Piazza dell'Esedra; it was my own private little revelation, my adventure on the way to Damascus. It had been making itself felt occasionally, ever since we reached Southern France and saw for the first time some of the ruins of ancient Rome and the sensation had been strengthening since we had crossed the Italian frontier at Ventimiglia and made a leisurely progress down the peninsula to Rome.

Classical form. I now knew what I liked, at least in architecture: Roman, Romanesque and early Renaissance buildings evoked a warmer response from me than any others. But why? One could not honestly say that the Pantheon of Rome was more beautiful than the dazzling Gothic cathedrals of France, those incantations of lacy stone that, in the moister air of Northern Europe, seem to reach their goal in heaven. The Pantheon is earth-bound; indeed, like most of the ancient Roman edifices still standing, it is now below the present ground level. Nor does it in any way confound itself with heaven for through the hole in the centre of the great dome one can see the sky and sometimes feel the rain. The Pantheon expresses stability, not aspiration, and offers shelter to men rather than a ladder to heaven. But why should I prefer to be earth-bound rather than sky-borne? Could one trace it all back to those solid bluestone foundations of my childhood which had seemed to offer some promise of permanence in a world of flux? I could not find a reason, but knew that I was the kind of person to whom classical form is more congenial than romantic, not only in architecture but in painting, sculpture, music, literature, dancing, even landscape. I can admire waste and solitary places, high mountains and deep, rugged gorges strike awe into my soul, but I cannot love them and am only happy in scenes made to the measure of man and humanised by his long habitation of labour in them.

V

Rome was the end of a long holiday and the end, for me, of the sheltered home of my minority. Lorna and I parted from Mother and John, who went off to Naples in the Clyno, and we took the train to Paris. Lorna had been entrusted with the power of the purse and the duty of equipping me for life at Somerville College. We boarded at a pension on the left bank of the Seine, in the rue Vaugiraud, which was patronised by cultured people who did not have much money, a good many of them from Boston. It was an extremely frugal establishment. Sometimes a single sardine, looking very lonely on a large plate, constituted a whole course and dessert was either a tiny pot of jam or two small, misshapen apples, often badly bruised, probably windfalls bought cheap at the market. Day after day Lorna and I went forth into Paris to buy my linen and wardrobe for Somerville. I fear that Lorna must have exceeded the budget, for she knew no more about household matters than I did, and in a lordly manner ordered several sets of pure linen sheets, which were of such a quality that they lasted me half a lifetime.

Sheets and towels, though necessary, were boring, whereas the acquisition of a Parisian wardrobe was bliss. I insisted that I must have a tweed suit, because in books English girls were invariably attired, during the daytime, in such garments, and it was stressed in the literature that although they might be old and shabby, they simply must be well tailored. So we found a tailor whose window bore a notice stating that 'all our suits are cut and signed by Monsieur himself'. The suit proved to be almost excessively English, in brown tweed, a colour which did not suit me and made me look anaemic, but it was well cut, although I was rather disappointed by Monsieur's signature which turned out to be no more than an ordinary sewn-in label. Very delightful, however, were the beige jumper suit, the black dinner dress and the pink silk afternoon one, all crowned by the very latest hair style, the Eton crop, for which all my waves were shorn and I emerged '*en* boy', with short back and sides. It was the height of fashion in 1926 for girls to look as much like boys as possible without actually wearing trousers, a style which was still to come.

Mother and John arrived back from their travels in time to see me off to Oxford. It was the first journey I had ever made alone in my life and I was very apprehensive, not, as it proved, without reason, for I have never felt so lonely as during my first term at Somerville College. I had never been separated from my family before and I was terribly homesick, especially for Lorna, who had been my chief support in life ever since I could remember, as she was to remain for the next half-century, although we were to live twelve thousand miles apart. For the first ten days at Somerville none of my new companions addressed a single word to me. Meals were a terrible ordeal, especially the protracted dinner. The food was badly cooked and served half cold but what worried me more was that my neighbour on the right spoke to hers on the right and my neighbour on the left to hers on the left, while I sat between their cold shoulders in total silence. I learnt later that this was not deliberate unkindness. English people of the upper and middle-class simply lack the easy sociability of colonials and Americans. Some are shy and feel you may have as little wish to know them as they have to know you. Others are snobbish and unwilling to commit themselves to a social relationship which may prove uncongenial. But should the barriers fall and friendship eventuate, English people, I found, make firm, faithful and frank friends, more willing to confide and share their lives than Australians and Americans who are superficially cordial but, in fact, keep themselves to themselves.

My study-bedroom appalled me. I had never had such an ugly room, which was also rather dark and principally furnished with a mean iron bedstead and a washstand. It was an unusually cold October, with lower temperatures than I had ever experienced and as England was in the grip of the coal strike there was a shortage of fuel and our rooms were heated only by coal fires. We were given a ration of coal and told to eke it out by sharing fires with our friends but as I had no friends I usually had no fire either. I developed a raging cold and, as I was also not getting enough to eat because I was shirking the embarrassing meals in hall, I soon began to look so queer as to attract the attention of the Principal, who sent for me and asked what was the matter. I replied that through change of hemisphere I had had two summers in succession and was not yet acclimatised to the cold. Miss Penrose was splendid. She wisely did not increase my coal ration, a favour which might have aroused hostility, but moved me from the coldest part of the college, my natural home as a fresher, to a small, bright room next door to a bathroom whose hot water pipes raised the temperature of my living quarters.

The room was minute but snug and cheerful and whereas the outlook from my first room had been bleak I now had a charming view of lawn and trees. I plucked up heart and bought a cover for the ugly bed and a pair of beautiful curtains, with a flowing Jacobean design in rich reds and blues, warming even to behold. A thaw set in on the social front and I began to make acquaintances. My health improved and I ceased to feel and look like a character in a play by Ibsen. I began to find my way about Oxford and to discover that although it was not as pretty as Cambridge because the colleges were less concentrated and were interspersed with commercial buildings, it was larger and grander and struck a more imperial note than Cambridge, which seemed provincial in comparison. I loved to go to lectures at Christ Church, entering by Tom Tower, crossing the noble quadrangle and, never failing to look upwards, when passing under the marvellous fan vaulting of the great staircase. It was a delight to pace the perfect Gothic cloisters of New College, the meticulously tended lawns of St John's and the charming paths through the woods at Magdalen. It was a privilege to study in the dusky recesses of Duke Humphrey's Library and in the Bodleian and to feel oneself a drop in the great stream of folk, which has, for so many centuries, flowed into Oxford seeking and finding knowledge there. And when, at last, the bitter winter was over and done and I could go further afield it was a joy to discover the sweet English countryside about Oxford as it was half a century ago, to walk through the water meadows towards Godstow Lock in spring, marvelling at the intense green of English grass, the gold of a myriad of kingcups and the illusion of distance created by great drifts of misty blue forget-me-nots or, choosing the Iffley way instead, to come on the little, ancient, Norman church which seems rather to have grown out of the earth than to have been imposed on it.

Although my memories of Oxford are not altogether happy, as I count over the beads of my experience there I recognise the value of some of them. Perhaps the most important, in leading ultimately to self-knowledge and the best use of my own talents was my learning, once and for all, what is meant by scholarship. Real scholars, I believe, are born as well as made and what was given, in my case, did not add up to the potential of a real scholar. There was, however, enough of this strange creature in me to enable me to recognise and appreciate the real thing and later to give all the furtherance in my power to those of my own students in whom I detected the rare gifts that make a true scholar.

I have always loved literature as well as history and it was at Oxford that a new world was opened to me by my meeting with the work of Henry James, of whom I had never heard during my three years of literary study in Melbourne. I owe this introduction to an American graduate, who was studying for her doctorate at Somerville: she became a Professor in her own country afterwards and is now dead, so that it is too late to thank her by name for having enriched my life. Almost every one of Henry James's many books – for I have never succeeded in finding copies of some of his early non-fictional works – are on my shelves today and most of them are well-worn. I have never ceased to delight in him as an artist and as a moralist he has been to me a life-long teacher and support: many have been the occasions I have turned to him for help when the problems of the conduct of life were too difficult for me to solve unaided and I have never failed to find in his wisdom a guide and in his example an injection of courage.

Another gain from my time at Oxford was my arrival at political consciousness. Hitherto I had taken up an attitude of detachment from politics: the subject did not interest me and I refused to concern myself with it. This attitude had been challenged from the moment of our arrival at Liverpool and rudely shaken by the experience of being in London soon after the general strike of 1926. The contrast between the unemployment, hardship and distress of some people and the life of privilege and luxury led by others made me uneasy but was not, I thought, my business, a comfortable view encouraged by the confusing mass of impressions I was receiving.

At Oxford, however, I was not a mere observer and a transient but part of a community and I could no longer dismiss the social problem from my consciousness. Oxford half a century ago, was still the almost exclusive preserve of the rich, and instances of the extravagance and arrogance of many of the undergraduates and of the cringing servility of shopkeepers and others in dependent situations were everyday experiences. During my first few weeks when, in Fuller's tea shop or the café of the Super Cinema, I witnessed encounters between gilded youths meeting after the Long Vacation, I was sickened by overhearing their exchanges of anecdotes of derring-do when, as volunteers, they had helped to break the General Strike. What had been a tragedy to millions of their fellow-countrymen had been a mere lark to them, of the same order as a treasure-hunt or a debagging. It is difficult for anyone today to realise how frivolous the English upper classes were in the 'twenties, but Frances Donaldson in her *Edward VIII* caught the tone of the time perfectly when she related how 'large sections of society spent their time in the pursuit of pleasure with a single-mindedness which marks this generation off from almost every other in history'.

It began to dawn on me that there are circumstances in which the posture of neutrality is indefensible. I was twenty-one now, a responsible adult, and had no right to avert my eyes from human suffering. Clearly, a revolution in favour of social justice was needed in this country and perhaps, for all I knew, in my own too. Short of violence, only by means of political action could reform be effected, and I should therefore support whatever political action was appropriate. But I was terribly ignorant both of what was wrong and of the various proposals for righting it. I ordered the *Manchester Guardian,* read it conscientiously, and from its solid, informed and fair-minded columns began my political education. I also had the good luck, early in my Oxford time, to make a friend for life – Isobel Addison, who was a socialist both by conviction and, as it were, by birth, as her father was a Labour politician and her mother was a Christian Socialist who practised what she preached. At Isobel's suggestion I joined the Labour Club where, it is ironical to recall, our guru and high hope was a brilliant, radical young economist, Colin Clark, who, after his conversion to Catholicism and migration to Australia, was to earn the reputation of a pillar of reaction. I never came to relish politics nor to be politically very active, but I did accept the view that politics is the business of every citizen and that I had no dispensation from the dust and heat.

It is not possible for a person of any sensibility to be unaffected by living for two years in a place of such beauty and antiquity as Oxford, so hallowed by centuries of distinction in the life of the mind. And yet, in later years, I was to listen almost with envy to male colleagues who, like me, had taken their first degrees in Australia and their second in Oxford and who looked back with evident nostalgia, which I could not share, to their blissful days in the Paradise Lost of Oxford. I too had been in Arcadia but I did not long to return and felt guilty of my failure to respond appropriately to a great opportunity by being in fact rather unhappy while there. For one thing, I had never felt really well. Although in general a healthy person, I had always been prone to colds and bronchitis and as fords are made in low-lying river places, the climate of Oxford, a sunken circle in the Thames valley, moist even in summer, was unsuitable for me, and my resistance to lowering minor ailments was not fortified by a good diet. Never before or since have I had to eat food as deplorably cooked and served as that of Somerville College. Breakfast and luncheon were not too bad but dinner was uneatable. After grace had been said and we had sat down the maids placed on the table vegetable dishes without lids, one containing potatoes and the other, usually 'greens' awash with water. Then they went back to the kitchen and fetched the soup. By the time that had been eaten and the soup-plates removed and replaced by the main course, a cut from a joint of unidentifiable meat, the vegetables were stone-cold and were carried out again, practically untouched, before the arrival of the final delicacy, the heavy, tasteless pudding, smothered in a dire sauce.

During my first year I suffered very much from the sudden severance of every link with my native land. No male Australian undergraduate would have been so isolated because there were always fellow-countrymen in Oxford on Rhodes or other scholarships, but I was not only the sole Australian woman undergraduate in Somerville but, as far as I know, in all Oxford at that time. Most English people, in those days, still liked having an Empire, but they did not like its inhabitants much and had little or no curiosity about the places on which the sun never set. Only one girl at Somerville ever asked me a question about Australia, although several told me that they had heard that New Zealand was a much nicer place, more like England. But although these English attitudes at first distressed me I was growing up and commonsense came to the aid of wounded *amour propre*. English people had not been brought up in the kinship myth in which colonials of my generation had been nurtured; we were not their long-lost cousins and they could not be expected to welcome and cherish us.

What I could never reconcile myself to was the position of women at Oxford. In 1926 when I arrived there, it was only a few years since women had been admitted to the full status of members of the university, on their way to receiving degrees like the men, and since this emancipation had been won with difficulty the authorities of the women's colleges were very anxious that their undergraduates should be as inconspicuous as possible and give no occasion for adverse criticism. To ensure this they subjected us to much stricter discipline than that dispensed to male undergraduates. Although I was not in the least unruly I felt the prison-like atmosphere of the college to be degrading. Outside the college, too, we were constantly reminded that we were not particularly welcome in Oxford. Some irreconcilable male dons refused to admit women to their lectures and others took the more subtle course of admitting but embarrassing them. All undergraduates were required to wear academic dress to lectures, but indoors the men took off their mortar-boards whereas women were required to wear their thick cloth caps indoors as well as out. I was at a lecture one warm spring day when a girl who was feeling the heat took her cap off. She was publicly reproved by the lecturer who told her that he would not have improperly dressed females in his lectures, as if the poor, mortified girl had stripped herself naked.

Many of the male undergraduates also made it clear that they despised the women students, thinking them a dreary, dowdy lot. Literary evidence abounds to show that this attitude prevailed among the male undergraduates at Oxford until the Second World War. Emlyn Williams was a clever working-class boy who won a scholarship to Christ Church, the most fashionable of the Oxford colleges. His autobiography records his speedy acclimatisation to the mores and opinions of Christ Church, which included despising women undergraduates. A decade later Nigel Nicholson spent three years at Balliol, the most intellectual of the colleges, without ever once entering a women's college or knowing a single inmate of one and does not think he was exceptional in this. Once, when he was attending the first lecture of a series the lecturer, noticing a few girls in the class, announced that he did not lecture to 'undergraduettes' and bade them be gone. They went but the men rose in a body and left too. At the next lecture the girls were there again and the don gave in and accepted them. However, none of the men ever spoke a word to the girls they had championed, considering resistance to tyranny one thing and social relations with women undergraduates quite another.

The prejudice of undergraduates against 'undergraduettes' was partly a matter of tradition and partly a result of the fact that homosexuality was widespread in that community of young men who had spent most of their lives in boarding-schools, but it also arose from sheer snobbery. The undergraduates who formed the smart set at Oxford in my day came from the gentry and the prosperous upper-middle class: they were, in the main, in Oxford in pursuit of pleasure rather than of learning. J.I.M. Stewart, who was an undergraduate in my time and returned as a don to a transformed Oxford in the second half of the century, found with relief that the colleges were no longer 'noticeably cluttered up with hopelessly thick or even incorrigibly idle youths from privileged homes.' Such youths had set the social tone before the Second World War and had naturally had no time for the girls in the women's colleges who came, on the whole, from the middle-class and tended to be hard-working and clever because, as Oxford could accept only one woman for every four men, they would enter only by a fairly rigorous entrance examination. Angus Wilson, who was at Oxford in the 'thirties, recalls that 'the smart Christ Church set... knew no women undergraduates, only debs from London and the shires' and J.I.M. Stewart, who was at Oriel, which was not a fashionable college, shows how this taboo was conformed to even by those not in the smart set: 'one risked ridicule by a bare mention of the women's colleges'. When balls were held in the men's colleges only a few women undergraduates, dazzlingly pretty or very well-connected, were invited, as the hosts preferred to be seen with extra-curricular debs, who would do them credit. During my two years at Oxford I never received an invitation to anything from an Oxford man. In Melbourne the men students had quite liked the women students and mixed freely with them, and I did not enjoy my new status as a frump, deprived of the male society I had taken for granted at home.

Gibbon wrote of 'that tender regard, which seldom fails to arise in a liberal mind, from the recollection of the place where it has discovered and exercised its growing powers'. My failure to develop a tender regard for Oxford arose, in the last analysis, neither from loneliness nor the sense of the loss of liberty I suffered at Somerville nor from resentment against sex-discrimination – although all three contributed – but from the fact that it was at Melbourne and not at Oxford that my mind had discovered and exercised its growing powers. I had come to Oxford with extravagant hopes of intellectual progress and partly owing to my own inadequacy and partly to circumstances beyond my control these hopes had been disappointed. There is probably no better system of university tuition than that practised in Oxford in my day, of the weekly tutorial in which one tutor and one undergraduate participated, but its efficacy depended on the quality of the participants. I was, once again, dogged by that absence of good teaching which I was not intellectually strong enough to overcome. With a single exception, I was unlucky in my tutors and one, with whom I wasted two terms, was hopelessly inadequate. The exception was the senior History don at Somerville, Maud Violet Clarke, a fascinating Irish woman, a fine scholar, reserved and aloof, with rare charm and wit. Unluckily, as Miss Clarke was a mediaevalist and as I was principally interested in Renaissance and post-Renaissance History, I enjoyed the privilege of her tuition for only one term. Lectures did not compensate for the mediocrity of my other tutors because at that time most Oxford historians took a rather off-hand attitude to lectures, merely discoursing in detail about their own research without much effort at elucidation or regard for the needs of under-graduates.

The Oxford undergraduate spends only twenty-four weeks of each year in Oxford, engaged in attending lectures and tutorials and writing essays. Because I was compressing the three-year course into two years I sometimes had to write two essays a week and led the life of a galley slave. Serious study, outside essay topics, is done in vacations and I had thought that, being already a graduate, I would have no difficulty in accomplishing it, but there was less overlap between my two courses than I had expected and my reading began to lag behind the required number of subjects. I increased my hours of study to the point of diminishing returns in knowledge but still I could not keep up and became nervy and depressed.

In deciding to study History at Oxford I had not had a professional end in view: I had thought no further than seizing the opportunity to become an educated person. But maturity was overtaking me and I was beginning to ask myself what the upshot of these protracted studies was to be and what I could do to justify using up so much of our family's resources for my personal enrichment. Clearly, I should begin to earn my living when I went home. But how? There were not many jobs for girls in Australia in those days and teaching seemed the only one for which I was fitted. I shrank from the thought of school-teaching because that would require a Diploma of Education, involving a further year of study and essay-writing. No further qualification would be required for teaching in a university; could I perhaps do that? I thought it would be a wonderful life and for a time it seemed possible because during my first year at Oxford my work was well regarded and I had heard that I was being spoken of as the likely future winner of a first-class degree.

As my course went on the quality of my work fell off and I doggedly – and stupidly – worked harder and harder. When the time for my final examinations came, in the summer of 1928, I was exhausted and beaten before the five-day long ordeal began. I remember looking hopelessly at the examination paper in my special subject, in which I was so well-prepared that I knew the answer to every question but was so enfeebled that I had to select the questions put in specially for the dolts, those which did not require thought or the organisation of knowledge but only information. I got a second-class degree. Although I had known that a first was out of the question I had still hoped for a miracle and was terribly dejected by having, as I felt, failed to justify the family's investment in me and also by the prospect of returning to Australia without the passport to an academic career in my hand.

VI

It was with heavy hearts that Mother and I packed for our return to Australia in the English autumn of 1928. John had gone home in 1927 and we were leaving Lorna behind because she had married an Italian engineer and was to live on the Continent. We travelled first-class in an Orient liner in a snobbish, pretentious environment we both disliked, so different from the merry simplicity of our voyage on the dear old *Nestor*. We did not contribute much to the gaiety of the scene ourselves. Poor Mother's grand design for our Europeanisation had miscarried; she had lost her beloved eldest child, the joy of our house, from whom she was to be separated for most of the rest of her life, her second daughter had taken up the stance of a figure on a funeral monument, weeping over her wilted academic laurels, and she herself had nothing to look forward to but the resumption of the role of a suburban housewife, which she had always detested.

The voyage seemed interminable but we did not really want to reach our journey's end. We arrived at Colombo and inspected it and Kandy like conscientious tourists, but our hearts were not in it. Mother cared only for Europe and although I would, ordinarily, have been enchanted by Ceylon, not even a first glimpse of the East could now rouse me from apathy. So on we went again, and on and on, through the endless rollers of the Indian ocean. One day as I was sitting on deck, gazing with sightless eyes at the waste of waters, a steward brought me a telegram which he said was from Australia. Why was it addressed to me and not to Mother? In my tragic frame of mind it could only be tidings of disaster. Perhaps Father or John was dead and I must break the news to Mother. But no, when with trembling fingers I opened the missive, it was signed 'Ernest Scott', and it said that owing to the sudden death of Arnold Wood, Professor of History in Sydney, a temporary vacancy for a lecturer would arise there in the coming academic year. Professor Scott had been asked for a recommendation and had suggested me. He was now authorised to offer me this appointment and requested an immediate decision.

I had made it before reaching the end of the telegram. Amazingly, I was to be given a second chance and despite all that had gone before I felt convinced that this time I would not muff it. The prospect before me was indeed awesome as I had just turned twenty-three and had never given a lecture in my life. Even if I had come home with a first-class degree I would have counted myself lucky, in those days when academic staffs were so small, to begin at the bottom as a tutor. And now I was to receive a princely salary, 400 pounds a year, which would ease my conscience of its burden of guilt as a waster of the family substance. True, the appointment was only for two terms but I was sure that, if I filled it adequately, the experience would help me, at some time or other, to gain another university post. So, in the event, it did, although it took ten years and many reverses of fortune before I got back to my starting-point as a lecurer in History at 400 pounds a year.

During the time that remained before we reached Fremantle I at last faced, accepted and profited by my Oxford dèbâcle. It is true that not all of those who receive first-class degrees at Oxford are people of real distinction: I might, with luck, have been one of them. But essentially the Oxford verdict was just. I was not first-class, not an original or profound thinker and I would never set the Thames of scholarship on fire. But I was a worker, loved my subject, had some imagination, some feeling for words and some gift for teaching. There was room, even in universities, for people with a vocation for teaching and now that I knew myself and my limitations I would never again aspire to a status beyond my capacity. As we drew near Australia I realised that it was not autumn but spring there, and the bare and bony land that greets the traveller at Fremantle was, in its own kind, beautiful in my eyes. I had been 'Home' and now was coming home.